Culture of Responsibility and the Role of NGOs

Culture of Responsibility and the Role of NGOs

Edited by
Tajeldin I. Hamad
Frederick A. Swarts
and
Anne Ranniste Smart

PARAGON HOUSE
St. Paul, Minnesota

Published in the United States of America by

Paragon House
2285 University Avenue West
St. Paul, Minnesota 55114

Produced for the World Association of Non-Governmental Organizations
http://www.wango.org by Paragon House

Library of Congress Catalog-in-Publication Data

World Association of Non-governmental Organizations. Conference (2002 : Washington, D.C.)
Culture of responsibility and the role of NGOs / edited by Taj I. Hamad, Frederick A. Swarts, and Anne R. Smart.
p. cm.
Papers presented at the 2002 Annual Conference of the World Association of Non-governmental Organizations (WANGO), held Oct. 18-20, 2002 in Washington, D.C.
ISBN 1-885118-14-7 (pbk. : alk. paper)
1. Non-governmental organizations--Congresses. 2. Social action--Congresses. 3. Social conflict--Prevention--Congresses. 4. Human rights--Congresses. 5. Responsibility--Congresses. I. Hamad, Taj I. II. Swarts, Frederick A., 1952- III. Smart, Anne R. (Anne Ranniste) IV. Title.
HN3 .W383 2003
361.7--dc22

2003016165

10 9 8 7 6 5 4 3 2 1

For current information about all releases from Paragon House,
visit the web site at http://www.paragonhouse.com

Contents

Part IV: NGOs and Environmental Protection

Part V: NGOs, the Family, and International Organizations

Part VI: NGOs and the Media

Part VII: Resources for NGOs

Part VIII: Excellence in the NGO Community

Part IX: Diversity of NGOs

Preface

In our time, we have witnessed a dramatic increase in the number, importance, and diversity of non-governmental organizations (NGOs). Internationally active NGOs have increased nearly thirtyfold in the past century, and the growth of national and local NGOs has been equally impressive. NGOs now impact policies and advance initiatives that once were nearly exclusively the arena of governments and corporations, and their humanitarian service has become vital to the well-being of individuals and societies throughout the globe. In many cases, NGOs have proven more adept than governments in responding to particular needs.

The umbrella-term "NGOs" refers to a broad, kaleidoscopic grouping of nonprofit organizations that espouse a variety of agendas, causes, and ideologies, and differ in size, resources, and organizational level. NGOs are involved in humanitarian relief, advocacy, educational and monitoring programs, conflict prevention, high-level mediation, and innumerable other tasks. They may focus on international agendas or local community affairs. They may be small, one-person operations or large international organizations, such as Amnesty International, which has more than 1 million members, subscribers, and donors in more than 140 countries, with an international secretariat staffed by more than 450 members and volunteers. Collectively, these not-for-profit entities are garnering increased attention as a powerful "third sector," forging an effective middle ground between the state and the corporate world.

With this increased impact comes increased responsibility. NGOs have the responsibility to be transparent, honest, accountable, ethical, to give out accurate information, and to not manipulate situations for personal benefit. NGOs have the calling to go beyond the boundaries of race, religion, ethnicity, culture, and politics. They have the obligation to respect each person's fundamental human rights. NGOs are to have a system of proper governance. They must be careful not to misuse public money for selfish purposes and to treat all public assets with utmost seriousness as a sacred trust. NGOs have a responsibility to not align themselves with, or stand in opposition to, any particular government for purely selfish or shortsighted means, nor to become controlled by a governmental body. In short, NGOs have the responsibility to dedicate themselves for the sake of others and do so according to the highest code of ethical conduct.

One fundamental truth about good and just government and society is that they depend on a culture of responsibility. The well-being of nations, corporations, media, and the non-governmental community depends on responsible citizenship, and each of these entities has a role to play in fostering a mutually beneficial culture. US president George W. Bush, in his 2002 State of the Union Address, explained that responsibility implies service to our neighbors and to the pursuit of "goals larger than self." We might conclude that a good and just global society will be based on universal respect for human rights, service to others, and responsible behavior.

The importance of fostering a culture of responsibility among people and institutions has particular relevance to NGOs. As they adopt the role of advocates of a more just and caring society, NGOs can help develop and nurture conscientious concerns in the emerging global culture. Similarly, NGOs also have a duty to stay the course in terms of their own founding vision of service.

The papers in this book have been selected from an international conference convened on the theme of "Culture of Responsibility and the Role of NGOs." This event was the 2002 Annual Conference of the World Association of Non-Governmental Organizations(WANGO), an international membership organization uniting NGOs in the cause of world peace and global well-being. For three days, from October

18–20, 2002, executive NGO officers from throughout the world as well as select governmental, intergovernmental, and corporate leaders, gathered in Washington, DC to discuss issues related to fostering a culture of responsibility as well as share innovative ideas and practices, and build strategic partnerships to help NGOs better fulfill their missions. In all, over 350 prominent leaders from 74 nations participated in this conference.

The conference's varied session formats included plenary sessions where leading authorities delivered presentations, panel sessions where NGO representatives introduced their organizations or discussed their activities or concerns, and workshops where experts provided guidance on practical topics of importance to NGOs. From the conference these forty-four papers were culled, in order to advance our understanding of the work of the NGO community, broaden our perspective of issues of global import, and discern where we, the NGO community, need to go to better address humanity's basic problems. Hopefully, this book also provides helpful practical information that can allow NGOs to be more effective in their vital activities.

These papers represent a variety of perspectives, reflecting the diversity of the conference participants. On the one hand, presentations were offered by prominent leaders of internationally known NGOs and governmental, intergovernmental, and corporate bodies: the Center for Strategic and International Studies, Worldwatch Institute, the Points of Light Foundation, Amnesty International, the World Bank, Freedom House, the US Department of State, the World Peace Centre, the World Family Policy Center, the University of Bridgeport, United Press International, *Tiempos del Mundo*, the Heritage Foundation, and the State University of New York, among others. On the other hand, smaller NGOs from the least developed nations, little known outside their own communities or countries, also had a voice at the conference and are represented in these proceedings. Furthermore, the attending NGOs encompassed the vast spectrum of human activity: humanitarian aid, conflict prevention and resolution, health care, the environment, economic and social development, indigenous people, religion, media, women's issues, and so forth.

Among the highlights of WANGO Annual Conference 2002

was the awards banquet, where recognition was given to NGOs that have shown remarkable leadership in their field of endeavor. In this way, WANGO recognized the spirit of service among NGOs and acknowledged particularly effective groups, whether they be internationally known, such as the Arias Foundation, the Inuit Circumpolar Conference, and the United Religions Initiative, or smaller NGOs whose valuable contributions may have been overlooked on the international stage. These presentations are also included in this volume.

One particularly valuable part of the conference did not make it into these proceedings in full because it was "off the record." Several roundtable discussions were designed to bring governmental representatives and NGOs together to discuss how they can best work together to tackle humanity's problems. Clearly, greater cooperation between these two arenas can advance solutions toward many difficult challenges with which each nation's citizens are faced. In each session, NGO leaders and governmental representatives examined how to increase cooperation between governments and competent NGOs that have substantial capabilities in their areas of focus and with which cooperation would be both appropriate and mutually beneficial. Official government representatives from the People's Republic of China (human rights), the Dominican Republic (families and youth), Germany (development issues), Japan (environment), and Italy (conflict resolution, peace, and security) began the discourse. Explored was how governments can integrate NGO experience, knowledge, and expertise into their operations to increase effectiveness in dealing with issues and priorities in their agendas as well as what mechanisms are in place for government-NGO cooperation and how to strengthen the process for government-NGO consultation and dialogue. These sessions proved to be quite productive and insightful. As a representative example, a report on the human rights interactive section is included in these proceedings. Hopefully, such discussions can lead toward a new compact, in particular between governments and civil society organizations, so govrenments treat them as allies rather than as adversaries and thus use their strengths to benefit citizens and deliver services.

The authors represented within these pages (as well as the WANGO participants) share a common concern for the well-being of humanity and our planet. They contribute information, offer insights, and propose solutions. Their presentations cross the spectrum from basic facts to concrete initiatives and are generally short, many limited by the time allowed to the authors in the conference sessions. Nonetheless, I believe they contain a great deal of worthwhile information that should be helpful to the NGO community and those interested in seeing the continuing evolution of the NGO community in playing a leading role in building a "culture of responsibility."

T.H. and F.S.

Part I
NGOs and Culture of Responsibility

Introduction

We live in a world of remarkable technological advances, but also extraordinary challenges. Approximately 800 million people suffer from malnutrition and 900 million are illiterate. Over 1 billion people live on less than a dollar a day, and an estimated one-quarter of humanity lives in poverty. Our environment faces unprecedented threats of pollution, species elimination, deforestation, declining fisheries, rising sea levels, and so forth. Wars, terrorism, weapons of mass destruction, and crime beset our planet, and child prostitution, slavery, and serious diseases remain a tragic reality. The three sectors of society—government, business, and non-governmental organizations—all share a social responsibility to address these and other pressing problems.

Many in the NGO community do take responsibility for the serious social, environmental, political, educational, and human rights issues with which we are confronted. Many also serve to foster such a culture of responsibility among governments and corporations. Corporations, which might see their sole responsibility to be making profits, are guided by NGOs to understand that they also have ethical responsibilities relative to protecting the environment, human rights, labor rights, and so forth. Likewise, NGOs address issues of governmental corruption, inequality in treatment of citizens, political prisoners, and so forth.

NGOs also have an internal responsibility. They are charged with the responsibility to exhibit the highest ethical behavior in their own activities: transparency, fiscal accountability, fairness, honesty, and so forth.

The papers in this section deal with this theme of NGOs and the culture of responsibility. Some also treat general issues related to NGOs and their importance today, including the accomplishments and constraints of the non-governmental community and recent trends in global non-governmentalism.

The Role of the Non-Governmental Community in Building a Culture of Responsibility

1

A Human Imperative for the Twenty-first Century

NOEL BROWN

It is a distinct pleasure to join in the task of exploring the role of the non-governmental community in building a culture of responsibility, a theme, which as I see it, is nothing less than a human imperative for the twenty-first century.

As we begin a new millennium, what some have termed "the global century," it is clear that we are entering a new kind of world, a world at once forbidding and exciting, creative and disturbing, humane and compassionate, yet brutal and cruel. It is a globalizing world where we become increasingly more conscious of ourselves as a global species, a world in which we are now able to become more conscious of each other as individuals, sharing and caring for each other, which is an essential ingredient for survival.

Ours is also an intricately connected world, a wired world if you will, where information technology now makes it possible for any event, anywhere on earth, to be covered live, and that is a remarkable achievement. We now have the capacity to build common heroes, common devils, common joys and sorrows, and common empathies; in effect, a closed-circuit world where it is always prime time.

It is a highly productive world, where the engines of wealth generation are now working full-time, and where it is now possible to eradicate the scourge of abject poverty and thereby engender a period of universal prosperity. The present pattern of distribution, however, raises some disturbing ethical questions regarding the state

---

Dr. Noel Brown serves as president of Friends of the United Nations and is a former regional director of the United Nations Environment Program, North American Region.

of the global social contract and the moral imperatives of a just society. This challenge is perhaps most glaringly reflected in the fact that the combined assets of our 450 billionaires are greater than the combined income of 40 percent of the world's poor. We have the capacity to eradicate poverty if the will is there.

Darker Side of Humanity

On the other hand, despite such potential, and great promises of a positive human future, a darker side of humanity seems to be coming to light as a specter of terror stalks the earth, leaving in its wake a growing culture of fear, insecurity, and anxiety, and here one can no longer claim immunity or sanctuary. No one can be nonaligned or be at the wrong place at the wrong time. There is no longer any wrong place at the wrong time. Global terror knows no bounds and shows no respect or sensitivity. It strikes at will wherever it wishes, in Bali, in Kuwait, in New York, in Manila, and even in Washington, DC.

Writing in a *New York Times* editorial entitled "The Sniper Next Door," author Patricia Cornwell states the situation in rather graphic terms when she begins to suggest that this culture of fear has begun to paralyze us. She observed that fear creates fear, and the more we fear, the more we will create fear, turning us into indoor creatures and eventually bringing ruin to our lives. Cornwell went on to list the social deficits of terror as evidenced by the sniper shootings in the Washington, DC area:

> We don't want to buy gas. We don't want our children going to school. We don't want to shop. We don't want to drive to work. We may deliberate for hours whether we go to the grocery store or pharmacy.
>
> These days we cringe beneath the shadow and roar of every low-flying passenger plane. We worry about opening our mail. At the office, we demand X-ray scanners and other high tech devices that might detect explosions or anthrax. We decide not to buy the new house or the new car. Really, we rationalize, we don't need anything right now. New clothes can wait.

A dinner at our favorite restaurant isn't a necessity. In fact, let's not go anywhere.

To some, such scenario may seem somewhat overdrawn or fanciful, and many others might think that this is certainly something that is exaggerated and that we are far from a state of social paralysis. Still the trends are, at best, worrying, and stand for a new kind of metaphor for what ails humanity in these first years of the millennium.

Sooner or later, we will have to confront the same fundamental question: What can we, as individuals and citizens, do about it? Do we simply yield to fear? How can we become more fully engaged in the safety and well-being of our society? Can the non-governmental community play a greater role in building a genuine human security community, where ethno-linguistic nationalisms and religious fundamentalisms are held in check and where people, ordinary people, are no longer the front line of this latest global scourge? Clearly these are questions that need pondering and demand some new approaches, and perhaps the time has come for us to broaden our focus.

Human Responsibility

For years, the non-governmental community has been in the front line in the fight to secure human rights and fundamental freedom, and our record of achievement has been quite impressive indeed. Most basic rights have now been codified in various conventions and constitutions, even in those societies where they may not be observed or their provisions implemented.

But what we need to do now is move beyond the question of rights, to human responsibility. Some years ago I was part of a study group in Trieste, Italy, that was established to write a Magna Carta of human duties. We wanted to come up with a document that would identify and list for us those duties that we as human beings owe to the earth and to each other. But we realized at the end of the exercise that the central challenge was not really a drafting problem. That is very simple. What we needed was a political and social culture that would infuse human beings with a set of values and attitudes, and that would make human beings more responsible for their conduct and for the way we go about the business of living in society. So what we need now is to focus on how we can inculcate in ourselves and in society a new sense of responsibility for each other and the earth. How we can build a new global political culture that is supportive of the culture of responsibility.

That is why the theme of WANGO Annual Conference 2002, "Culture of Responsibility and the Role of NGOs," and the gathering of NGO leaders from throughout the world to discuss this theme is such an extremely timely and relevant exercise. The purpose of WANGO 2002 is not simply to write a code of responsibility or a Magna Carta of human responsibilities, but to build, step by step, a new structure whereby human beings will assume responsibility for themselves, for the earth, and each other.

The timing may be right. Those of us who were at Johannesburg for the World Summit on Sustainable Development recognize that perhaps the single success of the conference was the acknowledgment of the role of the non-governmental community in becoming partners with governments in global problem-solving. In the past, the non-governmentals were simply guests of the process. We would invite you to make a statement, we thanked you, and you went about your business. Now we are partners in the process of global governance and global problem-solving.

But that role of partners carries with it a very basic responsibility. We will need to demonstrate that we can discharge these new opportunities responsibly. It is not enough to simply be confrontational, or to be critical, or to protest. These may gain us a few headlines, but they will not gain us a place at the table or access to the boardrooms. And so as we assemble to explore the question of a culture of responsibility, I believe that we have a very unique opportunity to help build a new kind of society, that we can indeed demonstrate to the United Nations and the world that non-governmentalism can be effectively *responsible non-governmentalism*, and that we are now in a position to cooperate in a very responsible way. If this were to be done, then I think the non-governmental community will have made a quantum leap forward.

Social Justice in Today's World

2

OSCAR ARIAS SÁNCHEZ

I come from Latin America, the region with the worst income disparities in the world. This gives me an unfortunate firsthand knowledge about what we are lacking as a world community when we speak of social justice and equality of opportunities. Fortunately, my country, Costa Rica, has one of the lowest levels of social inequality in Latin America, and so I also have some experience of what a more egalitarian society can look like. Of course, we are still far from achieving our goal: a society where everyone's basic needs are ensured and where all children and adults have ample opportunities to live in dignity and develop to their full human potential.

Because no society in the world has fully achieved this goal, we tend to become complacent, satisfied to say that we are trying, and perhaps believing that such a world is not really possible. If it is not, we may ask ourselves, why spend a lot of effort to try to attain something that is unattainable?

But I tell you this: there is no lack of resources in the world for fighting poverty. What we are experiencing is rather a lack of will. When entire economies enter into crisis, wealthy governments quickly gather the billions of dollars needed for a bailout. But when we see the crises of poverty and hunger, illiteracy and disease, that affect so many of our brothers and sisters, where is the rapid response? Where is the will to gather up the resources that could feed and house everyone, that could provide safe drinking water, basic health and sanitation, and at least an elementary education to the world's population?

Misplaced Priorities

We have been led to believe that it is unrealistic to think in terms of resolving the world's poverty crisis. But if we take a take a close look at

---

H.E. Dr. Oscar Arias Sánchez is former president of Costa Rica and the 1987 Nobel Peace Prize Laureate.

the priorities of our governments, we will see that the problem is not one of scale, but one of vision. In the year 2000 the world spent about $800 billion on weapons and soldiers, but only $56 billion on development assistance. It is estimated by the United Nations Development Program that an investment of $40 billion a year for ten years would be enough to provide basic education, health care, and nutrition, potable water, and sanitation to all of the world's people. That is, with just 5 percent of what we spend preparing for and fighting wars, we could eliminate the most elementary forms of needless suffering from the face of the planet.

So, why don't we? It is a tragedy that we are beginning the twenty-first century by building an expensive and unrealistic shield against missiles rather than a practical and much less taxing shield against poverty and inequality. Between ballistic missiles and social injustice, I am thoroughly convinced that the latter presents a much larger threat to the security of life on this planet. But we choose to focus on chasing after our enemies, otherwise diverting precious resources from the battle to be fought against poverty and therefore reducing our chances of winning it.

If the Bush administration forges ahead with its plans to build a national missile defense system, we have been assured by numerous experts that China's investment in military technology will increase dramatically, as will both India's and Pakistan's, among others. I need hardly point out that these are countries that cannot afford to waste resources on weapons. In India and Pakistan alone, more than 480 million people subsist on less than one dollar per day, and I am sure that I do not need to remind you that a large proportion of these people are children. Additionally, these two nations are home to over 500 million illiterate adults. Increased nuclear power will not help these individuals to live better lives.

Indian author Arundhati Roy called her country's nuclear bomb "the final act of betrayal by a ruling class that has failed its people." I believe that we could apply the same strong language to members of the government and military of leading countries around the world, such as North Korea, a country with an income per capita of just five hundred dollars. Indeed, for some leaders it is easier to make atomic bombs than to educate their nation's children.

The simple truth is, spending money on arms, and especially getting caught up in regional or global arms races, is the surest way to perpetuate poverty. And in my view, it also is a very poor method of guaranteeing security. For an arms race never has a winner, and the losers are numbered most heavily among the poor. It is not coincidence that poverty and violence so often go hand in hand. When will we learn that the best way to enforce security is to act to ensure justice?

Role of Civil Society

I have been speaking about governments, and now you may be asking yourselves how individuals and organizations fit into this picture. I want to make it perfectly clear that I believe social justice to be the responsibility of governments. Yet governments do not exist in a vacuum. At least in democratic societies they have to be an expression of the will of the people, and all of us have something to say about that. In every country there is a vital role to be played by civil society in the struggle for a more just and peaceful world. That role encompasses both immediate action to alleviate suffering and an advocacy and lobbying role to influence those in positions of power to keep the faceless and voiceless ever before them in their work.

There are many bright lights in the world, individuals and organizations, working toward both of these ends. As someone with more than thirty years of experience in government and politics, I can tell you quite confidently that while government provides the skeleton of our communities, it is civil society that constitutes the soul. Political leaders must look to individuals and organizations in order to find our true north, the manifestation of what is best in humanity, and the direction in which all of our laws and policies should take us. As examples to be emulated and as a chiding rod pushing us on toward real action, non-governmental organizations as well as outstanding individuals are invaluable. Truly, our societies would be lifeless without them.

It is incumbent upon all of us, from the individual to the NGO to the state, to be carriers of compassion and voices for social justice. As individuals we must begin with those around us and continue to search for ways to make a difference, always keeping a standard of fairness and justice in our hearts. When individuals come together to form organizations, the impact of our actions can be multiplied and the clamoring for justice grows ever louder. When we examine the level of government, whether from the point of view of a voter, an activist, or a public officeholder, we must face up to a complex challenge. For it is the responsibility of governments to look at the larger picture, but never to forget the human person, and to balance the needs of individuals and families with the greatest common good.

This is not an easy task, and I tip my hat to those political leaders who are making an honest effort to strike this balance. I tend to believe, however, that many of our governments and societies are leaning much too far in the direction of individualism today, and that we have a serious shortage of solidarity.

A Guide To our Actions

I would like to suggest that we take the words of Mahatma Gandhi as a guide to our actions as we strive to create a better world. Gandhi identified seven social sins to be avoided at all costs by political and community leaders, and we would do well to keep them in mind. They are: (1) politics without principle, (2) wealth without work, (3) pleasure without conscience, (4) knowledge without character, (5) commerce without morality, (6) science without humanity, and (7) worship without sacrifice. If we let these seven road signs mark the paths we do not want to take, then the path ahead to progress will appear much more clearly.

Everyone needs to be committed to a vision that promotes social justice, compassion, and solidarity. These are values that are going out of style, and they need as many defenders as they can get. I would like to encourage everyone to open your minds and hearts to an active examination of the important role that a culture of responsibility plays in fostering social justice. The challenges before us are great indeed, but I think we will find that when we open ourselves up—as a community—to all of the possibilities presented to us by our imagination and our intellect, our creativity and our logic, we will have taken a great stride further down the road toward a truly just and peaceful world.

NGO Core Values and True Responsibility

3

CHUNG HWAN KWAK

As human society has evolved, certain central institutional structures have come to be recognized as among the fundamental building blocks of any human community. Among these are, of course, family, the state, religion, and the marketplace. In the development of the modern West, two concepts for understanding human history and society have been viewed as primary. These are the individual and the state.

Throughout much of the twentieth century, the idea of the individual was affirmed by the democratic, capitalist West, and the idea of the collective or state was affirmed by the communist bloc. In the post–Cold War era, humanity has come to appreciate those "mediating institutions" that stand between the individual and the state, or what Hegel called civil society. These "mediating institutions" include the family, neighborhoods, communities of faith and worship, voluntary associations, clubs, and so forth. These are the locales where ordinary life for most of us is lived, where we learn and practice our basic virtues and values as human beings. For, as far as our primary identity and core values go, we are neither isolated individuals on the one hand nor parts of a political collective on the other. We are people who come into being in primary, face-to-face relationships with family, relatives, friends, neighbors, colleagues and associates.

We live our lives on many levels simultaneously, in families, in communities, in nations, in a world, and in the cosmos. Ultimately we exist and develop in a network of relationships. No being exists outside of a series of give-and-take relationships. This is a universal and cosmic principle. Moreover, while the structure of relationships is very important, in all human relationships the internal quality is more important. The highest forms of human relationship are characterized

---

Dr. Chung Hwan Kwak serves as chairman of WANGO's International Council.

by sincerity and true love. This potential for true love to form the quality or culture of relationships is what sets human beings apart from the natural or animal worlds.

In this respect, the family is potentially the most central, precious, and noble of all human institutions. For it is within the family that we can best develop and perfect the culture of heart and true love for others. In this sense, we can say that the family is the primary school of love. That is why the family has been understood as the fundamental unit of human society.

WANGO Vision

The term civil society is often used interchangeably with the movement of non-governmental organizations (NGOs). NGOs are set apart from governments and they are set apart from the realm of isolated individuals. This is why, especially in the post–Cold War era, NGOs are so important. They represent our human tendency to join together in forming constructive relationships with one another, centered on a purpose to contribute in some way to human well-being.

The founder of WANGO, Dr. Sun Myung Moon, has been a pioneer and advocate of NGOs for fifty years, beginning with an ecumenical association aimed at forging greater unity among Christian denominations. He also created NGOs to promote such goals as wider interreligious harmony, humanitarian service, fair and responsible mass communications media, peace research and activism, and so forth. The WANGO founder has played a central role in providing education and training in marriage and family for millions of couples and parents around the world; developing a very active HIV/AIDS prevention program in Africa; heading up conflict resolution initiatives in South Asia, the Middle East, and the Korean peninsula; and investing in sustainable ocean development to provide jobs, opportunities, and education for small island nations, just to mention a few of his worthy endeavors.

I mention these to illustrate a point that is at the heart and the foundation of the WANGO vision. That is, WANGO seeks not only to be a resource for NGOs worldwide, but also seeks to encourage the development of a "culture of peace" and a "culture of responsibility" among NGOs. One reason for the disaffection with politics, economics, and individualism among people around the world is their awareness of a culture of selfishness and self-interest that dominates many political systems, many corporate cultures, and many individuals.

Core NGO Values

If the NGO movement is not to suffer a loss of credibility, we must all affirm, uphold, and practice certain core values. These values are universal values that have been affirmed throughout history by saints, sages, philosophers, and ordinary men and women of conscience. They include the value of unselfishness, the value of a life lived for the well-being of others, such as the parent who sacrifices for his or her children or the patriot who serves the nation. If NGOs are characterized by unselfishness, then we will earn and deserve the confidence and respect of others. If we degenerate into special interest groups that have self-centered, narrow purposes, we are nothing more than one more competing voice seeking attention and resources. Let us live for the sake of others.

Secondly, NGOs must transcend the interests of any single race, religion, culture, or nationality. That is, even if our mission is explicitly focused on the well-being of a particular community, we must always also have a greater vision for the whole of humanity and its well-being. If any one of us succeeds at the expense of others, our victory will be short lived.

As we consider the theme of WANGO 2002, "Culture of Responsibility and the Role of NGOs," we are encouraged to reflect, not on how we can receive or benefit or on how we can cast blame or criticism toward others. Rather we are asked to take responsibility. This, I believe, is leadership. A true leader is one who takes responsibility, who takes on the burdens and tasks necessary to correct problems.

The modern era of human history has prided itself on technological advancement as well as rational and efficient organizational structures. However, the most unique value and potential of human beings lies in the realm of the heart, in the realm of true love. Structures without heart and relationships without true love are empty and lacking in lasting value.

We cannot find true freedom and well-being for humanity

through technology or rational organizational structures alone. True liberty and happiness are not based on our ability to satisfy our wants without limit. True freedom is related to true responsibility. By practicing true responsibility, we achieve true freedom.

True Responsibility

What is true responsibility? True responsibility is based on the principle of service, and the paradigm of true responsibility is found in parental love. The heart of a mother and father for their children contains three aspects. First of all, the parental heart willingly takes on the task of caring with unconditional love for one's offspring. Second, the parents have a heart to guide and educate the next generation in the way of truth and goodness. And, third, the parents have the heart to provide for and protect their family.

The parental heart is not an ideal that applies only within the family. The mature parental heart is also the paradigm of social responsibility. If we are to create a culture of peace and a culture of responsibility, it needs to be rooted in this parental heart.

The parental heart will not produce a culture of selfishness or individualism. Such a culture of selfishness will only lead to conflict. The NGO community must seriously consider this point about the moral and spiritual foundations of our work. If we cultivate this parental heart, we will not only prosper, but we will make a great contribution to world peace. Should we fail, and become agents of self-interest, we will decline.

Let this attitude guide us in the days ahead. Let the WANGO annual conference mark a day in the history of the NGO movement that we can look back on with pride, for we did not gather for a selfish purpose, but for the sake of others. We can look back and say that we gathered for the sake of world peace.

Volunteering—Reconnecting a Disconnected Society

4

The Volunteer Movement Creating a Culture of Responsibility

MEI COBB

I am always excited to address something I feel very passionately about, and that is volunteering. The year 2002 has been an eventful year in the United States, with volunteering being moved to the forefront of our national agenda, especially with President George W. Bush's most recent call for Americans to offer four thousand hours, or two years, of volunteer service. Our goal at the Points of Light Foundation, which promotes volunteerism, is to not only increase the number of volunteers, but also the quality of the volunteer experience as well.

While the span of society is great, you often hear people say that the world is getting smaller. It never ceases to amaze me how today you can travel the entire world in the same time frame that it once took you to explore your own community. Equally as impressive, it is hard to imagine that before the invention of the automobile, the average person never traveled more than twenty miles from their home. From the moment that first automobile left town or an international flight landed, there has been a rapid acceleration, which has been made even faster by global cell phones, the Internet, and broadcast satellite coverage.

With the international exchange of people and electronic signals comes the most important travelers of all, information and knowledge—knowledge that cannot be hidden or ignored. Now this may be a very simplistic explanation of globalization, but that information has set the global stage. Knowledge and technology have eliminated the barriers of distance and time, and now the world is the

---

Mei Cobb serves as senior vice president of the Points of Light Foundation, a national, nonpartisan, nonprofit organization founded by US President George H. Bush, who serves as honorary chairman.

community, leaving us much more aware of the similarities and differences of our own cultures.

For better or worse, whether we want them or not, we have up-to-the-minute updates on our successes, our triumphs, and our tragedies, and when we are able to see through the complexity of it all, we realize that we are all neighbors. The spirit of neighbor helping neighbor has been a critical factor in the success of our democratic government. What we learned from our ancestors, and what we continue to learn, is that the freedom and individual rights that are at the core of our society come with a shared responsibility for the health and well-being of our communities, and to each other.

We also believed early in our United States history that by uniting ourselves in principles, values, and government, our nation would become stronger by connecting ourselves to each other, that we could easily share the rich and abundant resources of new frontiers with everyone. On the basis of these beliefs, we created a number of social and economic systems to help us manage the distribution of resources more effectively.

However, not everyone was connected to these new systems of society. Not everyone was privy to the part of society where resources were traded freely and fairly. Unfortunately, from the United States' earliest democratic infancy, not all people were really "created equal." As a result of social inequality, some people and communities became disconnected from each other. Even an ordinary person in the eighteenth century, regardless of race or religion, may have become completely disenfranchised from the privileges offered to the elite. Women had no rights at all.

Overall, the society of the early United States was primarily a system of social and political separatism. Let me share a quote with you by a great British writer, and I must be thinking about children, because he is the author of the Winnie the Pooh books. But he said, "In the quiet hours when we are alone, and there is nobody to tell us what fine ones we are, we come sometimes upon a moment in which we wonder, not how much money we are earning, not how famous we have become, but what good are we doing?" The Points of Light Foundation was founded to keep this spirit alive. Our mission is to engage more people, more effectively in volunteer service to help solve serious social problems.

Points of Light

When do you first remember the expression "Points of Light"? Well, you may recall that in 1988, then vice president George H. W. Bush said in his acceptance speech for the nomination as presidential candidate that "we are a nation of communities, of thousands and tens of thousands of ethnic, religious, social, business, labor unions, neighborhood, regional, and other organizations, all of them varied, voluntary, and unique. A brilliant diversity spread like stars, like a thousand points of light, in a broad and peaceful sky."

In 1990 the Points of Light Foundation was founded as a national, nonpartisan, nonprofit organization. We work in partnership with local volunteer centers, and there are roughly five hundred centers across the United States today. The foundation supports and organizes the vital work of community volunteers, who help solve our nation's most serious social problems by bringing people and resources together. At the Points of Light Foundation and the Volunteer Center National Network, the essence of the work that we do is bringing people and communities, and the organizations within those communities, closer together. We connect people, to reach out sometimes to the extreme limits of our social boundaries and perhaps touch someone in a way that makes a significant difference.

So while the world is more connected within the confines of knowledge and time, there is an opposing force driven by the complexities of an unequal society that creates a disconnect, even isolation. Today, isolation—from each other, from our communities, and from fundamental resources—has created a complicated and interrelated set of social problems: poverty, homelessness, unemployment, violence, crime, drug abuse, discrimination, sexual harassment, child and spousal abuse, unwanted pregnancies, mental health crises, and environmental pollution. These problems are very difficult to prevent and difficult to solve, and none of them can be eliminated, as much as we would like, overnight.

A Disconnected Society

Today more than 85 percent of the United States' population believes that a disconnected society is at the heart of our most serious social problems. One in four of the world's people today live in a state of absolute poverty. Thirty-five thousand children die every day, directly because of poverty. One hundred and thirty million children do not attend primary school, 70 percent of them girls, and 1.3 billion people have no safe water or sanitation.

When people are separated from each other by values, principles, and social discrimination, the results are often serious and long-lasting. Unfortunately, more than two-thirds of our country's general public believes that social problems are getting worse. Even with our increased and collective sensitivity to the hardship of those around us, social problems are getting worse and we stay disconnected from each other.

We are certainly no strangers to diversity. After all, the United States is considered to be a melting pot of races, cultures, religions, and ideas. The Statue of Liberty reaches out to "the tired, the poor, the huddled masses," and welcomes every woman, man, and child to participate in our democracy. Every voice may be heard, every opportunity may be seized, every human right may be exercised. Our society has always yearned to explore the diversity of our planet, and now the universe in which it resides, and this natural diversity has posed no threat to us because we have always known how to conquer it. We have a good track record of facing our fears of the unknown, in order to capitalize on new discoveries. But simply identifying diversity does not offer us a culture of responsibility. In fact, it's more likely to create reasons for such a disconnect.

I and our organization believe that volunteering will play a major role in transforming simple knowledge of diversity into fully engaged global citizenship and thus give opportunities to exercise this unique perspective. The volunteer movement is stronger than ever as we enter the twenty-first century. More than half of the United States alone, 56 percent, volunteer; that is an estimated 109 million people over the age of eighteen. While this is a very impressive number, we are still concerned that nearly half of these people volunteer sporadically and consider it a onetime activity. Therefore, it is not enough to get people to engage in service. We seek to lead a movement.

Three Requirements for a Volunteer Movement

We believe there are three central requirements to sustain such a volunteer movement, to foster such a culture of responsibility. These are: one, an ethic of service; two, a delivery system through which service is extended, or an infrastructure; and three, a focus of that service.

We believe that the first requirement of a robust agenda of service is a system of values, or an ethic, where volunteering must be highly valued in the broader community. One of former president Bush's greatest contributions to this movement was his belief that there can be no definition of a successful life without service to others. Again: *No definition of a successful life without service to others.* This statement and the leadership around this idea were significant, because he could provide moral leadership for the nation, and he chose to elevate the importance of volunteering, by saying that every other previously prized attribute of success had to be rethought. Service to neighbors, according to his leadership ideas, was more important than financial or career success. This leadership positioning required people to consider whether they had created room in their own busy lives to offer assistance to those who need help.

Volunteering is not something that is simply nice to do; it is absolutely necessary. It is necessary because government alone cannot fill all of the tears in the social safety net that is left by poverty and illiteracy, crime, and violence, and the other social ills and pathologies that exist. It is necessary because our communities are strongest when everyone takes responsibility. There is an old Celtic saying that we warm ourselves by fires that we did not dig. There is a Native American saying that we sit in the shade of a great tree we did not plant. It is this sense that even the strongest and most successful among us will give great service to give thanks, at least in part, for our own comforts and our own success. Likewise, an old Irish proverb says it is in the shelter of each other that people live. This means that when life's burdens are greatest, we can and should turn to our neighbors for assistance.

Former President Bush also said every problem in America is being solved someplace in America, because the belief in the power and role of volunteering is not a matter of partisan politics. There was great agreement with the value of the ethic of service by former president Clinton as well. He said words that were very similar. He said there's nothing wrong with America that cannot be solved by what's right with America. So we need to ask, how will our volunteer force change to address society's needs? Who will volunteer and how will we get people to make volunteering a regular part of their lives? Who will help carry this torch?

This leads us to the second essential component for this movement, a delivery system, or an infrastructure. It depends upon the realization that service does not take place from a national leadership position. It happens locally. People receive services from the hands of volunteers at the community level and not from some national plateau. NGOs must play a leadership role in effecting change. The Points of Light Foundation and our partners in the national network of volunteer centers face major challenges in the near future as we work to mobilize volunteers, to address the serious social problems that exist in our local and global communities.

Volunteering has the greatest chance of becoming an integral, valued, and sustained part of a community or a society when there are NGOs in place that assume leadership roles in promoting and supporting it. The success of these organizations is critical to the long-term success of volunteering, to this culture of responsibility. Simply put, someone must make it their primary priority to ensure attention to the promotion of volunteering and the creation of an infrastructure that supports volunteering, and the development of skilled, knowledgeable national and local leaders. Without this resource, volunteering will remain undervalued, poorly organized, and in a margin of community life.

It's no mystery that since September 11, 2001, citizens of the United States have found a renewed spirit of giving and spirit. This past January, in the 2002 State of the Union address, President George W. Bush called for citizens to give four thousand hours, the equivalent of two years of our lives, in service to others. The Unity and the Spirit of America Act, which he signed on January 10, 2002, called for the Points of Light Foundation and the Volunteer Center National Network to identify and organize volunteer service projects across the United States, each in tribute to one of the victims of the September 11 attacks. Since June 2002, over nine hundred projects have been registered for over nine hundred thousand volunteers in honor of victims.

Some people say that September 11 changed the nature of

volunteering in the United States. But perhaps a better explanation is that this horrible event created a connection between members of our society through a common and shared experience. Volunteering has been a natural manifestation of that newly rediscovered connection. The future of service in the United States has been boosted by the spirit, but the role and purpose of volunteering remains the same. The days following September 11 provided people in the United States a prime example of how volunteering and the spirit of service can bridge great divides in our society, even when we are asked to explain the unexplainable. In the aftermath of the tragedy, one of the few positives is an opportunity for volunteer leaders to ride a surge of interest and make volunteer service a central part of the life of every citizen.

Twenty-five Years from Now

So how do we take this enthusiasm and create a movement? This leads us to the third and final element: focus of service. During our preparations for the new century, we asked three thousand attendees at our Conference for National Service and Community Volunteering to create a vision for their work in the future. What would they take from the past to sustain their efforts? What would be different, and what strategies would they need to achieve their vision?

The group agreed that a necessity for the future was the spirit of neighbor helping neighbor, with people rising above their differences and having a shared sense of mutual responsibility and personal commitment. There is agreement about what had to be different: more young people must be involved in service and instilled with a lifelong commitment to serve. And a major strategy to achieve this vision was strengthening service as a core value for families and individuals.

Our team looked forward some twenty-five years, into the year 2025, when US high school students would be forty-something middle-aged men and women and, because of their service efforts as teenagers, they will be deeply committed volunteers in their communities. And on the other hand, they would now have raised the bar and have higher expectations about the benefits they and their communities can reap through volunteer efforts. Young people will be the most sought after potential volunteers because of their known dedication and perseverance in achieving goals. Service learning will be part of the school curriculum in every school district, and each school will have its own volunteer center with a trained professional staff. Organizations of all types will reach out to youth, realizing the importance of creating opportunities with them, not only for them to address community needs.

In this vision of the future, families will introduce their children to volunteer activities. Parents and grandparents will encourage children and teens to get involved, to feel empowered, and learn new skills through volunteer opportunities. Schools, houses of worship, and workplaces routinely will offer family volunteering days. The older-than-sixty-five population will nearly double during the next twenty-five years, exceeding the younger-than-eighteen generation. With more people retired and living longer, healthier lives, seniors will continue a trend of increased volunteering first observed in the late 1990s. Volunteer opportunities for seniors fit their busy, diverse lives, tapping their wealth of knowledge and experience while promoting self-benefits. Likewise, the commitment and dedication of the world's senior volunteer force will ensure that the resources they provide to their neighbors and communities will be available to them, if needed.

We expect that one day virtual volunteering will be commonplace. Millions of adults and young people will be recruited and will volunteer online. Virtual volunteering will open the door to an entire new cadre of volunteers. They include the homebound and the disabled, who now will enjoy the benefits of connecting with others as they eliminate their own sense of isolation. And with more people working at home, companies will use their volunteer programs more strategically to bring employees together with customers, vendors, and one another.

It is our hope that a model like this will be customized for other parts of the world. Volunteer centers will be synonymous with volunteer action in every community throughout the world. They will be known for their ability to tap the best available resources to mobilize volunteers and help make communities healthier places to live. Volunteer centers, through their partnership with the Points of Light Foundation, are at the core of a burgeoning movement spearheaded by the foundation that encourages neighbors, neighborhoods, and entire communities to connect to one another, creating a dynamic volunteer force. That is our vision. Our challenge is to make that vision a reality.

A responsible citizen helps address concerns and finds effective solutions to poverty and injustice, and volunteering helps people take action. Ultimately, we the people, the global citizens, are the ones who make choices about our future. If we are the solution to serious social problems, then our responsibility must be to each other. If we are successful in building a better society for the future, then perhaps today's social problems will be remembered simply as the growing pains of our past. In the end, the spirit of volunteering may be one of the most effective ways to change the world, to address the world as global citizens. I am deeply encouraged by our progress, but there is still much more work to be done.

So remember, in the quiet hours when we are alone, and there is nobody to tell us what fine people we are, we come sometimes upon a moment in which we wonder, not how much money we are earning, nor how famous we have become, but what good we are doing.

Good Governance and Civic Engagement

5

WILLIAM REUBEN

Good governance and civic engagement are two key ingredients in the creation of a new civic culture of responsibility. Good governance and civic engagement need to address the fact that the wealthiest fifth of the world's people consume 86 percent of all goods and services, while the poorest fifth consumes 1 percent. Good governance and civic engagement need to address the fact that 1.2 billion people live on less than one dollar a day. Good governance and civic engagement need to prevent income disparities in countries like Guatemala, Paraguay, and Brazil, where the lowest 20 percent of the population receives only 2 percent of the income while the highest 20 percent of the population receives roughly 60 percent of the income.

Good governance and civic engagement need to prevent conflict. Eighty percent of the world's twenty poorest countries today have suffered from a major conflict in the past fifteen years. Conflict in Africa is causing a loss of 2 percent of annual economic growth across the continent. Good governance and civic engagement need to stress public accountability in order to address the positive correlation between high corruption and low per capita GDP.

But how are these two terms tied together in a meaningful and effective way? I would like to share some thoughts about this linkage and its implications for civic organizations

Contradictory, Not Antagonistic Relationship

There is a fundamental misunderstanding regarding the role of civic engagement in development resulting from what I would consider an Anglo-Saxon interpretation of civil society and a prevailing new

---

William Reuben serves as coordinator of the NGO and Civil Society Unit at the World Bank and as senior civil society specialist.

classical understanding of the role of the state in development, which perceives the state and civil society as antagonistic elements. Civil society and the state have a contradictory relationship. They do not necessarily play antagonistic roles in development—neither one replaces the other. The existence of a strong civil society does not preclude the existence of a robust state. Moreover, there is strong evidence that an effective and sound public sector depends very much on the existence of a dynamic civil society and strong citizen involvement in the public realm. By the same token, the existence of a robust public sector, with its capacity to enforce the rule of law, set clear rules of engagement for civil society, and promote sound public policy, has proven to provide an appropriate environment for civic engagement.

Any governance crisis expresses a fundamental contradiction between citizenry and the state. The fact that the power exercised by the states through law, coercion, and the demonstration of public resources is the result of the takeover of citizen sovereignty permeates the entire range of tensions that characterizes this relationship. This contradiction has existed since the emergence of the state. It takes on different shapes and grows by several degrees according to the characteristics of the political regimes and the level of disjuncture between ruling institutions and citizens.

The smaller the extent to which citizens feel represented and received by public institutions, the larger the governance crisis. The greater the degree of separation between the action of rulers and citizen's expectations and control over rulers' actions, the greater the governance crisis. However, this statement is not as simple as it appears because it embeds two distinct elements on the same side of the equation: expectations and representations.

The majority of citizens may feel that their values are represented and respected by a given government, yet that does not inevitably mean that their expectations are fulfilled. Representation encompasses the existence and functioning of democratic institutions and mechanisms of control over those who exercise power. Fulfillment of expectations is linked to the capacity of public institutions to manage and deliver public goods. There is a struggle between these two basic elements and a tension between decisiveness in fulfilling expectations and accountability in holding public power.

The point of encroachment of these two contradictory elements defines the type of regime, and therefore the likely political solutions, to address the governance dilemma. Tyrannies will tend to exhibit high levels of decisiveness with low levels of accountability. Deadlock regimes will tend to exhibit the opposite. Other regimes will use a more balanced mixture of the two elements to work out the governance equation.

New Set of Accountability Mechanisms

I would like to discuss briefly a new set of social mechanisms of accountability, characterized by their vertical nature and the exercise of direct participation of civil society organizations and citizens at large. We in the social development department of the World Bank have identified and are promoting four types of social accountability mechanisms that express the demand side of accountability and that occur at different stages of the policy sequence. These mechanisms operate along the budget and public expenditure cycle, understanding that budgets and their execution more thoroughly reflect actual policy decisions and their implementations. The assumption is that even though budgets and actual expenditures are covered by the mystical views of public accounting, they are dressed down relative to the rhetoric attached to policy statements and declarations. In that sense, they are more trackable and subject to public scrutiny.

(1) The first mechanism is *participatory budget formulation,* such as seen in Porto Alegre, Brazil. (2) The second is *budget analysis and demystification,* which has been implemented in many developing and developed countries by independent NGOs and dependent civil society groups, who analyze budgets and try to demystify the budget composition and share their views with the rest of the population to raise awareness about budgets.

The need for a third mechanism, (3) *budget tracking,* arises from institutional weaknesses such as opportunities for patronage, and leakages, and the failure of disbursed funds to reach all the intended beneficiaries. By identifying the elusive bureaucratic channels through which funds flow, civic groups can highlight bottlenecks in the flow of resources and other systemic differences. There is a recent experience in Argentina called the Social Monitor, by which a consortium of civil society organizations, NGOs, are monitoring public expenditure in the social emergency programs of the government of Argentina.

The fourth type of intervention is (4) *service delivery monitoring*, in which the performance of selected publicly funded agencies is assessed by the beneficiaries through a specific mechanism of survey called Report Cards.

Evidence so far indicates that the use of appropriate mechanisms of social accountability may become a promising alternative to both enhancing controls over public institutions and the use of public resources, and rendering those institutions more effective and responsive to the needs and aspirations of the board.

Institutional Capacity

However, social accountability systems do not occur in a vacuum. This is probably the most important challenge for these mechanisms to work. There is an ongoing debate about the conditions that enable effective and sustainable civic engagement and social accountability. Almost all parties agree that the context and the civil society capacity to exercise social agency are the two most important factors. In other words, effective civic engagement requires the prevalence of an enabling environment and the exercise of institutional capacities in civil society organizations to influence public debate in order to hold public institutions accountable.

The existence of institutional capacity of civil society organizations is key in this process. The presence of resilient responsive and credible organizations is a critical component of civic engagement. This entails building the capacity of these organizations to become financially sustainable and adequately skilled. It also implies the development of attributes and flexibility to learn from and communicate with the external world through the establishment of regional and global networks. But, as I stated before, the most important factor is fostering the credibility of civil society to mobilize social adherence and support, while spreading credibility is key for the role of civil society in social accountability.

The old conundrum of clinical studies deserves particular attention when civil society engages in social accountability initiatives. Transparent management of their representation, and the acceptance that poor and excluded groups do not necessarily enjoy the same access to resources, information, voice, and negotiation as do other well-established civil society organizations, are the bottom line of any substantive step toward creating sustainable and effective systems of social accountability.

Different levels of access to powers and economic resources can be found within civil society and among all civil society organizations. It is likely that the lower levels of institutional development, an influence characterized by civil society organizations of the poor, lead to what I used to call "civic exclusion." Many hurdles, such as lack of access to information, resources, and political leverage, prevent these organizations of the poor from engaging in public debate and public policy implementation. Major efforts in supporting the enabling an environment for civic engagement and civil society capacity building should focus on helping the poor and other excluded groups to develop their own presence in policymaking processes and service delivery activities.

As indicated above, civic inclusion should be at the core of any strategy geared toward increasing social accountability and the effectiveness of civic engagement, and international NGOs play a key role in this process.

Standards for NGOs

6

NGO Legitimacy, Integrity, Accountability, and Responsibility

JERRY JOHN RAWLINGS

It is a great pleasure and an honor to share with leaders of the NGO community my very heartfelt desires and aspirations. I have attended so many meetings where we have had to mouth all kinds of political language that makes a lot of sense, but which does not carry as much of the sincerity of the heart. But the WANGO annual conference is one meeting that has made me feel very much at home because most of the speakers that I have listened to, starting from the initial group, and the various participatory ladies and gentlemen who interacted with the various speakers, have made me feel very much at home. I have to admit that you are going to have a problem to peel me off this group. I intend to apply and to become a very active member of WANGO.

Let me take this opportunity to introduce to you my wife, Nana. [Editor's note: Nana Agyeman-Rawlings is president of one of the largest NGOs in Africa, the 31st December Women's Movement, which has a membership of about 2 million. Among many activities, this NGO has set up over nine hundred preschool facilities in its bid to empower women of Ghana, established cottage-type industries, acted as a pressure group to outlaw certain customs such as female genital mutilation, and encouraged women to enter into politics.] Quite frankly, without her efforts throughout Ghana, we would not have many of the parliamentarians who ended up in our legislative assembly. This is a lady who has won my heart since I was fifteen years old. It took me an additional seven years to get as close as holding her hand. As she latter put it to me, her father sent her to school to learn how to

---

H.E. Flt. Lt. Jerry John Rawlings is former president of the Republic of Ghana (1981–2000). In 2001, Flight Lieutenant Rawlings was designated by UN Secretary-General Kofi Annan as a United Nations Eminent Person for International Voluntarism, and he is a joint recipient of the 1993 World Hunger Prize.

study and not to get acquainted with boys. I am a Catholic and she is Protestant, and I was almost excommunicated locally in the school by my Catholic father, Father John, a very tough Irish father, because I walked out of the Catholic Church and went and joined the Protestant Church, because she was a member of the choir group.

Freedom and Morality

Let me start with a very interesting incident that happened in 1992, when we had to transform our government from a military government into a multiparty democracy. During the 1992 election campaign period, a lady was invited to climb onto the platform, and she was showering us with so many praises about how much we have done for her, and for women in general, and so forth and so on. When it came to my turn, and I climbed onto the platform, I had to disappoint this lady in the sense that I told her, "Madame, as much as I appreciate all the beautiful things you've said about my government, and what we've done for you, quite frankly the truth is that we didn't do all those things for you. All we did was to unchain you culturally, traditionally, and free you, and all that was achieved was done through your own free will, because you obtained your freedom, your freedom that had been deprived from you all those years."

If we are talking about the power of responsibility, it has a very strong moral basis. The spirit of volunteerism derives its power from a freedom, or a sense of freedom, or the quality of freedom that is related to morality. We have denied our people that level of freedom for so long. When we untied those ropes around womanhood in Africa, or in my country of Ghana, the freedom gave expression in such a constructive way that there was no way I was going to stand up there and take credit for what womanhood had been able to achieve for themselves and for their children. For me, that is just one little classical example of the exercise of a sense of responsibility, and its need for an atmosphere or an ambience of justice.

The absence of political justice undermines economic and social justice. In other words, for anybody to want to make any progress of any kind, whether you want to live in your little area of riches or I have to live in my little corner of poverty, what we want to see is that justice must permeate society. This is why I stated that I felt so much at home, particularly when I heard the first four speakers: WANGO Secretary General Taj Hamad, the Honorable Oscar Arias, Mr. William Reuben from the World Bank, and Ms. Mei Cobb from the Points of Light Foundation. Listening to them, I realized that if I had been a member of the panel, I would not have had anything more to say because they understood the roots of what gives birth to the spirit of volunteerism and the spirit of a sense of responsibility.

NGOs and Volunteerism

NGOs foster a culture of humane responsibility in present times between the "haves" and the "have-nots" in this global village of ours. In recent times there has been a very remarkable growth in the number of NGOs as people bind together to address a wide range of human needs such as poverty alleviation, sustainable development, human rights advocacy, and HIV/AIDS awareness, amongst others. If we had time, I would discuss a lot more on the extent of damage that HIV/AIDS is doing to the global community and especially in Africa. But we will have to deal with this some other time.

NGOs by their very nature epitomize the spirit of volunteerism, fueled by their desire to make a positive contribution to human society. However, the spirit of volunteerism does not emanate out of a vacuum, but is based entirely on a clear understanding of the role of civil society in a process that fosters real achievements and improvements in the economic, social, and political life of a people.

My personal experiences have proved time and again that the spirit of responsibility and volunteerism is, for the most part, based on the prevalence rooted in the issue of social, political, and economic justice. This is achieved only through the process of empowering and not disempowering civil society. It is my candid view that if civil society loses its empowerment process, it loses its moral sense of belonging and its sense of responsibility.

The growth in both the number and the achievements of NGOs worldwide is very heartwarming. Ghana, for example, is a country of numerous successful rural development projects carried out by NGOs in collaboration with local communities. And in the area of preventive health initiatives, we have received critical support for child immunization programs to the extent that we have been able to bring polio to its knees, with many more such successes.

Legitimacy, Integrity, and Accountability

While acknowledging the strides that NGOs have made over the years in alleviating pain, suffering, and supplementing the role of governments, it is imperative that we become conscious of NGOs that are essentially one-man or one-woman operations. With little more than a letterhead, an e-mail address, and a superficially convincing promotional line of advertisement, they have succeeded in securing funding projects from reputable international donors. These NGOs ultimately raise serious concerns bordering on their legitimacy in terms of whom they speak for, and how differences in opinion are resolved where grassroots communities can strengthen resources. These NGOs raise questions bordering on their integrity and accountability in terms of who enjoys the benefits and who suffers the costs of their actions, primarily at the grassroots level in the areas that receive aid, as well as in the communities that donate.

A third concern borders on the substance of structure, and by this I am referring to questions on how to deal with the challenges of genuine international governance, decision-making, and the issue of vital communication links vis-à-vis the intended target groups in broad project planning and implementation, as well as their evaluation.

In addressing these issues, I strongly urge all NGOs to address a fundamental question that mimics the desire to move from their role as unhappy agents of a foreign aid system in decline to where we want to be as real peoples working for international cooperation in the emerging global arena. We must maintain our integrity to ensure that when we feel that governments are going wrong, our criticisms must be constructive in much the same way that our criticisms of the populace must be constructive.

So also must the feedback be with the donor community. We must not be seen as an appendage of the foreign policy of a foreign power that provides the wherewithal. I am sure that every NGO will interpret this challenge in a different way. This does not matter so long as you are an NGO whose qualities are transparent, you are accountable, and you do everything to demonstrate the issue of propriety in what you do.

I have highlighted some of the prospects and problems of NGOs, not because I doubt the dedication, commitment, and compassion of the great majority of NGOs, but I do so in the ultimate sense of goodwill to ensure the optimum contribution of NGOs to global development and social justice, the very desire of each and every one of us.

Recommendations

I would like to make a few suggestions or recommendations. In order to forestall some of these problems, we must make it possible to bring to the attention of our very governments what we can do, in order to prevent them from unduly regulating our activities in our countries. In this respect, I would like to call upon WANGO to come up with a standard, or criteria, for operating procedures as guidelines for NGOs worldwide. I say this because I think it is very important for us to maintain our integrity, because the global community is going through a transition.

In this respect, I would like to go on to suggest a few guidelines that could be included. One is that the NGO stroke the government interface management, and coordination of NGO programs and projects with local and national development programs must be done in such a way as not to create areas of antagonism. I would also like to suggest that a standard on the proportion of NGO budgets for administrative purposes should be well-examined, making sure that we leave the bulk of the amount of donations for the fieldwork, for the projects, and not for administrative luxuries.

Another point that I would like to make, and thankfully we have made a bit of progress in this respect, is that we must also ensure that as we move into the communities, we should not allow religious and political interference in local affairs to divide us.

The last point I would like to make is that the standards of subcontracting NGO work to local NGOs and consultants and their verification must be made as efficaciously and as efficiently as we possibly can in order to maintain integrity.

Global Togetherness and Responsibility

In conclusion, I hope that the phenomenal increase in NGO activities worldwide will foster a culture of global togetherness and responsibility among the peoples of the world toward each and every one of us, and that we all will help each other to achieve and realize a new world social and economic order.

I would like thank the executives of WANGO, the organizers of the annual conference, and those who made WANGO Annual Conference 2002 successful and our stay so comfortable, and to assure them that for this kind of efficient organization they should not be surprised if they should find us here the next time around.

Let me also take this opportunity to say a big thank you and to congratulate especially the WANGO 2002 award winners for their vision, or rather their visions, and their tenacity of purpose, which make it possible for them to lead so many of our people to support them in achieving this very recognition that led to their winning of these awards.

I would like to say a big thank you to Almighty God. I want to say, Good Lord, that I hope most sincerely that You will give us the strength and the energy to continue the work that we have started and to build upon what we have already achieved and to make those who have eyes to see, but refuse to see, who have ears to hear, but cannot hear, a mind to recognize what needs to be done and are closing their minds, that You open up their eyes, their ears, and their minds to the fruits of what we are doing. It is only for the benefit of humanity.

Part II
NGOs, Human Security, and the United Nations

Introduction

Among the most pressing contemporary crises facing humanity is the menace of terrorism. The September 11 terror attacks in the United States demonstrated that a small, committed group of individuals can thwart even the world's strongest national defense, and that national security is not confined within national boundaries. One-third of the people killed on September 11 were non-Americans, citizens of more than sixty countries. While the cost of the attack was perhaps less than $1 million, the economic and social impacts were global, resulting in billions of dollars in worldwide economic loss. Likewise, the world continues to face threats from weapons of mass destruction, whether nuclear, biological, or chemical. There is an urgent need for the building of a human security community.

NGOs have an important role in any broad-based vision of human security for the twenty-first century. Understandably, the definition of NGOs is broad and thus includes even extremist organizations. Even those NGOs with good programs can hinder peace and security when promoting self-interests over those of the people they serve. However, most NGOs play, or can play, important roles that can advance human security. Certain NGOs address and help relieve the underlying conditions in which terrorism is spawned, such as poverty and lack of democracy, by providing services and humanitarian relief, health care, advocacy, and so forth. Some offer educational and monitoring programs. Others are directly engaged in conflict prevention and resolution, high-level mediation, land mine clearance, helping refugees, and infrastructure building. Still others provide expert analyses and consul, and early warning mechanisms. As a third sector between governments and corporations—and what some call the fifth estate—NGOs can provide some comparative advantages, such as highly motivated staff, regional expertise, and organizational freedom and flexibility.

The papers in this section provide some perspective on the

current and potential role NGOs play, good and bad, in combating terrorism and weapons of mass destruction—and more broadly in building a human security community. Since the United Nations is a central intergovernmental institution for combating terrorism and advancing human security, this section also includes discussions on the relationship between NGOs and the United Nations. Furthermore, the papers in this section examine perceptions of humanity's security future.

It should be emphasized that a diversity of viewpoints is represented in these papers. Since there is a lack of unanimity on many of the issues raised, and the topic of terrorism in general and the Middle East and Kashmir in particular can touch the emotions of many people, some of the papers generated a lot of debate when presented. Regardless of one's own position, these papers are quite helpful in shedding light on an important topic.

Legal Personality and the Role of Non-Governmental Organizations and Non-State Political Entities in the United Nations System

7

RUTH WEDGWOOD

The reach of international legal personality beyond the nation-state is a formal question that may interest analytical lawyers more than legal sociologists. In whatever way one chooses to pose the question, nonetheless, the evolving role of non-governmental organizations (NGOs) and non-state political entities within the international system requires critical scrutiny.[1] In particular, one must judge whether giving voice and standing to these new actors will help or hinder the primary tasks of the United Nations system in resolving internal and international conflicts, and enforcing human rights.

Non-governmental organizations have, lately, been celebrated as the soil and seed for a new international civil society—to democratize the conversation about international matters beyond the sometimes self-regarding concerns of nation-states. In an era when civil rights and democracy are regarded as fundamental, autocratic governments may seem unsatisfactory representatives of their populations. And when transnational processes of the economy and movements of population often have their own tempo outside the control of governments, the pertinence of ambassadors and foreign offices may seem questionable.

The entry of NGOs into international fora predates the UN system, of course. Foreign antislavery societies, conferences for

---

Ruth Wedgwood is professor of law at Yale Law School and director of the Program on International Law and Organizations at the School of Advanced International Studies at Johns Hopkins University. Ms. Wedgwood also serves on the United Nations Human Rights Committee, the implementation body for the International Covenant on Civil and Political Rights.

world peace, and other gatherings of the flock have long competed with governments in seeking to claim legitimacy and mobilize support. At San Francisco in 1945, public-minded associations pushed to have human rights included in the UN Charter as one of the new organization's charged purposes. In Article 71 of the UN Charter, NGOs were acknowledged as useful partners in the proceedings of the UN Economic and Social Council (ECOSOC),[2] a role that may have seemed especially important at a time when the future preeminence of the Bretton Woods international financial institutions was not yet clear. "Consultative status" was available to properly qualified international NGOs, allowing them to attend ECOSOC proceedings, to place items on the agenda of the council, and to submit written statements for official circulation. These privileges are also available in ECOSOC's subsidiary bodies, including the Commission on Sustainable Development and the Commission on the Status of Women.[3]

Wariness of the nature of private associations—the acknowledgement that private power can be as problematic as public power—was built into the seminal ECOSOC Resolution 1296. This framework resolution required that NGOs have a democratically adopted constitution and policy set through a "conference, congress or other representative body." The enigmatic role of money in politics, including international politics—that the free marketplace of ideas can be cornered when policy campaigns are bankrolled by interested parties—brought a matching prescription of financial transparency. Any financial donations and any government support of an NGO had to be revealed to ECOSOC's Committee on Non-Governmental Organizations. And a concern for the efficiency of ECOSOC (showing an early innocence, perhaps) brought the stricture that consultative arrangements should not "overburden the Council" or "transform it from a body for co-ordination of policy and action…into a general forum for discussion."[4]

The New World of NGOs

The number of NGOs engaged at the UN has grown exponentially. In 1948, 41 NGOs had consultative status with ECOSOC; in 1968, 377

NGOs; in 1998, 1350 NGOs had consultative status with ECOSOC.[5] Another 1,550 organizations are associated with the UN Department of Public Information, with a right to receive UN documents and enter its halls freely. The NGO role of intermediation may be bypassed in a new age of the Internet and websites. But until recently, with little reporting of UN proceedings by the news media, an archaic documents system that made UN business largely impenetrable, and a recondite political structure, the work of the UN has been opaque to most ordinary citizens. It was necessary to have a familiar at court to assure that one's interests, including public interests, were represented. The role of NGOs in following UN proceedings and expressing the views of sectors of the public was useful to all sides.

NGOs have been important to the UN, both to member-states and the Secretariat, as a way of mobilizing publics. The independent sources of legitimacy of many NGOs, in their affiliation with church groups, with widely held political philosophies, or with public professions, and their grassroots structure, have allowed NGOs to summon public support for formal UN decisions and emerging proposals, complementing and challenging the direct voice of governments.

In aid delivery, NGOs have become an integral part of the UN administrative apparatus. The High Commissioner for Refugees and the Department of Humanitarian Affairs, for example, solicit financial support and aid packages from member governments, but much of their work on the ground is necessarily subcontracted to international and national NGOs.[6] In conflict situations, when national governments have been reluctant to deploy their civilian and military personnel, NGOs have remained in exceedingly dangerous conditions, sometimes in a formal arrangement with the United Nations, but often simply assisting ad hoc in the distribution of aid and organization of relief efforts.[7] The key role of NGOs in the relief and refugee sector is shown in the new arrangements of the UN emergency relief coordinator. The International Committee of the Red Cross, the International Federation of Red Cross and Red Crescent Societies, and three consortia of NGOs—InterAction, the International Council of Voluntary Agencies, and the Steering Committee for Humanitarian Response—serve with the heads of UN agencies such as the UN

Development Program, UNICEF, and the World Food Program, on the UN Inter-Agency Standing Committee. This is the "central humanitarian policy-making body in the UN system."[8] UNICEF, the UN Development Program, and the World Food Program also invite NGOs to attend and speak at agency executive board meetings.[9] The new UN program to coordinate work on AIDS, the Joint Program on HIV/AIDS, permits NGO representatives to serve on its coordinating board together with the representatives of twenty-two member states, UN agencies, and people with HIV/AIDS.[10]

In human rights monitoring, the role of NGOs has also been central.[11] Groups such as the International Commission of Jurists, Amnesty International, the Lawyers Committee for Human Rights, and Human Rights Watch have provided close-to-the-ground monitoring and reportage with a single-mindedness and independence that few national governments can afford. Human rights groups have been willing to break through the stifling etiquette that inhibited governments from criticizing each other in formal proceedings. The era when countries could not be criticized by name in UN fora has passed, but the public reproof of countries by the UN Human Rights Commission still requires assembling the votes of government representatives, whose countries have many fish to fry. The NGOs provide a useful corrective to this trimming and tucking. As Felice Gaer notes, the ultimate tribute to the power of NGOs in the human rights monitoring process is reflected in the competition of violator countries for election to the Commission on Human Rights and the ECOSOC/NGO committee, seeking "to protect themselves from a negative vote and to reply to and often intimidate the nongovernmental organisations."[12]

Formal consultative status has permitted NGOs to propose agenda items and submit statements to the UN Human Rights Commission, and its Subcommission on the Prevention of Discrimination and the Protection of Minorities.[13] The subcommission's Working Group on Indigenous Populations has extended the same privilege to many NGOs, largely consisting of indigenous groups, even where they lack formal consultative status. Regionally, NGOs have been permitted to lodge complaints with the Inter-American Commission on Human Rights,[14] and have been able to provide legal and investigative assistance.[15] Plainly, a premier contribution of human rights organizations has been their skill in bringing human rights complaints to public attention through the media, with investigative reports, public platforms for victims and dissidents, and cultivation of a public voice.

In the norm-building exercises of international conferences and in treaty negotiations, the NGOs have gained perhaps their most prominent new role. The Women's Conference in Beijing, for example, defied the Chinese government's wish to diminish the influence of attending NGOs. Though the NGO meeting was held at a considerable distance from the states assembly, the impact on Chinese society was widely remarked. NGOs played a prominent role in the environmental negotiations at Rio, with a formal role preserved for future review conferences.[16] In the campaign against land mines, the NGO community is given credit for accelerating the political process, successfully seeking the transfer of negotiations from the UN Committee on Disarmament in Geneva to a convocation of "like-minded" states in Ottawa. This yielded a Treaty on Anti-Personnel Landmines in 1997,[17] a signal achievement in so short a time, though a cautionary tale as well, since the negotiations failed to accommodate the expressed military needs of the United States in defending South Korea, and also failed to gain the adherence of land mine manufacturing countries such as the Russian Federation and China.

NGOs were extraordinarily prominent at the Rome negotiations for a permanent international criminal court in June and July 1998, lobbying national delegations and claiming to represent the sense of the meeting by keeping a tally of announced country positions on the treaty draft's difficult details. (These tallies were important to the UN Conference Bureau in the formulation of the final treaty draft, presented for an up-or-down vote without amendment on the final day of the conference.) In the view of some, the Rome experience may show the solipsistic danger of a close relationship between NGOs and international personnel. Mutual agreement between NGOs and like-minded states, or between NGOs and secretariat officials, does not mean that a treaty will reflect the real political forces necessary for its successful implementation (the contrast between Chile's vote in favor of the international criminal court and its reticence about the arrest of Pinochet, is one case in point). Nonetheless, it is indisputable that the tone and tenor of the Rome conference was in large part set by NGOs.

In international adjudication, NGOs have also found an increasing role in providing information to the decision-makers. The International Court of Justice (ICJ), designed to resolve state-to-state complaints, has not yet followed the practice of some other courts in permitting nonparties to advise as amicus curiae in contentious cases. But several of the judges have expressed private interest in the practice. In the recent case on the Legality of the Use by a State of Nuclear Weapons in Armed Conflict,[18] the Court refused a formal request for participation as amicus curiae by a nongovernmental group (Physicians for the Prevention of Nuclear War), yet the government of Zimbabwe included information from the International Committee on the Red Cross as part of its filing. Professor Shelton has argued that the ICJ is entitled within its existing statute and rules to allow amicus participation in such advisory cases[19] (indeed, the ICJ did so in the South-West Africa case, though the NGO in question failed to file on time). Amicus filings in contentious cases would arguably require an amendment of the Court's rules.

Amicus curiae, including NGOs, have been permitted to appear before the International Criminal Tribunal for the former Yugoslavia,[20] and have appeared before the European Court of Justice,[21] the European Court of Human Rights,[22] and the Inter-American Court of Human Rights.[23] In the European Court of Justice, intervenors have included trade associations such as the Federation of European Bearing Manufacturers Associations as well as more classical "public interest" group,[24] a latitude that the UN system might bear in mind when UN activities come to affect commercial and industrial practices.

Even in the Security Council's deliberations on international peace and security, NGOs have newly been permitted a role. The Council has traditionally been an opaque political organ, conducting its most delicate discussions in private. (Indeed, some of the pressure to "democratize" the Council and make it more representative of member countries has stemmed from the Council's discreet practices.). Yet on two recent occasions, to gather information and advice on the crisis in the Great Lakes region of Africa, the Council has engaged in consultations with NGOs. These were informally dubbed "Arria" consultations, after the former permanent representative of Venezuela who initiated the practice. Technically, the Council adjourned its session and continued in an informal meeting. But parliamentary technique aside, the Security Council recognized that NGOs working in remote areas have a unique pool of information on local conditions and political currents. So, too, recent UN peacekeeping operations and UN force commanders have discovered that NGOs working in the area provide one of the few reliable sources of local intelligence concerning political conditions, refugee flows, and relief needs.

Another unique security role for NGOs in the international system is evidenced in mediation work, in particular, mediation by the faith community of Saint Egidio in Mozambique. Saint Egidio *(Comunità di Sant'Egidio)* had particular stature with the Renamo insurgents in the former Portuguese colony after many years of humanitarian work in the countryside, also because a widely noted audience with insurgents against Portuguese colonial rule was held in the Vatican in the mid-1970s. Their success in facilitating peace accords in the Mozambique conflict was notable. Saint Egidio has also attempted mediation in Algeria and in Albania. The informal political groupings of states that have been of assistance to the secretary-general in resolving civil conflicts—such as the Friends of the Secretary General for Haiti, El Salvador, and Georgia—may be mimicked in the future by nonstate mediators that have equal standing with the warring parties.

Non-government actors have also entered the field as military forces. One may decline to use the term NGO, for these actors are for-profit companies solicited by state parties to strengthen their security. Operators such as Executive Outcomes and Sandline International have been involved in African conflicts including in Namibia, Sierra Leone, and Zaire, and are often paid through swap transactions involving mineral concessions.[25] Military Professional Resources, Inc. (MPRI) was similarly recruited to train the Croatian forces for Operation Storm in 1995, helping to end the Bosnian war (though allowing a brutal swath of Croatian ethnic cleansing in the Krajina). MPRI has also operated the "train and equip" program for the Federation armed forces in Bosnia as part of the Dayton package. This privatization of the core security functions of the state is highly problematic, to be sure—it challenges international law's traditional strictures against mercenaries and decouples any link between military strength and the popularity of a government. The private forces have not always been delicate in their methods, and lack the direct responsibility of a government under the Geneva system of humanitarian law. But they appear to be a new feature of a period in which the juridical state may not command loyalty among varied groups, and in which the limits of postcolonial state-building have become evident. In theory, there is no reason why a third-party security function must be for-profit. Volunteer forces could operate as well.

The new importance of NGOs and actors is thus undeniable. Though NGOs do not enjoy the legal accoutrements of states—they cannot sue in the ICJ, have no vote in the General Assembly, and do not enjoy the protections of territorial integrity and political sovereignty—and hence may not be said to have full legal personality, nonetheless NGOs are real actors in international systems, affecting outcomes, mobilizing publics, and constraining states.

Problems of NGOs

The problems posed by the newly active role of NGOs are also apparent. First, NGOs lack the political legitimacy of the state itself. To be sure, states are often undemocratic and do not have to pass any minimum test of popular participation in government in order to take their seat in the General Assembly. The UN's most recent step toward reaffirming an international right to democracy was, unhappily, a rather timid document.[26] But states do purport to speak for their whole population, even if the method of measuring general will is deficient. NGOs on the other hand are avowedly limited membership organizations, in which policy may be set by a few people. The strength of an NGO's voice may not reflect a breadth of membership, but instead be amplified by the deep pockets of a few members.

NGOs' direct political operations at the international level may also seem an evasion of the ordinary give-and-take of democratic national politics. Every position that an NGO espouses could be presented at the national level, seeking reflection and inclusion in the official positions of a state member of the UN. If a particular minority group is systematically excluded from national political participation or lacks the strength to have its interests reflected,[27] or if there is a majority that has difficulty mobilizing politically (often observed of women because of their responsibilities in the family), the pursuit of a direct voice at the international level is more understandable. International voice provides a form of proportional representation, allowing small minorities and interest groups in many countries to aggregate their power to achieve effective influence. But the ground level challenge still remains: why shouldn't most NGO interests be mediated through the representation of the nation-state? The theory of pluralism and interest group politics presumes that even when a group cannot succeed in electing its own member as a direct representative, it may succeed in tipping an election to favor the more moderate of majority candidates. Its interests may be represented indirectly. Certainly the enfranchisement of blacks in the American South in the last thirty years has given weight to this claim. The availability of direct participation in the international arena may distract some interest groups from focusing reasonable efforts toward the achievement of influence in national politics, preferring to bypass the more local forum.

The "sheer number"[28] of NGOs is another reason for valuing the intermediation performed by nation-states. The General Assembly is thought to be a less efficient body than the Security Council for crisis response by dint of its 185 members. Yet NGOs number in the thousands; any obligation to include them in deliberations, other than through a representational scheme, would pose obvious problems.[29]

The direct intervention of interest groups at the international level creates a puzzle on what decision rule should be employed. In matters requiring a vote of the General Assembly or Security Council, the nation-state will continue to reign supreme, with votes tallied according to Charter requirements. But there are a great many discretionary decisions that rest with the Secretariat and specialized agencies. Many UN activities are funded through voluntary contributions and these can come from private sources. Private contributions may distort the choice of priority areas, and may even influence policy itself. Certainly in the operation of UN organs where the appearance of neutrality is essential, such as international war crimes tribunals, the receipt of private monies is troublesome. And there are concerns voiced, from time to time, that NGOs may seek greater influence within UN councils by providing undue material consideration to delegations from member countries.

The incompleteness of NGO representation of public society is also apparent when one sees which groups have chosen to take part in international proceedings. To be sure, industry and business took an active role at the UN Conference on the Environment at Rio, and the chemical industry has been deeply involved in the implementation of the Chemical Weapons Convention. Groups such as the National Rifle Association and the American tobacco industry have become newly involved in a defensive posture in UN affairs as UN agencies have begun to entertain the idea of regulating small arms traffic and controlling the use of nicotine as a pharmacological agent. Still, the bulk of NGOs espouse positions that may be considered liberal rather than conservative. The requirement that NGOs enjoy nonprofit status may have favored, at least initially, the representation of certain points of view. In the politics of Washington and Brussels, industry groups understand the importance of making their views known through lobbying and informational meetings with legislators and administrators. But in the multilateral arena of the UN, conservative groups have more often relied on the celebration of national sovereignty as a premier means of resisting UN actions, rather than attempting to enter interest group politics at the international level. UN delegations and Secretariat personnel must understand the truncated nature of the representation provided by NGO activity—that the voices of civil society at the international level are incomplete and typically give little weight to the private market sector.

Southern countries have also complained that NGO representation favors the North. Available financing for NGOs is more common in the industrialized economies of the North rather than the developing economies and emerging markets of the South. Just as the South has complained of the practice of using "seconded" personnel within the UN to help the organization carry out such critical functions as planning for peacekeeping operations, because such personnel come predominantly from developed nations, so too the South entertains a suspicion that its voice is inadequately heard through NGOs not indigenous to the region.

There are, as well, NGOs supported by government funds, directly or indirectly. Though this support is subject to disclosure in NGO filings with the Economic and Social Council, a so-called "Quango" (quasi-autonomous non-governmental organization) may appear to multiply the influence of a single nation in the UN's deliberations.

Certainly, in the dissemination of information to influence debate, NGOs have wielded a power that dwarfs some nation-states. Many First World NGOs are highly skilled in the use of the media and in the techniques of building a grassroots campaign to influence public opinion. The attractive aims of these campaigns may justify overlooking the question of appropriate influence. But one has to worry when the net effect of a campaign is to propound standards that nation-states have no intention of observing. International law's crab-wise progress has depended on maintaining a strong link between aspirational norms and the actual behavior of states, especially states with a stake in the subject matter. This state compliance is part of legitimacy, evidencing state consent, and of relevance, allowing international law to describe the international community as it is rather than as a political philosopher would have it be.

In recent multilateral negotiations, such as the treaty banning antipersonnel land mines, reached at Ottawa, or the Rome statute for a permanent criminal court, some would argue that the prominence of NGO voices distracted a number of "like-minded" governments from paying sufficient heed to useful compromises to bring along other key national actors, such as the United States, Russia, and China at Ottawa, and the United States and China at Rome. NGOs may create an inward turn, in which it is forgotten that a multilateral negotiation is designed to engineer a compromise among states rather than a perfect product that lacks widespread adherence. The emergence of the caucus of so-called "like-minded" states has brought this problem to the fore. Vocal support by international NGOs has at times seemed to distract the like-minded from the desirable task of gaining large power adherence.

Another question about NGOs is accountability—whether they should be bound by the same principles of legal responsibility and financial liability that attach to nation-states. One example mentioned in the literature is the boycott campaign conducted by Greenpeace against Royal Dutch Shell when the oil company proposed to scuttle an oil rig on the floor of the North Sea. The consumer boycott was highly effective, reducing Shell's sales in Germany by 30 percent, and Royal Dutch Shell abandoned the Brent Spar rig scuttling, even though Shell had received the necessary approvals from national and international agencies. Such a boycott might give rise to financial responsibility on the part of a state, Professor Spiro has suggested, but an NGO such as Greenpeace lacks any direct responsibility under international law[30] (any potential responsibility under national law faces limitations of the prescriptive and adjudicative jurisdiction of national courts). Without international personality, NGOs may avoid any adequate schema of responsibility.

So, too, when NGOs are used for program implementation by the UN, such as by UNHCR, methods of assuring their financial responsibility remain important. Recent criticism of the relief operations of UNHCR has centered on the question of whether monies distributed through some African NGOs were well-spent or not.[31]

The Future of NGOs

Despite these questions of legitimacy, it is hard to deny the function of NGOs in helping the arguably archaic structure of the UN adapt to a changed international system. In a time when the nation-state is less relevant to international transactions, NGOs help create a reasonable isomorphism between the structure of formal international organizations and the real actors in international politics. The state is no longer able to control the information received by its population with the exception of a few autarkic countries such as North Korea. The state is no longer in effective control of the economy, facing the attractions and the debilities of opening itself to global investment. So, too, the state is facing a competition for legitimacy and the loyalty of its citizens with the reemergence of substate actors such as ethnic groups and nations that demand autonomy or even independence. The state-to-state system of representation created at the UN thus no longer reflects many of the most powerful determinants of international and internal conflict. The NGO system allows some mitigation of this inadequacy as interests other than those of the state can make themselves known.

So, too, with the undemocratic structure of many UN members, it is attractive to allow dissentient and minority groups another bite at the apple, making their case directly when official diplomatic representatives will not deign to pass along their views. The UN Charter's preamble speaks of the representation of "peoples" of the world, and a voice for many indigenous minorities can only be obtained by bypassing the formal seating of state delegations. Special rapporteurs appointed by the Commission on Human Rights and the secretary-general can help fill out the portfolio of interests in other ways; for example, there is a special rapporteur for internally displaced persons—a group that cannot expect to wield much direct political power. NGOs also speak, if only indirectly, for groups that lack a national voice, and help to cure the representational inadequacies of an intergovernmental organization.

In a political system that still has some faith in "scientism"—use of expert knowledge to aid the resolution of problems—the NGOs will retain a role as well. Whether in environment, regulation of hazardous substances, refugee flows, or small-arms control, national governments may be goaded by parochial interests. The availability of expert information from NGOs can supplement the record that governments provide, and bolster the assurance of objectivity.

Finally, NGOs provide international organizations with a political opportunity that is as old as it is effective—the ability to appeal to ordinary people over the heads of government. There may be times when most governments fail to represent the preferences of their populations. The schemes of the Progressive era in American politics, the notion that elected representatives should be subject to check by referendum, recall, or direct instruction, can be mimicked through the use of NGOs. The mobilization of interested citizens through NGOs can give international organizations the chance to create their own constituency and allow them to show national governments that popularity can subsist with internationalism.

The Role of Non-State Political Entities

Substate political units have gained a new importance in international organizations since the end of the Cold War. With the outbreak of civil conflicts, the Security Council has felt compelled to address its decisions on peace and security to the real combatants on the ground, including insurgent forces such as the FMLN in El Salvador,[32] the PDK in Cambodia,[33] UNITA in Angola,[34] and "local Serb authorities" in Bosnia.[35] So, too, in the Dayton Peace Accord, the international community created new governmental entities close to nineteenth-century forms of demisovereignty. The peace settlement recognized the Muslim-Croat Federation and the breakaway Bosnian Serb polity, Republika Srpska, as so-called "entities" (a solecism whose Serbo-Croatian equivalent was not agreed upon at Dayton), each enjoying its own police force and army, and its own educational system, self-governing except for required deference to a national parliament and presidency on issues of foreign relations, national security, and national economic policy.

The absence of any formal international personality for these entities can be troublesome. It has created problems in aid distribution. For example, aid to Republika Srpska from the World Bank and the International Monetary Fund has to be distributed through a sovereign state, the overall national government of Bosnia and Herzegovina, which has not been functioning except when it is pushed by the international community's high representative. Republika Srpska is not permitted to take direct international responsibility for a loan even though its credit is at stake in making repayments. So, too, the distrust of the national government has led the Bosnian entities to pursue their own foreign policy interests through "special parallel relationships" with Croatia and the Federal Republic of Yugoslavia—creating an ethnic "near-abroad" and challenging the multiethnic ambition of Bosnia and Herzegovina. Direct international personality, at least in limited ways, might avoid the entities' crippling dependence on the international voices of more awesome neighbors.

Non-state political entities have also not shared the direct responsibility of governments under the conventions of humanitarian law. Although individual actors who commit grave breaches can and must be arrested by the territorial sovereign, the non-state political entity functioning as a local government may avoid direct international financial responsibility, even where it has instigated the acts. The effective observance of international humanitarian law in a conflict may also require backdoor negotiation if the warring parties include an insurgent or belligerent that has succeeded in displacing the international sovereign.

The invisibility of non-state political entities within the international legal system was designed, of course, to allow each nation-state the latitude to decide for itself how to implement its international obligations. But the insulation of such entities from direct international responsibility may also encourage behavior that takes international law lightly. In the United States, for example, Virginia declined to delay the execution of a Paraguayan defendant named Breard despite an admitted violation of the Vienna Convention on Consular Relations in the failure to notify the Paraguayan consul of Breard's arrest for murder. The ICJ ordered as a provisional measure that the United States "should take all measures at its disposal" to assure that the execution be delayed until a decision was made on the merits of the treaty claim.[36] The secretary of state requested Virginia to delay the execution, but the US solicitor general took the position in the Supreme Court that there was no direct power to order Virginia to do so.[37] Within a system of federalism, such incomplete power in the national government creates the possibility of unconstrained action—a subnational state can act without considering the question of financial responsibility. A lack of international legal personality on the part of substate political entities thus can detract from compliance with international law.

On the other hand, there is an argument that allowing direct international address to substate entities may at times make it harder to solve civil conflicts. In the former Soviet republic of Georgia, for example, there is a long-standing conflict between Tblisi and Sukhumi over the status of the Abkhaz region in the north. The Abkhaz consider themselves a distinct people, but enjoyed independence only for a brief period following the Russian revolution, making do thereafter with an "autonomous republic" within Georgia. In 1991, after the rupture of the Soviet Union, the Abkhaz declared their independence, and despite a population that is too small to be viable and the fierce fighting and embargoes that have shut down the economy, they have declined to return to any form of union. Though the wrongs and rights of the dispute are hard to untangle, one could argue that Abkhaz resistance to settlement is strengthened, rather than weakened, by the attention they have received from the international community, with a special representative of the secretary-general present in the area, and UN military observers. An Abkhaz political representative who was fluent on the Internet went so far as to set up a home page for the "Permanent Representative of Abkhazia to the United Nations"—using self-help to claim a formal international personality. It is an empirical question whether an international presence is likelier to salve or exacerbate civil war conflicts, but one should at least consider the possibility that giving international address to insurgents may delegitimize the current national government and give new confidence to the rebel group. Certainly in bilateral diplomacy, giving direct address to insurgent groups by foreign diplomats is seen as derisive of the authority of the existing government. Though the UN Security Council and secretary-general have a broad security responsibility, it needs to be carefully considered each time whether addressing the insurgent groups may create an undesirable form of moral equivalency.

Conclusion

The matter of international legal personality is best not answered as a formal question. We can easily agree that NGOs and non-state political entities do not enjoy the full panoply of rights and responsibilities of nation-states. But the interesting inquiry each time is whether according rights of participation and address or imposing some limited form of direct responsibility for non-state actors in the international community will usefully increase the capacity to resolve conflicts and enforce standards of human security. The test for the "privatization" of the international legal order must be a functional one. In the case of non-governmental organizations, their role has been seen as beneficial and creative, subject to suitable cautions. In the case of non-state political entities, the international community has treated with them from necessity where the nation-+state did not have full control of its own domain, but it remains to be seen whether these political imperatives may require a more formal status outside the state orientation of the Westphalian system.

Endnotes

1. The topic has won new attention from foreign policy analysts and the popular press. See P.J. Simmons, "Learning to Live with NGOs," *Foreign Policy,* vol. 112 (1998), 82; Jessica Mathews, "Power Shift," *Foreign Affairs,* vol. 76 (1997), 50; Paul Lewis, "Not Just Governments Make War or Peace," *New York Times,* 28 November 1998.

2. Article 71 UN Charter.
3. See generally Dianne Otto, "Non-governmental Organizations in the United Nations System: The Emerging Role of International Civil Society," HRQ, vol. 18 (1996), 107.
4. *Resolution 1296 of the Economic and Social Council, 1986,* UN Doc. E/4548. This seminal resolution has been revisited by the Council on several occasions, see, e.g., *ECOSOC Resolution 1993/80 of 30 July 1993* and *Resolution 1996/31 of 25 July 1996.*
5. Report of the Secretary-General, "Arrangements and practices for the interaction of NGOs in all activities of the United Nations system," General Assembly, 53rd session, UN Doc. A/53/170 of 10 July 1998, para. 2.
6. See generally Mark Duffield, "NGO Relief in War Zones: Toward an Analysis of the New Aid Paradigm," in: Thomas Weiss (ed.), *Beyond UN Subcontracting: Task-Sharing with Regional Security Arrangements and Service-Providing NGOs,* 1988.
7. The new *Convention on the Safety of United Nations and Associated Personnel,* UN Doc. A/RES/49/59, Annex, adopted by the General Assembly on 9 December 1994, does not protect private relief personnel unless their work is performed under formal contract with the United Nations. Some relief organizations have noted that such a formal link may be inconsistent with their necessary neutrality in the field. See Antoine Bouvier, *Convention on the Safety of UN and Associated Personnel: Presentation and Analysis,* IRRC, 1995, 638, 655.
8. See Report of the Secretary-General, "Arrangements and practices for the interaction of NGOs in all activities of the United Nations system" (note 5), para. 36.
9. *Id.*, paragraphs. 17–20.
10. *Id.*, paragraph. 30.
11. See generally Felice D. Gaer, "Reality Check: Human Rights NGOs Confront Governments at the UN," in: Thomas Weiss/Leon Gordenker (eds.), *NGOs, the UN, and Global Governance,* 1996, 51-66.
12. *Id.*, 53.
13. See generally Dianne Otto (note 3).
14. American Convention on Human Rights (Pact of San José), ILM, vol. 9 (1970), 673, Art. 44. For example, the human rights clinic of the University of Minnesota School of Law has prosecuted complaints concerning the practice of juvenile capital punishment before the Inter-American Commission. See generally Martin Olz, "Non-Governmental Organizations in Regional Human Rights Systems," *Columbia Human Rights Law Review,* vol. 28 (1997), 307.
15. Cecilia Medina Quiroga, *The Battle of Human Rights. Gross, Systematic Violations and the Inter-American System,* 1988.
16. *Report of the United Nations Conference on Environment and Development,* Rio de Janeiro, 3–14 June 1992, UN Doc. A/CONF.151/26, para. 27.4.

17. "Convention on the Prohibition of the Use, Stockpiling, Production, and Transfer of Anti-Personnel Mines and on Their Destruction," ILM, vol. 36 (1997), 1507.

18. 1996 ICJ, 66 (Advisory Opinion of 8 July 1996).

19. Dinah Shelton, "The Participation of Non-Governmental Organizations in International Judicial Proceedings," AJIL, vol. 88 (1994), 611, 628.

20. See Decision on the Defence Motion for Interlocutory Appeal on Jurisdiction, *Prosecutor v. Duško Tadi a/k/a Dule,* International Criminal Tribunal for the former Yugoslavia, Case No. IT-94-1-AR72, Appeals Chamber, 2 October 1995, Decision on the Objections of the Republic of Croatia to the Issuance of Subpoenae Duces Tecum, *Prosecutor v. Blaški,* Case No. IT-95-14-PT, Trial Chamber II, 18 July 1997, reversed in part and affirmed in part in Judgment on the Request of the Republic of Croatia for Review of the Decision of the Trial Chamber II of 18 July 1997, *Prosecutor v. Blaški,* Case No. IT-95-14-AR108 bis, Appeals Chamber, 2 October 1997.

21. See Protocol on the Statute of the Court of Justice of the European Economic Community of 17 April 1957, Art. 37, 298 UNTS 147, as amended by Council Decision 88/591, 1989 O.J. (C 215) 1; Shelton (note 19), 628.

22. See Protocol No. 11 to the Convention for the Protection of Human Rights and Fundamental Freedoms, ETS, No. 155 of 11 May 1994, Art. 36 (third-party intervention); Council of Europe: Explanatory Report and Protocol No. 11, ILM, vol. 33 (1993), 943; *Andrew Drzemczewski/Jens Meyer-Ladewig*, Principal Characteristics of the New ECHR Control Mechanism, as Established by Protocol 11, HRLJ, vol. 15 (1994), 81.

23. See Martin Olz (note 14), 359; Shelton (note 19).

24. See Shelton (note 19), 628, n. 114.

25. See David Shearer, "Outsourcing War," *Foreign Policy*, vol. 112 (1998), 68; Al J. Venter, "Market Forces: How Hired Guns Succeeded Where the United Nations Failed," *Jane's International Defense Review, 1*998. Executive Outcomes advertises its services on the web to interested countries and clients, see http://www.eo.com/about/about.html. See also "Report on the question of the use of mercenaries as a means of violating human rights and impeding the exercise of the right of peoples to self-determination," UN Doc. E/CN.4/1996/ 27 of 17 January 1996, paras. 85, 96, 98.

26. See Boutros Boutros-Ghali, *An Agenda for Democratization, UN* Doc. A/51/761 of 20 December 1996.

27. See John Hart Ely, *Democracy and Distrust,* 1980.

28. Report of the Secretary-General, "Arrangements and practices for the interaction of NGOs in all activities of the United Nations system" (note 5), para. 34.

29. The growth of representational government within the NGO sector itself is evidenced in the Secretary-General's optimistic remark that "By forming alliances, networks and caucuses, NGOs also demonstrated that their fast-growing numbers do not necessarily lead to increased logistical or political difficulties for the organizers of UN conferences." *Id.*, para. 58.

30. See Peter Spiro, "New Players on the International Stage," in: James E. Hickey, Jr. (ed.), *International Legal Personality,* Hofstra Law & Policy Symposium, vol. 2 (1997), 26-27, 34.

31. See Jimmy Burns/Frances Williams, "Refugees' agency lost in wilderness of bungling and waste," *Financial Times,* 29 July 1998: less than 50 percent of required audit certificates for 1995 received from NGOs for "necessary assurance about the propriety of the expenditure"; Letter to the Editor from Soren Jessen-Petersen, Assistant High Commissioner for Refugees, *Financial Times,* 30 July 1998; and related articles in *Financial Times,* 1, 3, 4, and 7 August 1998.

    The Secretary-General voiced a more general concern to an annual conference of NGOs at the United Nations, see Secretary-General Calls for New United Nations-NGO Partnership Amidst Ongoing Human Rights Revolution, UN Press Release SG/SM/ 6697, PI/1079, 14 September 1998: "we are convinced that there are no limits to what a strong civil society can achieve in partnership with governments. But that is why I am so troubled when the NGO idea is abused; when NGOs are established to procure funding and nothing more; or when NGOs are used as fronts claiming to be one thing when, in fact they are another. . . . it may be time for NGOs to consider ways to protect your own invaluable franchise."

32. S/RES/888 of 30 November 1993, urging government of El Salvador and the Frente Farabundo Marti para la Liberacion Nacional (FMLN) "to prevent political violence and accelerate compliance" with the peace accords.

33. S/RES/792 of 30 November 1992, "[c]ondemn[ing] the failure by the PDK to comply with its obligations" under the peace plan.

34. S/RES/1045 of 8 February 1996, urging Government of Angola and UNITA to maintain ceasefire and conclude talks on integration of armed forces.

35. S/RES/981 of 31 March 1995.

36. Case concerning the Vienna Convention on Consular Relations *(Paraguay v. United States),* 1998 ICJ, Provisional Measures Order of 9 April 1998.

37. See Agora: Breard, AJIL, vol. 92 (1998), 666–712.

Rights and Duties in a New Challenging World

8

SHIREEN T. HUNTER

I find it heartwarming to see so many people from so many different parts of the world gathered for the WANGO annual conference, and I think that this is really very fitting for the new world we are facing. The term "globalization" perhaps has become somewhat overused, almost to the point of being trivialized. But trivialization of a word does not necessarily mean that excessive usage has caused it to lose its validity in many ways. We are increasingly becoming a global village. If you detect in some of my language and terminology terms like "global village," "interdependence," and so on, you have to blame it also on my experience with multilateral diplomacy in a previous incarnation.

I always had an ongoing debate with my husband about where the balance of rights and responsibilities lies in general. I think that this is an existential question not only for groups such as NGOs, nations, subnations, and so on, but also for individuals. In our own daily lives we have to say, "Yes, as a human being we have certain rights but also as a human being we have certain responsibilities and certain duties." It has been said that in the Victorian Age the emphasis perhaps was too much on duties. But some people now say that we may have gone a little bit too far to the other extent and have forgotten our responsibilities. Clearly, striking the right balance between rights and duties is something that we have all to struggle with, both at the individual level and also at the collective level.

I am going to try to link this very important philosophical question with something that is much more urgent—two really major questions and themes that unfortunately seem to be moving in a direc-

---

Dr. Shireen T. Hunter is director of the Islam Program at the Center for Strategic International Studies (CSIS) and author of *The Future of Islam in the West: Clash of Civilizations or Peaceful Co-Existence?*

tion where they intersect. This second theme is the issue of terrorism, particularly international terrorism of a level that goes beyond the confines of either a particular country or a particular region, and acquires international dimensions and, of course, increasingly deadly weapons. The nexus of this terrorism and weapons of mass destruction is a new challenge that I think not only individual countries are confronting at some level, but the international community is also facing.

In the United States we all experienced with great shock and sadness what happened at the Pentagon in Washington, DC and in an even more tragic and heart-wrenching way the events in New York City. For the United States, as the leader of the world for both good and bad depending on peoples' perspectives, these issues are no longer a type of philosophical and esoteric discussion. It is something that is very serious and deals with very challenging policy issues as well as questions about our own political culture, and our relationships among each other and among various groups. This is where the role of NGOs is coming to play a vital role, not just in the United States, but also around the world.

Nothing New?

I believe in putting current circumstances and situations in some form of historical context. I read a lot of nineteenth-century novels. That's how I remain sane after working on all these fairly complicated issues. In one nineteenth-century English novel there was a quote attributed to a great American: "There ain't nothing new, ain't nothing true and it don't signify." But it does signify. What is important in that quote is "it ain't nothing new."

One thing we have to understand is that the use of terror to achieve political purposes is nothing new. What has happened, however, is that in the last decade it has acquired much greater dimensions and has created linkages between groups and states. I would not refer to them as "loose groups," but rather networks that may have relations with certain states but are not necessarily controlled by those states or completely directed by them. This has acquired a level of seriousness and a level of danger that bypasses anything that we have seen in the past.

Without falling too much into excesses of historicism, it is important to note that one act of a single individual can cause calamities for millions of people from which it may that take generations to recover. Ultimately the triggering event for the First World War was the assassination of Archduke Ferdinand in Sarajevo by one person, whether he was a nationalist or an anarchist. I am not suggesting that that single act was the cause of the First World War, but definitely it was the triggering event. It set it in motion dynamics that led to war.

Thus, an individual such as Osama bin Laden or someone like him, even if they lack the wherewithal and organization, by one or two acts can really hit a particular nerve and do extraordinary damage. Such concerns have to be taken very seriously.

The quest for more and more deadly weapons is again something that is not new to human history. As a graduate student, my interest was European politics in the interwar period, between the First and Second World Wars, so I studied the arms race in Europe. In an arms race the relevant parties want to have more sophisticated weapons. And then those on the other side want to get those weapons as well because otherwise the equation changes. The first time that poison gas was used on a massive level was in the First World War. In fact, while one could say that the First World War was the first of many global wars, still in my opinion it remains the Great War due to the vast number of people who died and the novelties and the thresholds that were crossed in terms of massive harming of civilians and so forth.

It has become somewhat disingenuous to say "underlying causes" in terms of assessing why there is terrorism, but such underlying causes do exist. What are the factors that cause people to resort to terror? Some of it, frankly and very plainly stated, relates to the fact that there is such a thing called evil in this world. I think that we cannot ignore the fact that there is evil. Sometimes you almost feel it in the air, sort of like *frisons* (French for goose bumps). There are people who are evil. And they do evil things. It has been pointedly stated that the devil often comes in the best of shapes and forms, and seductively, even tries to dress himself in higher ideals.

There seems to be no limit to how far an evil person will go in terms of harnessing ideas and ideals that have nothing to do with it for its own purposes. I think that this is what we see in religious extremism—I do not like to refer merely to "Islamic extremism." There is an Islamic extremism, and Muslims and others have to realize that it is a threat, perhaps more so to Muslim societies and countries themselves. We have to come to terms with its reality and fight it. And as we all know, other religious extremist elements exist as well.

One part of the equation of culture of responsibility is to take responsibility for the bad aspects of one's own culture as well as for its good aspects. Islamic extremism is not really inherent to the Islamic religion. A Muslim should not say, "No, I have to defend everything that is there, no matter what." You have to defend what is defensible and, for your own sake as well as for the sake of others, you have to admit what is wrong. Once you recognize what is wrong, then you can fight that with the tools that exist within your own culture.

We have to fight this cancer of extremism within Muslim societies because this is something that ultimately is going to be more damaging to Muslims. I am proud to say that I was a lonely voice during the 1980s when I used to say we do not have to fight Khomeinism with Saddamism. We did help Saddam, let us face it. But he has done more damage to Iraq and Arabs than perhaps anybody else could do. Khomeini did more damage to Iran than any external enemy, even the Soviet Union, could do. So we have to accept that as one element of a culture of responsibility. We have to take responsibility for that.

This should apply also to the other side, to those in the West. We also have to take responsibility for our acts. This is a very difficult thing to do for a great power and in particular for America. One of the things that I have always noticed is that for some reason, when you assume a mantle of the great power—the only great power and the leader of the world—at the same time you also assume all the sins and the misdeeds with which you had nothing to do. For example the US has come to inherit the guilt of other colonial powers. But that is something we have to live with. It comes with greatness. It comes with responsibility.

Immediate and Long-Term Tasks

President Bush, in a speech in March 2002 at the International Conference on Financing for Development in Monterrey, Mexico, addressed the issue of terrorism. And when he talked about our war on terrorism, it is quite obvious that we have two tasks. One is the very immediate task: to dismantle terror networks. Whoever says that we can delay this task, I think is wrong. Such a delay is not doing a service either to America or to other countries. The options remain in how we do it: whether it is drying up the funds, whether it is catching the terrorists, whether it is preventing the sort of laxities in intelligence activities to which others have referred. This is something that has to be done. It is a very, very difficult job.

The other task is to be humble and have a long-term vision. When you are taking an action, hindsight is a great thing. But nobody has four eyes and a crystal ball and so forth and so on. When the immediate task is done, it is important to try to discern the long-term ramifications of our actions.

We had to do certain things in Afghanistan, for example. But the war in Afghanistan created the kinds of circumstances that gave rise to a breeding ground for certain things, including the Taliban and Osama bin Laden and his terror network. So whatever we do as nations, we also have to look into the long-term, unintended consequences of our actions.

This is where NGO involvement is particularly important: fostering debate, providing background for policymakers and others, providing as much information as possible, providing various scenarios. We can never be sure that we are always going to make the right choices. I certainly have called things in the wrong way in many cases and we have to be humble enough to admit that. But let us try to have as much debate, as much discussion, as we can.

Another issue that is very important is that of weapons of mass destruction. We cannot be complacent on this either. In particular, biological weapons are very frightening in many ways if indeed they get into the wrong hands. And unfortunately, there is a risk that they could fall into the wrong hands. Again, NGOs can be of assistance in this matter by alerting the public and assisting in conflict resolution.

I mentioned the question of evil. If an evil person wants to do something, there may be very little we can do to dissuade him other than to get rid of him. And there are cases in which that is probably the only solution. How to go about getting rid of such a person or organization is another matter.

On the other hand, I also think that we have to see what is it that drives peoples or countries to acquire these weapons. Conflicts! So issues of conflict resolution are vital, and I think that the NGOs' role in this regard is very important. Sometimes people kill one another because they dehumanize one another. Somebody sitting in a cave in Afghanistan thinks of New York as if it were the new Babylon, and they believe it. They think they are doing a good deed! They do not understand that 99.9 percent of these people get up in the morning, get into that horrible subway, work, and go back home, then maybe watch a little television and go to sleep. So we have to humanize one another, and I think that the NGOs' role in this regard is very important.

Therefore, do not underestimate your role as an individual or as an NGO. All of us, even single individuals—like a little ant that carries something and contributes to the creation of this food reserve that will keep the ants from dying—can contribute in some way or another. As members of the human species, we have to live together. And to live together, we have to begin to see one another as human beings. Individuals have a very important role to play. And NGOs have an even greater role to play.

Iraq, Terrorism, and the Culture of Irresponsibility

9

LAURIE MYLROIE

As a Defense Department consultant on terrorism, I was involved with a briefing by a very smart Defense Department official, a general. He told this panel on terrorism that the most important thing we can provide them, the Pentagon leadership, is what he called "situational awareness." What he meant was to understand what is going on, because if you do not understand what is going on you cannot respond to it properly and deal with the problem effectively. So that is one of my first objectives of this talk, to provide some situational awareness to help in understanding what is going on.

Then the other part of it deals with the theme of this conference, "Culture of Responsibility." That is terribly important, the concept of a culture of responsibility. What I am going to describe this morning is the very opposite, a culture of irresponsibility. The tragedy of September 11 happened in the United States and in Washington, DC. And if it could happen in Washington, DC, it could happen anywhere in the world because this is about as good as governments get, in my view. But there are things that are sorely lacking. Let me start and explain what I mean by those introductory remarks.

World Trade Center 1993

Back in 1993, the World Trade Center in New York City was bombed. It was an attempt to topple one tower onto the other and bring them both down. Previous to that, in the 1980s, it was assumed that major terrorist attacks against the United States were carried out by terrorist states. For all practical purposes, that meant Iran, Iraq, Libya, and

---

Dr. Laurie Mylroie is publisher of *Iraq News*, an adjunct scholar at the American Enterprise Institute, and is author of *Study of Revenge: Saddam Hussein's Unfinished War Against America*.

Syria. Elsewhere in the world, it was also assumed that many major terrorist attacks were carried out mainly by terrorist organizations, very tightly knit, secretive, conspiratorial groups. If one thinks of Britain, the IRA; if one thinks of Spain, the Basque Separatists; if one thinks of Sri Lanka, the Tamal Tigers.

But with the 1993 World Trade Center bombing, the viewpoint of the United States changed significantly. The argument was made that there were no longer terrorist states attacking the United States, but so called "loose networks" of militant Muslims. It was felt that this represented a new terrorism, and this viewpoint was stated repeatedly.

However, as regards the 1993 World Trade Center bombing, that viewpoint was not true at all. New York law enforcement, and particularly the New York office of the FBI, which was headed by a fellow named Jim Fox, who has passed away, offered another perspective. Fox's background was counterintelligence, and he believed that Iraq was behind the '93 bombing of the World Trade Center.

Why did Jim Fox believe that? For one, there are Iraqis all around the fringe of that plot. One of them, a fellow by the name of Abdul Rahman Yasin, came in from Baghdad and returned to Baghdad after the bombing. He is still there. CBS News interviewed him in the summer of 2002 in Baghdad and he is still there.

Second, the Trade Center bomb was huge. The 1993 bombing, which was meant to topple the tower, left a crater six stories deep in the basement floors of that building. Within a week of the World Trade Center bombing, the FBI arrested a twenty-six-year old Palestinian, Mohammed Salameh. Remarkably, he went back to the truck rental agency for his deposit on the van that carried the bomb and got arrested. Jim Fox recognized that these people, who implicated Salameh and his friends, were not capable of carrying out such a massive attack alone. Furthermore, the fact of the ease of their arrest suggest a conspiracy masterminded by others, with these people left behind, meant to be caught and to take the blame.

Ramzi Yousef

So Fox suspected that Iraq was responsible. But one can go even further. One can demonstrate to the very high standard of "beyond a reasonable doubt" that is used for criminal convictions in the United States, that Iraq was behind that bomb. That demonstration is based on tracing the identity of the mastermind of the plot, Ramzi Yousef. He was arrested as a result of a failed plot in the Philippines, and he is sitting in a jail in Colorado right now. Yousef came into the United States with an Iraqi passport under the name of Ramzi Yousef, so that is why he is referred to by that name, but he left on a Pakistani passport in the name of Abdul Basit Karim. All of this comes from the evidence that was introduced by the prosecution in the World Trade Center bombing trials. It is all documented.

The name Abdul Basit Karim—the name on the Pakistani passport with which Yousef left the country—refers to a real person. Abdul Basit Karim was born and raised in Kuwait, where his father worked. He went to high school in Kuwait, graduated, and went for further training in Great Britain. After receiving his degree in June 1989, he returned to Kuwait where he got a job in Kuwait's Planning Ministry. He was in Kuwait a year later, when Iraq invaded in August 1990.

As a routine matter, Kuwait maintained an alien resident file on Abdul Basit Karim, and that file was tampered with. There was information missing from the file. There should have been copies of the front page of the passport, with his signature, the picture, and that kind of information. That was taken out, and all the Kuwaitis said, "Oh, this is because Iraq was here." There was also information in that file that should not have been there, above all the notation that Abdul Basit Karim and his family had left Kuwait on August 26, 1990, traveling from Kuwait to Iraq, and crossing from Iraq to Iran at Salamcheh, a border crossing point, on their way to Pakistani Baluchistan where they live now.

This information was reported to me by a former ambassador. I went to school at Harvard with the fellow, who was an ambassador from Kuwait to the United States in the mid-1990s and as a favor, he got that information for me. As he read it to me in his office and I scribbled it down, I looked up and asked him, "What's that information doing in your file?" His jaw dropped. As you all know, when you cross a border, you do not provide the authorities with your entire itinerary. You say you came from this point, you went to that point, you took this plane, on such and such a date. Moreover, on August 26, 1990, it says in the file, "They left Kuwait on August 26, 1990 traveling from Iraq to Iran, from Kuwait to Iraq, Iraq to Iran." On August 26, 1990, there was no Kuwaiti government. There was an Iraqi army of occupation. The Kuwaitis did not put that information in the file.

Finally, Yousef's fingerprints are in Abdul Basit Karim's file in Kuwait. We all have our own unique set of fingerprints. They're ours, no one else's. So that can only mean one of two things. Either Ramzi Yousef's real identity is Abdul Basit or someone took the original fingerprint card with Abdul Basit's fingerprints out of the file and put in a new card with Ramzi Yousef's fingerprints. Now, Yousef and Abdul Basit are two different people for a zillion reasons, one of which is Yousef is six feet tall and Abdul Basit is five-foot-eight. That means the fingerprint cards were switched.

There's only one party that reasonably could have done so, and that is Iraq, while it occupied Kuwait. It is a standard practice for Soviet-style intelligence agencies to develop false identities for people involved in what they call "wet operations," like terrorism. False identities are standard practice, and this little trick is too clever by half, because it ties Iraq directly to Ramzi Yousef with his fingerprints and therefore to the 1993 Trade Center bombing as well as the 1995 plot to bomb a dozen airplanes in the Philippines.

New Targets

Iraq was behind the World Trade Center bombing in February 1993. It is known that Iraq tried a few months later, in April 1993, to kill former president Bush, when he visited Kuwait. A third thing happened that spring. After the Trade Center bombing, the New York FBI began an operation to teach the Islamic militants a lesson: you do not carry out jihad here. They had an Egyptian informant who was also working for the Egyptian government go around proposing jihad, and a Sudanese immigrant picked up the bait to make jihad.

His original target was an armory in Manhattan, which is not very nice, but it was not as bad as what that plot eventually became, because this Sudanese fellow had two friends at Sudan's UN mission, intelligence agents. They said to him, "We're going to give you diplomatic plates so you can get your bomb into the UN parking garage, and blow that up." Then they added other targets, New York's federal building and two tunnels. Of course, these people were not building a bomb. They thought they were, but the FBI does not let you make explosives in the middle of New York City, and when the FBI had the evidence on these people—above all video—of their making what they believed to be a bomb, it arrested them early on the morning of June 24, 1993.

Two days later, on June 26, US president Bill Clinton hit Iraq intelligence headquarters with cruise missiles, and he said it was for the attempt to kill George Bush, and it was. For Clinton's 1992 presidential campaign, I served as his adviser on Iraq. During the campaign he was hawkish on Iraq, but this changed once he became president. Nonetheless, I was still dealing with the Clinton people at the time of his missile strike on Iraq in 1993. When Clinton hit the Iraqi intelligence headquarters, he publicly said it was meant as retaliation for Saddam's attempt to kill Bush, but it was also meant as a response for the terrorism in New York. He believed that it would deter Saddam from all future acts of terrorism and be a response to the second plot as well, where Sudan became involved in picking the targets.

The United States was King Kong. We could hit any building on the face of the planet. Clinton believed that to do that, and demonstrate that we were prepared to do it, would stop Saddam from future acts of terrorism. And it would take care of the problem without telling the American people what had happened, because the American people might demand he do an awful lot more.

False Explanation for Terrorism

In the process was born this false and fraudulent explanation for terrorism, that it is carried out by loose networks of Islamic militants, with the most recent manifestation being al-Qaeda. In reality, Iraq and al-Qaeda work together. They are inextricably linked. Iraqi intelligence was involved in September 11. Iraq trained Islamic militants to take over airplanes, as the Czechs have stated repeatedly. Iraqi intelligence met with the leader of the hijackers, Mohammed Atta, in Prague on at least one occasion.

If this is true, why does not the administration say it, that Iraq is working with Islam militants who attacked the United States? Actually, part of the administration does—the Pentagon. I wrote about this in a book that appeared in the fall of 2000, *Study of Revenge: Saddam Hussein's Unfinished War Against America* (American Enterprise Institute Press, 2000). Among those offering a blurb for the book was Deputy Secretary of Defense Paul Wolfowitz, who was then head of the Johns Hopkins School of Advanced International Studies (SAIS). It seems, although this was not told to me, it comes from my reading of the news, that Wolfowitz explained this to his boss, Donald Rumsfeld, prior to September 11. Thus, on September 11, 2001, when everyone else might have thought it was al-Qaeda alone, they had a different viewpoint, and they prevailed and won the debate about Iraq. This is why the United States began preparing for war with Iraq.

Why does not the United States acknowledge this? Iraq and terrorism is the missing link. Talk about a culture of irresponsibility. The CIA accommodated Clinton's desire not to hear that Iraq was involved in terrorism in any of these attacks. And now it has its feet in cement because of that. It acts as if it is Saddam's lawyer, dismissing every piece of information brought forward to suggest Iraq's involvement in 9/11. For example, there are suggestions that Iraq may have been training people to hijack airplanes , because there is a photograph of an airplane sitting in an Iraqi terrorist training camp. But the CIA responds, "How do we know they aren't doing what we know we would do, which is counter-hijacking training." That is an example of how they dismiss evidence.

Culture of Irresponsibility

There are consequences because of the pervasive culture of irresponsibility. I believe that the United States president understands that Iraq was likely involved in 9/11 or might have been, and that to leave Saddam and his biological weapons program in place is too dangerous. So we are preparing for war, but we are not taking the civil defense measures that we should be taking against biological terrorism in the United States. Why not? Without making the strong argument for Iraq's suspected involvement in 9/11, you risk alienating the public, so you do not talk about all the potential dangers. I expect that at the first biological terrorism attack, we will take the necessary measures, but it is too bad that such seems quite likely to occur.

You do not want your own institutions to be caught up in this culture of irresponsibility. The danger posed by Saddam was evident, not only through terrorism, which is a little complicated to explain, but through his weapons programs, too. When his son-in-law, Hussein al-Kamel, defected in August 1995, it was learned that huge amounts of unconventional weapons had survived the Gulf War bombing campaign, including those in a large biological weapons program. These biological weapons are so dangerous that someone in Iraqi intelligence could dump a pound of anthrax in the subway system of any US or British city and many people would die. The danger is evident. But some "Iraq experts" were just as bad as some of the "terrorism experts." They accommodated Clinton's desire not to hear that Iraq was a problem. I pushed one of them, a former colleague—we used to be friends—very hard in November 1998: "Where does responsibility lie if Saddam did something terrible because he's been left there? If he developed a nuclear weapon and used it? If he carried out a biological terrorist attack and many people here died? And this colleague, from a very prestigious institute in Washington, said to me, "The times are very cynical and everyone must do what he must do for his career." This is a culture of irresponsibility that can and has the potential to impact each one of us.

Women and Peace in South Asia 10

V. MOHINI GIRI

Mahatma Gandhi had said, "If only the women of the world came together, they could display such heroic nonviolence as to kick away the atom bomb like a mere ball. If the women of Asia wake up they will dazzle the world. My experiment in nonviolence would be instantly successful if I could secure women's help."

Everyone knows that ours is an age of conflict. The present century has been riddled with all sorts of wars. Most ironically, even two world wars were fought as "wars to end all wars," and to "make the world safe for peace." But there is no war that can end wars. As the spiritually enlightened have always known, evil cannot overcome evil. Not surprisingly, over two hundred wars of varying scale and intensity have been fought since those wars of peace!

In an effort to shape a better future, some of the women in South Asia wanted to focus—in a small way—on women's strengths. We tried to gather women of South Asia on a common platform and discuss ways to put into action strategies promoting a "culture of peace." We felt that the women's role in peace included addressing family and societal violence, and trafficking in women and children, as well as strategies for the removal of political and social inequalities, economic empowerment, and education of women.

Peace in its narrowest sense implies absence of war, terrorism, and armed conflict. In its broadest terms it implies an environment of just development and equal society. This would mean a reversal of racially motivated development that perpetuates the mechanics of patriarchal framework and leaves the means of development in the hands of the very perpetrators of violence. It is these perpetrators who have given rise to a distorted image of civilization that has contributed to the absolutely unjust picture of progress in the South Asian region.

For me, peace is a personal agenda, too, since as founder and

---

Dr. V. Mohini Giri is chairperson of the Guild of Service, India.

president of the War Widows Association of India, I have seen agony at its most scaring intensity; and, since governments are deaf to women's cries for peace and systematically keep them away from participating in conflict resolution, all I could do is pray and hope that conflicts were resolved through dialogue, not through bombs. This led to our observing an interfaith peace prayer for the past twenty years at Amar Jawan Jyothi on International Women's Day, March 8.

Women Taking Initiative for Peace

I was convinced that, since women and children are the worst victims of war, it is women who had to take the initiative for peace. And in the summer of 1999, when the guns boomed on the Kargil front and war rhetoric was at its highest pitch, many women in their separate places found themselves increasingly disturbed. The naked aggression and untold suffering on both sides was unnerving. While in the foreground there were drumrolls and bugles of valor and victory, through the lens of television cameras the devastation of smoking guns, body bags, and grieving mothers and wives was seen by all. A few women came together with their shared yet unspoken grief. From this event was born the Women's Initiative for Peace in South Asia (WIPSA).

The year 1999 saw the culmination of three programs on Peace involving WIPSA, which exemplified women's intervention and initiative in creating peace. On August 6, the anniversary of the day Hiroshima exploded, peace gatherings were held at many places in South Asia. In India several hundred women and men gathered at Gandhi Smriti, where Gandhiji [Mahatma Gandhi], the universal symbol of peace, fell to an assassin's bullets. On August 10 a conference focused on "Women's Initiative for Peace" and the idea of a "Bus of Peace to Lahore" originated. On December 19 women and men were mobilized all over India and in several countries of South Asia to form human chains for peace. Their slogan was "Peace for Empowerment, and Empowerment for Peace."

A number of people-to-people initiatives were mobilized, beginning with Lahore. On March 25, 2000, 41 women, comprising activists, lawyers, writers, teachers, artists, and so forth, went to Lahore and Islamabad to meet "sisters" in Pakistan. We met at Lahore and Islamabad and discussed common areas of interest; and met the then-CEO of Pakistan, Gen. Parvez Musharaf. A return delegation of sixty-four women from Pakistan visited Delhi, Agra, and Jaipur to interact with women's educational institutes, the Women's Study Center, minority groups, and members of the government.

These visits were indeed the beginning of people-to-people contact. This was the beginning of us getting to know each other so we could discuss the issues and problems that beset the South Asian region. From our talks we could discover that where there is understanding, there is no conflict. And as a part of a careful strategy to comprehend ground realities that obstruct peace, WIPSA India visited Jammu and Kashmir. This strategy called for an educational campaign that would dispel ignorance about Kashmir.

The fourth initiative of WIPSA widened the personal people-to-people contact, which was comprised of academics, professors, teachers, and leaders from universities. The aim was to enhance opportunities for youth to youth exchange, so that future relationships could be built upon the pillars of authentic information about one another.

India and Pakistan

Needless to say, Kashmir has been the core issue at the negotiating table that prevents the peace process. In order to build up confidence amongst women, we have started the first ever empowerment home in Jammu and Kashmir. We want to break the half-a-century-old distrust and approach the subject with vision and the offer of a vibrant democracy. We realized that the vital need of the day is to build a cohesive South Asian identity that will ensure a greater power at the negotiating table.

Throughout our initiative we felt that we must formulate a common culture to be shared by humankind. To do so it is necessary to find common threads of universal values that are embedded in the existing civilizations. Threads of these common and universal values will enable people to live in peace, avoid conflicts, and promote mutual respect and cooperation among various cultures.

To further our interaction for peace, on August 14, 2002, at 5:00 P.M., about 2,000 Indians and 5,000 of our Pakistani brothers and sisters met to celebrate our Independence Days respectively at the Wagah border. Music filled the air. Women on either side of the border looked at one another with great curiosity. We lit candles for peace and the scene that filled the Wagah border confirmed the belief that leaders on both sides can delay peace, but they cannot stop it. When the overwhelming mass of humanity is clamoring for peace, for exchanges, for sharing, then how long can governments plug their ears to our demands?

Wagah is not the achievement of a handful of people from Delhi. It is the victory of people of India and Pakistan that have galvanized their voices in protest to the complacency residing in the corridors of power. From this coming together we felt there were definitely some solid achievements. The personal warmth and the bond between people were evident. And the very fact that it has been sustained for a period of time shows that the women's movement is gaining strength. Our belief in the power of collective voices had strengthened, and we were happy that there was equal reciprocity on both sides. It was heartening to note that the movement was not confined to the Wagah border, but had spread to the Husainwala border, and as far away as the United States where Indian and Pakistanis were also lighting candles.

Outcomes

I. The Women's Peace Initiative has given an impetus to the process of peace. The warm welcome that the initiative has received bears witness to the fact that most women on both sides are committed to peace and reject the prejudices that have partly been state-sponsored.

II. There is the vital realization that both governments of India and Pakistan must end the rhetoric of violence and aggression.

III. Responsible media will continue in their effort to promote peace and will urge those who have glorified war and violence to play a positive role for the healthy survival of this region. There will be an effort made to form networks of responsible media. WIPSA noted with concern that this propaganda of violence has also infected popular media such as film and television serials. In this regard, the language used in the electronic media to communicate news and information has become incomprehensible and should be made intelligible to the people it addresses.

IV. There is a resolve to put an end to violence against women, be it on cultural, political, or economic grounds.

V. There should be a free exchange of newspapers, magazines, and books between Pakistan and India.

Steps for Peace

I am convinced that in order to restore the people's peace of mind, there is an urgent need for confidence-building among the governments and among the peoples of both countries. To achieve this, several steps need to be taken.

a. Intolerant militant forces in India and Pakistan have to be marginalized; and the governments of Pakistan and India urged to remove all government patronage to such forces.

b. The arms race and nuclearization of the subcontinent must come to an end. There are misplaced priorities in a region where injustice, illiteracy, hunger, disease, and child and maternal mortality are a rule rather than an exception.

c. All educational curricula must be purged of inaccuracies, biases, and prejudices. Our future generations should be educated primarily to recognize themselves as citizens of the world in order to promote peace among all human beings regardless of nationality, religious belief, caste, class, or sex.

We must ask: Who can take responsibility for today's world? Can the military or the politicians? Can businessmen or people with new technology? I strongly feel that if women take the initiative, many issues can be resolved, because women communicate as women, not as nationalities—since women have the greatest stake in the security of the progeny.

In the spiritual context, peace must be seen as synonymous with healing. Our hearts and minds need to be cleansed. Our historical memories need to be healed in the magnanimity of forgiveness. Individually and collectively we need to relocate our existential roots from the rationale of violence to the call of peace. This is a costly and demanding journey, a pilgrimage of faith. The Dalai Lama said that the difference between pilgrimage and tourism is that the former transforms while the tourists return unchanged. Our generation has been assiduously schooled in the alphabet of hate. It is time we switched over to the rhymes of love, that we may learn to dream yet again of peace and, having dreamt, pursue that divine dream through the annals of history.

The Right of the Ukraine to Call for Nuclear Disarmament

11

LEONID M. KRAVCHUK

The Ukraine Peace Council is a well-known NGO in the Ukraine that has for over fifty years united people of different nationalities, professions, and political and religious convictions in order to bring peace in the Ukraine and in the world. The Ukraine Peace Council is part of the worldwide movement for peace, which cooperates and networks with other international NGOs, foundations, and peace movements.

The Ukraine is Europe's second largest country in area (604,000 sq. km.), as large as Poland, Hungary, the former Czechoslovakia, and Austria combined. With a population of 52 million, the Ukraine is the fifth largest nation in Europe. By declaring its independence,[1] the Ukraine changed forever the situation in the Commonwealth of Independent States (CIS)—created after the dismantling of the Soviet Union (USSR).

Nuclear Arms

With the collapse of the Soviet Union, the Ukraine gained the third largest nuclear arsenal in the world (after the US and Russia), which consisted of approximately 4,200 tactical nuclear warheads, 176 intercontinental ballistic missiles with 1,240 warheads (aimed at the United States), and also 42 heavy bombers with 300 warheads.

As far back as the Chernobyl catastrophe in 1986, which resulted in hundreds being irradiated, the majority of Ukrainians have a deeply negative attitude to all that is nuclear. In July 1990, the Parliament of the Ukraine adopted the Declaration on State Independence, which included provisions of a nonnuclear status for the Ukraine. After independence, the Ukraine reinforced its efforts to convince the

---

Leonid M. Kravchuk is the first president of independent Ukraine (1991–94) and president of the Ukraine Peace Council.

international community that it has no nuclear ambitions.

On November 16, 1994, the Ukrainian Parliament adopted the resolution to pass the Treaty on Nonproliferation of Nuclear Weapons. This confirmed Ukraine's consistent course of diminishing the nuclear threat for humanity. And on December 5, 1994, the Strategic Arms Reduction Treaty (START Treaty) was signed, marking the successful completion of the final phase of reductions in strategic offensive arms; and the removal of all nuclear warheads and strategic offensive arms from the Ukraine—as well as from Belarus and Kazakhstan.

An Unprecedented Step

By adopting this decision the Ukraine has made a major contribution to strengthening the international regime of nuclear weapons nonproliferation. From the beginning of independence, the Ukraine has taken a peaceful direction in its policy. The voluntary refusal by the world's third largest nuclear arms owner is an unprecedented step in current history. The Ukraine took this important step because it fully acknowledged that nuclear weapons proliferation is one of the most dangerous sources of instability on the Eurasian continent and in the world.

All people have equal rights for a peaceful and comfortable life. Nuclear weapons pose an extreme problem for all of humanity. In order to control the threat of nuclear weapons, NGOs and other social organizations should be united. The role of NGOs throughout the world is rising to a new level. By unifying under an international structure and making international networks, NGOs can become stronger and can help form policies that can solve important problems for humanity.

Endnotes

1. On December 1, 1991, in a national referendum, 90.3 percent of Ukrainians voted in favor of confirming the declaration of independence from the USSR, adopted by the Ukrainian Parliament on August 24, 1991. Leonid M. Kravchuk was elected president on the day of the referendum.

Conflict Prevention in Europe and the Economic Dimension

12

MIHAELA DIMITRESCU

This is a time of deep social, economic, and political change, especially in some parts of the world. Though some changes are over, others are about to begin. This is because social conditions affect economy, economic conditions affect politics, and political conditions affect civil society. Consequently, everyone has to learn to better manage these sectors of life so as to avoid other problems.

Conflict is wasteful for people's lives and resources. Viewing the conflicts in Europe, one asks:

- Why do conflicts occur in transition countries and in poor countries?
- Why does globalization affect social psychology and increase resentment toward neighbors, or toward "those who are not like us"?
- What could international organizations do in conflict prevention and in efforts to develop an effective plan where countries work together?

The world changed dramatically during the twentieth century, as noted by former US vice president Dan Quayle in January 2001 at the Dialogue and Harmony among Civilizations convocation in New York:

> You can look at this past century and marvel at the great successes. We have had tremendous economic growth, we now have the Internet, and high technology is the sign of the times.... We have made great progress. But on the other hand, you can look at this

---

Professor Mihaela Dimitrescu is vice president of the Romanian Association for European Integration and Democracy (RAEID).

> last century and say that it was a century of conflict. World War I, World War II, we are now beyond the Cold War. It was a century of great genocide and starvation and disease and economic chaos and dysfunctional families.

As we look around us, we see that economy and security are in a painful transition. Everywhere in the world, a transformation process has proven to be much more complex than initially thought. Policy is important, but policy itself depends on conditions and preconditions at the economic level. And from this point of view, countries in the vicinity of the European Union remain pretty fragile, institutionally and economically.

Though the last few years show some progress in the southern European regions, there is more work to be done addressing income inequality; improving low rates of savings and investments; extending life expectancy; and reducing infant mortality numbers. All of which is challenging in the context of poor public governance and a weakened state that is also in transition.

Most conflicts start from at least one of these elements, and policymakers and analysts must decide in what order they should address these concerns. I would say that most transition economies reveal a combination of features found in both rich and poor countries. The example I would mention relates to the level of education and skills in the Balkans versus the degree of competitiveness of most of their industries.

I use the Balkans as a reference because a decade of wars and interethnic strife have complicated the task of reform. Under these circumstances, a fragile economy continues to mark the life of these countries. Globalization affects social psychology, and it could increase fears and resentment toward neighbors, or toward those "who are not like us." There are many examples. The effects of this mentality can be seen if we look at:

- Economic decline and rising poverty
- Huge unemployment rates (more than 30 percent of the active population)

- Massive migration numbers
- Decaying educational and health care systems

We can say that Europe is making efforts to implement a new mentality, a new economic dimension, and a way to provide reasonable and empowering cooperation at all levels of economic, political, and social life. And they seem to be committed, even if these reforms take a long time to implement.

European Integration

It is known that European integration is a process that has consequences for the relationship between economy and security, and brings extraordinary benefits for all players. Financial and trade liberalization does not make everyone happy, but we need to apply the "open door policy" in order to support countries in transition and help poor countries gain credible reform related to world trade policies.

This past year was a time of dialogue and effort at the level of the European Union in trying to minimize conflict in Europe. The European Integration Process and the Stability Pact does exert a positive influence on the region, and these strategies may become increasingly stronger. Moreover in Europe, both NATO and the European Union are supporting important projects that redefine the security and economic map of Europe. Furthermore, the OSCE plays an important role in stimulating the political will to promote and implement adequate legislation, such as: the governance and anticorruption programs of the World bank, the convention of combating bribery, and the UN convention against transnational organized crime.

A working group was established in Vienna last year that prepared a declaration on combating terrorism, and a plan of action was adopted by the OSCE Ministerial Council in Bucharest. Romania is the host of the SECI Regional Center for Combating Transborder Crime. Located in Bucharest, the Center has been successful in Southeastern Europe and could serve as a model for improvements in other regions.

United Nations

Romania applauds the United Nations' efforts to organize training programs promoting Building Capacity for Conflict Analysis and Resolution, in which forty NGOs working at the national level have participated. As a result, a newly trained team of negotiators is ready to share their experiences in their territories. In this way the United Nations Development Program, and the UN Department of Economic and Social Affairs are important partners in conflict prevention in Europe.

After the UNDP and partners' Foundation for Local Development TOT training in 2002, the Romanian Association for European Integration and Democracy (RAEID) continued the program and trained eighteen attorneys from the Safety and Mediation Community Center from eastern Romania, who requested that the course be repeated in their towns. If more NGOs become involved in such projects, the world will have more peacemakers. By learning to negotiate and respect both sides, we will also respect ourselves and we will achieve our goals.

Now WANGO, like the United Nations, works in a common effort for conflict prevention and peacekeeping in the world. The WANGO message will be heard all over the world through our voices. Likewise, more peacekeeping projects in our region, and more training courses on negotiation skills and conflict prevention and resolution would benefit our nation. We could be a credible partner for international organizations offering their expertise and goodwill. WANGO could participate by monitoring peace agreements.

RAEID has had a good experience working with the Interreligious and International Federation for World Peace (IIFWP)–Romania; with the Family Federation for World Peace and Unification International (FFWUI), and with the Collegiate Association for the Research of Principles (CARP), starting a project together based on character education in high schools. My partnership with women's organizations last year, with members of Parliament, and mostly with two US officials and an American volunteer resulted in an organizational management manual for women entering politics.

RAEID sponsors artistic camps for children, supports poor children and artists, is a partner in European projects, and maintains protocols with five major Romanian NGOs. It is a member of the Dialogue Group of Human Rights and works with the Equal Opportunities Commission of our Parliament. Our last project was started to assist a very poor village of approximately 6,000 people, of whom 2,000 are children. We started a campaign to buy winter shoes and boots so that they could go to school. We wanted to make them happy in this small way.

As part of the Ambassadors for Peace initiative, begun by the IIFWP, it is a great honor to work for the goal of peace. If we want to live in areas of stability, economic performance, good governance, and social and regional cohesion, we, the representatives of world NGOs, should support the actions of our nations and of international organizations that work for peace. Our cooperation will bring added value to peace initiatives everywhere.

Part III
NGOs and Human Rights

Introduction

The Universal Declaration of Human Rights, adopted in 1948, recognizes that every person has inalienable rights and fundamental freedoms that cannot be denied. Nonetheless, human rights violations occur all over the world. From disappearances and arbitrary arrests and detentions to the use of torture and police abuse, to abrogation of the freedom of religion, peaceful assembly, and association, to enslavement of people, and to violations of the rights to education, food, and housing, many human beings are denied the full extent of their recognized rights.

NGOs have often been at the forefront of promoting human rights around the globe. Indeed, the existence of the Universal Declaration itself is due in large part to the determination of NGOs. As advocacy, humanitarian, and monitoring organizations, human rights NGOs have influenced the human rights practices of governments and corporations, impacted the popular perceptions of human rights, and helped care for victims of human rights abuses. They have been involved in lobbying political officials, international financial institutions, and intergovernmental organizations; mobilizing public opinion; advancing treaty negotiations with governments; investigating and reporting on human rights violations; monitoring labor practices; providing services and training programs; and increasingly directing humanitarian assistance to disaster areas.

The papers in this section assess the impact of NGOs on human rights around the world as well as examine some of the significant human rights NGOs and the agendas and strategies they employ.

Human Rights NGOs as the Motors of Change

13

CLAUDE E. WELCH

In 1999, James Shand Watson published *Theory and Reality in the International Protection of Human Rights.*[1] He asserted that the academic community would be well advised to stop making extravagant claims about what international law could do for the oppressed, and instead analyze the reasons for the lack of success of the human rights idea. Well, we at this conference take issue with such a bald assertion. Probably all of us would say, "Professor Watson, you are wrong. The human rights idea has had a great deal of success." Much of this success is due to the role of the NGOs of the type represented here.

Without question, human rights NGOs have been significant for more than 150 years. One can consider examples from the nineteenth century such as the antislavery movement, efforts at women's suffrage, and attempts to broaden the rights of workers through expansion of the franchise itself and the development of trade union rights. However, it has been in roughly the last fifty-plus years that human rights have become fundamental parts of international politics. Human rights were central to the establishment of the United Nations, itself created in the horrendous shadow of World War II. One may look, for example, at the 1945 Charter of the UN, whose preamble reaffirms "faith in human rights, in the dignity and worth of the human person, [and] in the equal rights of men and women and of nations large and small..." Even more detailed is the 1948 Universal Declaration of Human Rights (the subject of an excellent recent book by Harvard Law School professor Mary Ann Glendon)[2] and the 1976 International Covenants on Civil and Political Rights and on Economic, Social and Cultural Rights. These three documents form the International Bill of Rights, which also includes other major treaties on abuses such as torture, racism, genocide, and dis-

---

Dr. Claude Welch is director of the Human Rights Center of the State University of New York at Buffalo and author of *NGOs and Human Rights: Promise and Performance.*

crimination against women or children.

A half century after the UN General Assembly adopted the UDHR without a dissenting vote, the scholar-activist William Korey published *NGOs and Human Rights*. Its rather odd subtitle, *A Curious Grapevine*, came from Eleanor Roosevelt, who considered the UDHR and its provisions for human rights as a sprouting ground from which much fruit could come. In 2002 we can fairly say that an extraordinary arbor has sprung from this curious grapevine, well beyond what Mrs. Roosevelt thought was possible.

Role of NGOs versus the Role of States

Professor Ruth Wedgwood and others asked us earlier to think about the respective roles that NGOs play compared with the roles of states. When we look at the roles of promotion and protection, the contrast is generally clear. (I am leaving aside those horrendous instances of failed states, where anarchy is paramount and law and order have broken down.) It is primarily the responsibility of NGOs to promote human rights, to try and build awareness, to make rights the fourth "R," if you will, to go along with reading, writing and "rithmetic." Education is thus a crucial responsibility of human rights NGOs. It is the essence of promotion. But, as I shall show below, they carry out other tasks, through which they gain the moral and political persuasiveness with which we are all ultimately concerned.

Under international law, states—or, more specifically, governments—focus on protection of human rights. They fulfill three obligations in international or regional treaties: 1) drafting them (usually multilaterally, under the auspices of the United Nations or a regional entity such as the Council of Europe or the Organization of African Unity); 2) ratifying them nationally (generally through constitutionally specified processes); and, far and away most important, 3) enforcing them. Treaties are thus formal legal obligations, as contrasted with non-binding declarations.[3] Drafting involves more than the usual political give-and-take (at least relative to declarations), since states may be obliged to accept responsibilities for which they are not eager. As a result, the lowest common denominator of agreement is reached, since consensus is the preferred means of operations. Ratification usually requires legislative assent—in the United States, "the advice and consent" of sixty members of the Senate—followed by executive implementation. Enforcement of human rights, to the extent this involves duties beyond what domestic laws already require, is the duty sine qua non of ratifying governments. They must devote the necessary resources to meet their obligations.

Just as we know that states protect human rights through their systems of laws, courts, justice, police, and the like while NGOs promote human rights through their bringing of information, and just as states negotiate and ratify treaties while NGOs press for stronger restraints on governments' actions, so we must recognize the dark side: states are major abusers of human rights.[4] Documentation and monitoring by NGOs are among their central responsibilities—and ones that frequently lead to tension with governments. NGOs have played significant, direct roles at all the stages just mentioned. Be it helping in drafting, pressing for ratification and enforcement, calling for effective enforcement, or publicizing abuses, entities such as Amnesty International, Anti-Slavery, Human Rights Watch, the International Campaign to Ban Land mines, or the World Federalist Movement (which pulled together the Coalition for an International Criminal Court) have met with increased success. Marginal actors in the mid to late 1940s when the UN Charter and UDHR were drafted, their significance has risen over time.

Legitimacy

Relationships between NGOs and governments remain contentious, however, fraught with ambiguities and difficulties and certainly needful of regular attention. Central to this is the very important question of legitimacy. How legitimate are human rights NGOs? How can the organizations represented at this conference counter the frequently heard argument that they espouse values derived from narrow legal, philosophical, sectarian, or other heritages? The organizations represented here have doubtless been criticized that they were unrepresentative of their societies' basic values and culture. How can we as scholars and activists counter such accusations?

Mike Dottridge, associated for many years with the Africa division of Amnesty International and later executive director of Anti-Slavery, has suggested eight important considerations that, taken together, bestow on human rights NGOs a special moral authority and legitimacy.[5]

First of all, they proclaim their independence, at least in relationship to their own government or to governments in general. Human rights NGOs stress their independence by emphasizing autonomy from outside influence in deciding what they do and how they do it. They are not beholden to states, in many and probably most cases not accepting funds from them. They are not government sponsors, nor government sponsored, nor apologists. Although Dottridge does not mention this, human rights NGOs are leery of foundation funds or individual gifts that have inappropriate strings attached. They have the right to comment, to criticize, to take issue; they are entities free to speak their own mind because they are independent.

But with independence also goes a second necessary characteristic: NGOs themselves must disseminate accurate information. Information that they provide must be carefully gathered, scrutinized, and verified time and time again to ensure that there is no error. A minor slip can undercut months of serious effort and even years of telling the truth. We have to be able to speak in a dispassionate manner, even about horrendous things.

Human rights NGOs thirdly claim to be nonpartisan, not supporting the agenda of a particular government or political group. They present their work as balanced, reporting on abuses committed by governments with opposing ideologies or by opposition parties to a particular conflict or dispute. I would supplement Dottridge's criterion here lest it seem narrowly political. Many of the worst human rights abuses are systemic in nature, resulting from maldistribution of economic resources (globally, regionally, and nationally, as His Excellency Oscar Arias discussed for Latin America), centuries of discrimination (as against Dalits in India and elsewhere in South Asia), from where economic imperatives intervene (as in child labor on farms in poor countries), or where long-standing practices (such as foot-binding in China or female genital mutilation in parts of Africa) may have been or still are justified by arguments of cultural relativism. Resolving them will require efforts considerably greater in cost and longer in duration than most governments, and human rights NGOs, are able to deploy.

Legitimacy is buttressed, as Dottridge fourthly notes, through the standards of international human rights law and often of national law. Such standards are crucial in calling for remedial action to end abuses.[6] This leads directly to the fifth point: human rights NGOs operate on the foundation of a rule of law. They are neither revolutionary nor radical (though the powers-that-be or vested interests may see them as such), but rather reformist in nature.

Sixth, human rights NGOs traditionally focus on abuses committed by specific and hence potentially identifiable individuals or authorities, rather than (as I noted above) on more general long-term patterns of inequality or discrimination for which no single actor is responsible. With responsibility goes culpability: abusers are to be found and brought to the bar of justice. Although impunity may seem politically necessary as a means of ending rights-abusive situations, it is corrosive, and human rights NGOs seek to end it.

Dottridge's penultimate point about advocacy brings us to the various mechanisms functioning in Geneva (at the European headquarters of the United Nations, where its various human rights treaty bodies convene), in headquarters of regional organizations, or in national capitals. Human rights NGOs work within institutions and procedures that have been well established, utilizing national and international bodies of law. They bring publicity to bear in courts at the domestic level; at the global level, it means they take the case to the Human Rights Committee, to the Committee on Economic and Social Rights, to the Committee Against Torture, to the Committee on the Elimination of Racial Discrimination, etc.

And, finally, human rights NGOs perceive the remedies they seek as consistent with the rule of law. The changes they desire, Dottridge asserts, mean they would not pay bribes or ransoms to secure solutions. Human rights NGOs perceive themselves as speaking with unchallengeable moral authority based on these characteristics, as well as the fact that the abuses they criticize are considered wrong—and perhaps even evil or immoral. It is this special legitimacy of which we need to be both aware and proud.

Useful Sources

To conclude my presentation on the functions and legitimacy of human rights NGOs, I would like to discuss a few other relevant scholars. Margaret Keck and Kathryn Sikkink recently published a very interesting book, *Activists Beyond Borders,* which I recommend highly.[7] They focus on networks among NGOs: in unity is their strength. NGO networks use four different strategies to increase their effectiveness: information politics, symbolic politics, linkage politics, and accountability politics. Three other American scholars, Jackie Smith, Ron Pagnucco and George Lopez, asked NGOs, "What do you do?" Ninety-two percent of the human rights NGOs they questioned provided information. Ninety percent of them supported human rights campaigns initiated by other groups. Over four-fifths used programs to educate the public about human rights. Three-quarters lobbied governments and almost the same percentage lobbied at intergovernmental meetings.[8]

My 1995 book *Protecting Human Rights in Africa* provides a convenient mnemonic device. Based on my field work in Namibia, Ethiopia, Nigeria, and Senegal, I said human rights NGOs work on issues of education, empowerment, enforcement, my three Es, as well as the three Ds of documentation, democratization, and (certainly highly significant for Africa) development.[9] Finally, Canadian scholar-activist Laurie Wiseberg, cofounder of Human Rights Internet, said that human rights NGOs have eight functions: gathering information as well as evaluating and disseminating it; advocacy to stop abuses and secure redress; legal aid, scientific expertise and humanitarian assistance; lobbying national and international authorities; pressing for national legislation to incorporate or develop human rights standards; education, conscientization or empowerment; delivery of services; and keeping the political process open.[10]

Three Gaps

In conclusion, I wish to comment on three gaps, some of which have been alluded to already at this conference. First is funding. Professor Wedgwood talked in very provocative fashion about big northern human rights NGOs sucking up the oxygen. The Ford Foundation has given over $200 million in the last few decades to human rights organizations.[11] I suspect that the bulk of this (for good reasons, I hasten to add!) has gone to NGOs based outside the developing world.

Second, we must stress the need for advocacy. Human rights organizations and academics can write great reports, but unless they enter the public consciousness, all their research will in a sense go for naught.

Finally, what do we as NGOs do with those parties, those belligerents, if you will, that do not recognize the rule of law or human rights? I am tempted to say it becomes the role less of human rights organizations than of humanitarian NGOs, a distinction perhaps without a difference. But there is a contrast in modus operandi between *Médécins sans Frontiers*/Doctors Without Borders, or the International Committee of the Red Cross, as contrasted with those of (for example) the Lawyers Committee for Human Rights. I see their roles as complementary, or overlapping in generally noncompetitive ways. But there are times when basic security considerations mean NGOs should largely bow out of the scene—though watching closely lest the reestablishment of law be accompanied by human rights abuses.

In conclusion, NGOs interested in human rights have a variety of responsibilities that they fulfill. Their numbers have grown extraordinarily; their legitimacy and importance cannot be minimized. Eleanor Roosevelt's curious grapevine has ramified widely. The existence of WANGO, and the scores of organizations represented here in Washington, bear witness to this.

Endnotes

1. James Shand Watson, *Theory and Reality in the International Protection of Human Rights* (Ardsley, NY: Transnational Publishers, 1999).

2. Mary Ann Glendon, *A World Made New: Eleanor Roosevelt and the Universal Declaration of Human Rights* (New York: Random House, 2001).

3. Prior to taking going through these processes, states often draft and adopt declarations. Just as the UDHR preceded the two International Covenants, various declarations on torture, children's, and women's rights antedated the respective treaties. Declarations are also used in areas in which international human rights law is evolving, or consensus has not been reached—witness the Declaration on the Elimination of All Forms of Intolerance and of Discrimination Based on Religion or Belief, or the Declaration on the Right to Development, adopted by the UN respectively in 1981 and 1986.

4. I do not intend to overlook the abuses that are rampant in civil wars, ethnic struggles, and the like, in which antigovernment forces may be equally or more guilty of atrocities. Reputable human rights NGOs cover abuses wherever their mandates permit, subject to the issue of accuracy to which I turn below. Nor do I wish to be perceived as neglecting the substantial abuses that come, for example, through domestic violence. Whether injury results from "private" or "public" agents, it nonetheless breaks domestic and potentially international law.

5. "Characteristics of 'human rights NGOs,' " unpublished paper on file with the author.

6. However, since there is in essence no governing international entity, enforcement lies in the hands of states. This is a fact of life that NGOs recognize, and likely rue.

7. Margaret E. Keck and Kathryn Sikkink, *Activists Beyond Borders: Advocacy Networks in International Politics* (Ithaca: Cornell University Press, 1998).

8. Jackie Smith and Ron Pagnucco, with George A. Lopez, "Globalizing Human Rights: The Work of Transnational Human Rights NGOs in the 1990s," *Human Rights Quarterly* 20 (1998): 379–412.

9. Claude E. Welch, Jr., *Protecting Human Rights in Africa: Strategies and Roles of Non-Governmental Organizations* (Philadelphia: University of Pennsylvania Press, 1995).

10. Laurie S. Wiseberg, "Human Rights Nongovernmental Organizations," reprinted in Richard Pierre Claude and Burns Weston, eds., *Human Rights in the World Community: Issues and Action* (Philadelphia: University of Pennsylvania Press, 1992, second edition), 374–82.

11. William D. Carmichael, "The Role of the Ford Foundation," in Claude E. Welch, Jr., ed., *NGOs and Human Rights: Promise and Performance* (Philadelphia: University of Pennsylvania Press, 2001), 252.

Human Rights Challenges, NGOs, and the US Government's Commitment

14

LORNE W. CRANER

I am honored by your invitation to speak to you at this important forum. As a former president of an NGO (the International Republican Institute, which coordinates programs outside the United States to promote democracy, free markets, and the rule of law), I consider non-governmental organizations to be an invaluable contributor to the advancement of human rights and democracy worldwide. NGOs not only provide a voice to advocate rights, but they provide a model for democratic participation. They help enable the practices of democracy to become a habit. This is as true for established democracies as it is for incipient democracies. It is also true for those who fight for democracy.

I know many NGO leaders are engaged in the betterment of this earth in many ways, and my admiration is with those who fight poverty, AIDS, hunger, illiteracy, environmental degradation, and other scourges that plague so many. At this time it is a particular kind of dignity, human rights, that I wish to address.

Since I became assistant secretary in June 2001, we in the Bush administration have been challenged by the consequences of disrespect for human rights and by the impact of those who look upon rights with disdain and disgust. But the new world we face also presents many opportunities to expand protections for human rights and democratic participation across the globe. We are working hard to meet the challenges and take advantage of the opportunities. As President Bush said in his 2002 State of the Union speech, America must stand firm for the nonnegotiable demands of human dignity, the rule of law, limits on the absolute power of the state, free speech, freedom

---

The Honorable Lorne W. Craner serves as United States assistant secretary of state for democracy, human rights and labor.

of worship, equal justice, respect for women, religious and ethnic tolerance, and respect for private property.

It is a worldwide task, one that must engage people in all countries from Africa to Latin America, and it is a task in which we have great allies in democracies from Mongolia and South Korea, to Mali and Senegal, to Mexico and Peru.

Let me address three of the opportunities to which others and I have been applying our energies in the first twenty months of the Bush administration. If our effort is successful it will not be apparent for a long time. The challenges faced in these three regions did not come about, and will not be resolved, overnight.

Middle East

The first is the Middle East. US Secretary of State Colin Powell has outlined a vision of the Middle East as a region where all people have jobs that let them put bread on their tables, provide a roof over their heads, and offer a decent education for their children. He said, "We have a vision of a region where all people worship God in a spirit of tolerance and understanding. And we have a vision of a region where respect for the sanctity of the individual, the rule of law, and the politics of participation grow stronger every day."

Throughout the region there are many countries, many political systems, that do not provide citizens an adequate say in how they are governed. They do not offer a way for people to peacefully work out competing needs and visions for their future. Helping to create new systems open to participation by individuals, men and women, and a healthy civil society, and ensuring such success is as important a task in countering terrorism as is direct financial, diplomatic, and military measures.

After September 11, we—and I mean not just the State Department or the Bush administration, but many of us in the universe of Middle East watchers—took a look at the Middle East, and we came to see a number of bright examples. Over the past year, for example, Bahrain has embarked on a series of political reforms. They promise a more representative government, and protection of the rights of citizens and workers. Bahrain's commitment to its constitution and the rule of law has been renewed, and NGOs have been legalized, labor protections have been promulgated. A modern Morocco, and soon Qatar, have also taken steps to expand political participation and to give elected representatives, including women, a greater voice in national and local affairs. I was especially pleased to see that WANGO is honoring the Bahrain Women's Society, a richly deserving organization.

Looking elsewhere in the Middle East region, we see more difficult challenges. We are reassessing how we address human rights issues in Egypt, for example, and are now meeting frequently with NGOs, civil society representatives, and government authorities in gathering the knowledge we need to determine the best approach. We have already expressed our great interest in the case of Egyptian-American human rights activist Saad Eddin Ibrahim. His is not the only issue, of course, but he is symbolic of our determination to integrate democracy and human rights objectives into our relations with Egypt and with other countries of the region.

Central Asia

The second area of opportunity is Central Asia. Although we have seen some positive steps over the past year, when our relations became much closer, human rights observance has been mixed at best, and in many cases downright poor. But, as in the Middle East, we are determined not to sidestep these issues. Indeed, this administration, from President Bush to Secretary Powell on down to each of our ambassadors, has made it crystal clear that expanded broader relationships with the United States will depend on political reform.

During the first half of 2002, we were heartened to see some small but significant steps to increase human rights in Uzbekistan. The first ever human rights organization was registered, and law enforcement officials were convicted to long prison sentences after being found guilty of torturing prisoners to death. However, a second human rights group was subsequently denied registration, and even more disheartening were further deaths of prisoners. While the censorship board there has been formally abolished, self-censorship remains a problem. Political pluralism will remain a distant goal as long as opposition political parties are not registered.

Tajikistan has made some notable gains this year. Freedom of the media was appreciably increased when the government licensed the first independent radio station and dropped criminal charges against exiled journalist Dododjon Atovulloev. When the Tajik government lowered the fees for registering NGOs this spring, the number of such groups increased dramatically. But in order for pluralism to flourish, we are urging the government to reform election and party registration in order to enable more parties to register and campaign freely.

Unfortunately, other countries in the region have not fared so well. Turkmenistan remains a country with an extremely poor human rights record. Government actions in Kazakhstan this year have raised serious concerns about their commitment to democratic reform. The year started off on a positive note with the formation of a new political party, but by late summer those opposition leaders had been jailed, and legislation severely limiting the ability of smaller opposition parties to survive has been inactive.

In Kyrgyzstan events of the past year have also raised concerns. A draconian presidential decree severely restricted media freedom. However, since then the government has taken steps to redress citizen grievances, including the formation of a constitutional conference that includes some members of the opposition.

Central Asia was an area for which many had great hopes when the Soviet Union fell. Those hopes were slowly extinguished throughout the 1990s, and by the end of the decade our diminished relations revolved largely around economics. Nothing good can be said to have come from September 11, but it has offered the opportunity of a second chance of relations with the region. The nations of the region have many incentives to take advantage of this opportunity. We intend to pursue it to advance democracy and human rights in the region.

China

A third area I want to address is China. This is a country where the government suppresses all groups that it views as a threat to its power. Unregistered church members, China Democracy Party activists, Tibetan Buddhists, and others have all been subjected to harassment or arrest. Human rights at its core is about human beings, and we therefore have welcomed a number of important releases of prisoners in 2002, including the recent release of Tibetan Ngawang Sandrol. We were also committed to the release of Xu Wenli, Rebiyah Kadeer, Xu Jian, Qin Yongmin, Jiang Weiping, and others.

At the same time there are seeds of hope in China. China is carrying out structural reforms in the areas of democracy and the rule of law. Direct elections at the village level are now mandatory nationwide, and momentum to move them to higher levels is growing. Economic reform has led to legal reform, generating pressure for judicial independence, consistency in the application and enforcement of law, and transparency. Individuals, especially workers, are increasingly demanding that the legal system protect their rights. Legislatures are experimenting with public hearings to incorporate public opinion into policy.

Beginning this year, the United States government is for the first time ever working with NGOs to substantially assist these structural changes, with numerous projects that seek to make the judiciary more independent, enhance rights awareness, increase citizen participation in government, and develop civil society. Our work in this area is an integral part of our China human rights policy.

Global Assistance

I do not mean, by highlighting the Middle East, Central Asia, and China, to imply that we are ignoring other areas of the world. The administration and my bureau are deeply involved in fashioning the $5 billion Millennium Challenge Account, which will offer the hope of further assistance to countries around the globe that are making progress in economic, social, and political reform. In the meantime, my bureau is funding programs in Africa, where, for example, we are expanding access to Angolan independent radio to 85 percent of the population. Elsewhere on the continent we intend to fund a program to aid women political leaders.

It is appropriate that WANGO is honoring Oscar Arias, one of the finest men this hemisphere has ever produced, and I look forward to telling him if I can that we are continuing work to enhance human rights and democracy in Latin America, including in Guatemala, Colombia, and Venezuela. Many of our objectives emphasize the establishment of legal norms and mechanisms to protect political and other rights.

We are keenly aware of the need to create space for civil society to exert positive influences. Governments that would thwart the expansions of rights and freedoms certainly understand the influence that civil society can have, which is why they try to curb and contain it. The duty of civil society's champions is to provide for civic participation, to push for open government, and to defend individuals from government infringement on liberties. We find, too, that societies that have vibrant civil spheres are stable and adaptable to change. They are uniquely able to respond to citizen's needs and accommodate multiple interests.

In opening remarks to the Afghan Reconstruction Group, Secretary Colin Powell emphasized the importance of human rights when he said, "Perhaps most important of all for the long-term stability of the country, we must help strengthen the country's fledgling institutions. In particular, we must provide resources and expertise to help the new Human Rights Judicial and Constitutional Committee lay the groundwork for a vibrant civil society, the rule of law, and accountable and transparent government." Afghanistan once pointed to the correlation between harsh rule and a weak state. With its negative lessons, and the positive lessons we have learned over the years, we are ready to push ahead and promote human rights and democracy there and elsewhere.

We look forward to being side by side with NGO leaders on the front lines.

Religious Freedom and the Role of NGOs

15

PAUL MARSHALL

I work for the Center for Religious Freedom of Freedom House, which was founded nearly sixty years ago by Eleanor Roosevelt and Wendell Willkie to serve as a clear voice for democracy and freedom around the world. My work focuses on religious freedom, and the mandate that I have been given for this presentation is to address NGOs and religious freedom in the world today.

Religious freedom in the world is obviously a very difficult thing to summarize. I have tried at book length to describe what is going on in the world, and I am all too conscious of the gaps that remain. But if we want to look at some patterns of religious freedom, I would point to four major trends, which, while they certainly do not cover everything, I think in terms of population cover probably over 90 percent of the problems.

Four Major Trends of Religious Repression

Where are there major problems of religious freedom? First, there are problems in the remaining communist and postcommunist countries. I am including as communist, in name at least, China, Vietnam, North Korea, Laos, and Cuba. I will not say too much, but if we take, for example, China, the world's most populous country, there is repression against the Uighur Muslims and other Muslim groups scattered throughout the country. There is continuing repression against Tibetans within Tibet and outside of it, and widespread repression of the rapidly growing Christian population, both Catholic and Protestant in the country. In Vietnam the repression mainly falls upon Buddhist and

---

Paul Marshall is senior fellow and coordinator for the Survey of Religious Freedom of Freedom House, and general editor of *Religious Freedom in the World: A Global Report on Freedom and Persecution* (2000).

neo-Buddhist groups, and on Christians in the mountain areas. The North Koreans repress any form of religious expression. In Cuba, the situation has eased somewhat in the last three to four years, but repression remains. In the postcommunist countries left in the aftermath of the collapse of the Soviet Union, religious repression is very common. It is most repressive in Turkmenistan and Uzbekistan.

A second trend is one that I will call religious nationalism. This refers to situations where governments or other sectors of the population try to identify a country with a particular religious heritage. This happens in a variety of areas, but a major concentration lies in South Asia, in India, in Sri Lanka, in Nepal, and in Burma. Burma is different in that the SLORC regime also persecutes Buddhists as well as others while trying to claim that it is the defender of Buddhism within Burma. In India there are radical Hindu groups who earlier this year took part in planned riots that resulted in the deaths of some three thousand Muslims in the state of Gujarat. There are also increasing attacks on other religious minorities, especially Christians. Religious nationalism is a trend and a growing trend.

A third trend, not as severe in terms of the destruction of people, but still a worrying one, is increasing repression of minority and unusual religious groups in Western Europe. It is not like the situation in China or, as I'll mention shortly, in Saudi Arabia. But this part of the world has a good record of human rights and religious freedom, and it is disturbing to watch the deterioration of such rights. We see this most markedly in France, in Germany, in Belgium, and in Austria.

The fourth major trend, the fourth major factor in repressing religious freedom, is extremist forms of Islam. This can take a wide range of forms, but breaking it down simply, we have repressive regimes or states such as Saudi Arabia, where in principle any non-Islamic expression is forbidden and in practice any non-Wahabi form of Islam is severely restricted. In Iran and Sudan, you get an equal kind of repression.

In other settings, it is not the regime that is causing most of the problems of religious freedom but militant groups or terrorist organizations. Let me just take one example, Indonesia. Indonesia has been in the news since the bombings in Bali on October 12. But what drew the world's attention was the fact that these terrorists killed foreigners. What has generally been ignored is that these groups and their allies have been involved in the deaths of probably over ten thousand Indonesians in the last three years. One could give other examples and other places where terrorist militant groups attack people whose religion they disagree with, such as Pakistan, Bangladesh, the Philippines, Nigeria, and Algeria. This last trend, extremist forms of Islam, is growing and is the largest one in terms of the number of countries it includes.

Are such trends likely to get better or worse? The first part of the answer is obviously that I do not know. The world is quite fluid and trends can change. The things we do and decide will affect those changes. But, if we are just looking at trends, then I would expect these situations to deteriorate over the next five years.

Another factor in deteriorating religious freedom is that many wars in the world today have an increasing religious dimension, sometimes sincerely felt, or sometimes just manipulated by politicians. One example is the conflict between Israel and the Palestinians. This has gone on for fifty years or more, but in the 1970s and into the 1980s the rhetoric from both sides was more nationalist, of people looking for a land. Now, particularly among the Palestinians, there is more religiously loaded language so that the fight is portrayed as between Jews and Muslims. This heightens emotions and makes it a much more difficult question to solve. We see similar trends in the conflicts around Kashmir or Chechnya or the former Yugoslavia.

This ends a far too brief summary of what I think are some of the major trends in religious freedom today.

Religious Freedom and NGOs

What might this mean for NGOs? Let me focus on one example in the United States. One problem for many human rights organizations is that they do not really have a mass or popular base. Amnesty International has a substantial membership, but human rights organizations generally are elite organizations. They receive funding from foundations or other groups, and they have boards of directors, but not very much daily contact with the general public. They tend to address themselves to other organizations or to the media or to the government.

In the United States as in many other societies, the mass organizations, the large population organizations within civil society, are usually very distant from them. The three largest types of organizations that exist in industrial society are political parties, labor unions, and religious organizations. The degree to which these or other groups can be mobilized in defense of human rights, the more likely a campaign is to be successful. So, for example, in campaigns dealing with apartheid, the mobilization of many in the African-American community was key. In many other issues, particularly those where questions of trade and jobs overlap, as for example in China, labor unions have been very active in coalitions with human rights groups.

Wide Coalitions

The question of religious freedom has in the last five years brought another, and I think a very good, dimension to the fore. About five years ago, for a variety of reasons, the issue of religious freedom and religious persecution began to draw much more attention within the United States. Interestingly, this issue drew together the major human rights groups but also liberal Jewish groups and conservative Evangelical Christian groups, Catholics together with Tibetan Buddhists, the Salvation Army together with the Ba'hai. It was a very wide and active coalition. But I think it is fair to say that the novel aspect of this mobilization around religious freedom was the involvement of churches, particularly conservative churches, because they have a membership of tens of millions and perhaps over 100 million, depending on how it is defined. If even a small proportion of these people become involved in this issue, they can flood their politicians. Indeed, that is what has happened. In terms of a mass-based initiative, this mobilization within churches proved to be the major factor that led to the passage of the International Religious Freedom Act in 1998.

This particular dynamic sometimes led to criticism that religious bodies were only being concerned with religious people. But I think that this accusation is incorrect. It is very important to realize that religious freedom is not just the freedom of religious people. Religious freedom affects everybody, whether Buddhists or Christians or

Muslims or atheists or agnostics. It focuses not so much on *who* suffers persecution but the *reason* they suffer persecution. So, for example, I believe it is still the case in Indonesia that it is in principle illegal to be an atheist. Belief in one God has been required in that country. Being an atheist in Saudi Arabia can get you executed. So there is no human being on the face of the planet who does not have a stake in the issue of religious freedom. It is the "why" of suffering, not the "who" of suffering that is highlighted.

Another feature of the wide coalition that has been brought together on the issue of religious freedom is that many of the people continue to work together. Very diverse people found themselves working together and realized that the others were not so horrible after all. This provided working relationships, networks, and patterns of trust, which have in turn led to several other actions. I will here mention four of them.

Continuing Coalitions

After helping pass the International Religious Freedom Act, many of these groups focused particularly on the country of Sudan as one of the world's worst violators of human rights. Strenuous lobbying led to the appointment of a special envoy to Sudan and to the passage of the Sudan Peace Act, which was signed by President Bush on October 21, 2002.

Many members of the same coalition also worked together on the relief of debts owed by countries in the south to countries and banks in the north. This is often regarded as a left-wing issue, but it is fascinating to watch Pat Robertson, a prominent conservative evangelical broadcaster, urging his television watchers to write to their members of Congress urging real action on debt relief.

The movement to end sex trafficking is another case. This movement has had many expressions, one of which was legislation passed in the year 2000. Many human rights groups have been very involved in this for many years, but there began an unusual coalition of feminists and Evangelicals, who are at odds over many things, but both agree that having women sold into sexual slavery is evil.

The fourth issue drawing such coalition partners is current legislation being considered on prison rape, an issue to which hardly anybody has paid attention in the past. It is not a glamorous issue; it does not have a constituency. But it has now drawn together bipartisan support from Senators Kennedy and Sessions in the United States Senate and Representatives Wolf and Scott in the House. These last two issues, sex trafficking and prison rape, involve appalling hardship but have no constituency of people in the United States who are directly affected by them. They simply reflect a deep moral concern.

This history of diverse coalitions, beginning with the issue of religious freedom and then mobilizing people in civil society to address a range of issues, is one that may have lessons for us. I hesitate to extrapolate from one issue to others, and I certainly hesitate to extrapolate from the United States to experience elsewhere. But I suggest that this history should lead us to push for at least two things. First, in human rights issues, to see to what degree it is possible to mobilize and work with the larger organizations in civil society and arouse their concern. Second, to see to what degree we can take those issues that can cut across political and ideological divisions and bring together people who disagree on much, but on this issue have a unified concern. This can transform our human rights advocacy.

Human Rights Challenges in the New Century

16

ALEXANDRA ARRIAGA

I am going to address the work that we do at Amnesty International, and then the challenges that I see that the human rights non-governmental community currently face. Amnesty International's main goals are to end human rights abuses wherever they take place and to promote human rights everywhere. We deal with the most horrific types of human rights violations. It is hard to imagine that today violations continue to take place, but they do.

As an illustration, I often think about one girl that Amnesty International interviewed. She was twelve years old. One day, as she was leaving her school, some soldiers, men in uniforms, stalked her. She was beaten up. She said that when they came up to her, all she saw was something coming at her suddenly; she recognized this as the butt of a gun. Then she just saw blackness. When she woke up in a dark cell, she did not know how long she had been out. For several days she was raped by she did not know how many men. She was twelve years old. This was in Liberia and this was not very long ago.

That is just one instance. We deal with individuals all over the world who have suffered horrendous types of violations, but also who have shown an enormous amount of courage in telling their stories. Often they do not want their names to be used or publicized. We have all the names, but we protect their right to privacy. Much of our work is to be a voice for them and to mobilize people to care and to make sure that we can try to make a difference.

Amnesty International

Amnesty International is a worldwide human rights movement. We

---

Alexandra Arriaga serves as director of government relations for Amnesty International USA.

have offices in over sixty countries around the world. Our headquarters are in London. In the United States we have a very large membership, and our worldwide membership is about 1.7 million.

Amnesty International was started as a result of an incident in the 1960s, when three students got together one night in Portugal, and they toasted freedom. This was in a public bar, and for that they were imprisoned, this being a time of Portuguese dictatorship. A gentleman in London heard about this case and put an ad in a newspaper and notified everybody of what had happened and asked people to write the Portuguese government. Suddenly the Portuguese government was flooded with letters about these three students. It really was not worth the trouble for the Portuguese authorities, so they agreed to release them. That was the beginning of Amnesty International, which took an interest in what was going on with individuals in other parts of the world and by holding governments accountable.

Amnesty International continues to be a membership organization. It is truly the most democratically oriented organization that I have ever known, and I have worked for both members of the United States Congress and for the United States administration. Amnesty International holds regional conferences around the world where all of our members come together and draft and pass their own resolutions, and at the annual conference they also pass resolutions. This serves as our guide for what our mission priorities are to be.

In the United States our tactics are part of a direct advocacy. I spend much of my time meeting with US administration officials and congressional leaders. But I also spend an enormous amount of time educating the public and our membership about what the issues are and providing them with the materials that they need to mobilize. Increasingly we are mobilizing people online. We have about one hundred thousand individuals who are registered online, and they take actions on a weekly basis.

Human Rights Campaigns

Among the campaigns we currently are engaged in are efforts to stop torture. Specifically, we are not only advocating before governments around the world to intervene in cases of torture, and to call for an end to such activities, but also we are looking at tools of torture. In the United States we have been looking toward regulation of certain types of crime control equipment to make sure that it is licensed when it goes abroad. And in those countries that are believed to be using that equipment for torture, we have been able to follow up on this. Also, certain types of equipment that are currently exported that we believe can only be used for torture, and we are looking to prevent the exportation of such torture equipment. I am happy to say that these activities have an enormous amount of bipartisan support as well as support by both the Congress and the current administration. So we are very hopeful that at an upcoming session of Congress we will be able to bring that to closure.

Amnesty International is involved in a lot of other issues related to human rights. Amnesty International is an abolitionist organization. We oppose the death penalty and seek to prevent executions; we are currently working on legislation to that effect in the United States and in other parts of the world.

Most of our work is country specific. Of course, we have researchers who go around the world and research situations and put out reports. This coming year we are also going to have a campaign on the problem of violence against women, in order to bring to light the types of situations that women face all over the world. We have been working very hard for ratification of the Treaty for the Rights of Women. One hundred and seventy nations have ratified this treaty, but the United States has not ratified it. We are also launching a more general campaign on discrimination, looking at the types of populations that are generally targets for discrimination and trying to bring that to light. Generally we try to support relevant treaty ratification.

Human Rights and the War on Terrorism

We have had quite a lot to do with the war on terrorism. I think this is a transition from what Amnesty has done, but is also relative to what the human rights movement as a whole is doing. We are very concerned that because of the war on terrorism much of the human rights framework that we know, and that we have supported, is at risk. Because there is a climate of danger and also a sense that this is a unique time, there is a temptation right now to go toward unilateralism and throw out the types of frameworks that have existed for quite some time. There is a challenge before us to try to maintain the multilateral system, to try to maintain support for universal standards of human rights and international systems of justice.

The United States played a key role in establishing international justice and human rights mechanisms early on, first with the Universal Declaration of Human Rights and then the covenants, as well as building on the Geneva conventions with the Nuremberg trials and others, leading eventually to the International Criminal Court. Right now, there is a tendency to say this is a unique time that calls for unique measures. We believe that, especially in unique times and especially in times of difficulty, it is then more important than ever to sustain and strengthen international norms. The United States as a world leader needs to set an example that it wants other countries to follow and to set a precedent that we are comfortable having other countries emulate.

What we are seeing now is a concern about compliance with international standards. We are concerned about possible erosion of international justice and the types of instruments that support it. We are also looking at incidents in which human rights abuses are taking place in the name of the war on terrorism. Take, for example, the situation in China where you have a crackdown in the Uighur Muslim community, a population that has suffered over many years and is now suffering in this climate. Likewise in Chechnya, we see abuses perpetrated by the Russians—also primarily against the Muslim community—but being viewed as part of the war on terrorism. And so we are spending much of our time trying to remind governments that there are international standards and our own standards.

Amnesty International is also looking at Afghanistan. Now that the war is over, it is very important that the United States follow through on its commitment toward reconstruction, and that necessarily includes human rights mechanisms. It needs to include education, the protection and defense of women's human rights, and the monetary support to allow these things to take place.

As we look at the possibility of intervention in Iraq, Amnesty International has been calling for strict compliance with the United

Nations Charter: in other words, first to exhaust all peaceful means and then, if necessary, to look at military intervention, to go to the UN Security Council and proceed under UN Security Council guidelines. If military intervention were to take place, of course, it is important to follow the commitments of international humanitarian law—those are the laws of war that must be abided by—as well as careful attention to the situation of refugees, that they should be able to leave the region and find safe refuge. In times of war, of course, it is essential that civilians not be targeted.

In the United States, Amnesty International has worked to look at the types of laws that the United States is putting in place relative to the war on terrorism and also to look at the treatment of those who are in detention. We, along with several other organizations, filed a Freedom of Information Act request seeking information on those who are currently being detained by the United States. What we have found is that, in many cases, in contrast to United States law, we have not been able to get information on the individuals, including such basic information as names, where they are being detained, charges against them, whether they have a lawyer, whether their family knows of their whereabouts—very basic information. We have won the first part of a lawsuit to obtain such information, but the United States government is currently challenging that, so it remains unsettled.

In the USA section of Amnesty International, we remain strongly opposed to the executive order establishing military commissions. We believe that the United States has a strong record of rule of law and that we have a justice system that ought to be tried. We maintain that the military order that was put out was in fact not only an embarrassment but it was also extremely harmful. The order did not provide for any kind of justice, and what was very shameful about it was that any dictator around the world could simply hold up the Bush administration order and say, "This is what I am going to do." That is what was harmful about it. Our hope is that it will never be used in the United States, but nonetheless the order itself stands as an erosion of justice.

These are some of the challenges that we are facing right now—challenges such as how to advance a human rights agenda in a time some government officials feel is unique and thus international standards can be put aside.

Time of Transition

We are, I think, in a stage of transition as we look at some of the changes in the world, such as globalization that puts everybody in touch with each other. A very good example of this is the World Conference on Women in Beijing, which brought together women from all over the world and put aside the north-south divide and cultural, religious, and other sorts of divides, and which demonstrated that the human rights movement can come together even when we have focused on different topics. But there is still a north-south divide. There remain divisions of cultural, religious, and universal rights groups. There is also a division between those groups that focus on international civil and political rights and those that focus on economic, social, and cultural rights.

During this past year, Amnesty International has moved from focusing specifically on civil and political rights to including in our new mandate economic, social, and cultural rights. This means for us that we will be looking now at issues of the right to education, the right to medical care—very important in terms of HIV/AIDS, for example—child labor issues, and other sorts of human rights.

Although human rights organizations have focused primarily on state actors, holding governments accountable, we find that increasingly non-state actors are the perpetrators. So Amnesty International is also working in that realm, to make sure that we are looking at violations or abuses taking place even in opposition groups, or in some instances perhaps in corporate entities that are impacting on human rights.

These are some of the challenges with which we are confronted as we strive to safeguard human rights throughout the world.

A Working Paradigm for Human Rights Discourse

17

Report on an Interactive Session on Human Rights

THOMAS J. WARD AND ALEXA FISH WARD

Toward the conclusion of WANGO Annual Conference 2002, a special interactive session was held on human rights. Participants in the session represented a variety of viewpoints and experiences in the human rights arena. Some of those in attendance spoke on behalf of Central and Eastern countries, which, over the past decade, have been adapting to a Western democratic model, stressing civil rights, pluralism, and the democratic process. Others who participated were from African nations such as Zimbabwe, where as little as two decades ago the vast majority of the nations' populations continued to be marginalized and disenfranchised by a racially determined oligarchy who were the sole participants in the "democratic" process. Represented as well at the session was the People's Republic of China, which, after decades of failed socialist experiments, and upon observing the stunning economic and political progress of neighbors such as the Republic of Korea and Chinese Taipei, determined that political freedom must be preceded by expansive economic development to insure the ongoing improvement of living conditions for the people of China.

This paper is a report on that session, which was done off the record. Although much of the interaction in the session focused on the status of human rights in China, parallel inquiries were made into how new working relationships could emerge between non-governmental organizations with human rights concerns and the governments that have been identified as repressive or remiss in protecting the human rights outlined in documents such as the United Nations Universal

Dr. Thomas J. Ward is vice president for international programs and dean of the International College at the University of Bridgeport, and Mrs. Alexa Fish Ward is president of the Women's Federation for World Peace (USA).

Declaration. A working paradigm aimed at fostering dialogue between NGOs and target governments, it was observed, would need to focus on projects that facilitate the conditions needed to build trust and long-term working relationships that can produce win-win results.

The new working paradigm that was discussed and, indeed, *experienced* differs sharply from the confrontational model that has frequently resulted in a breakdown of communication between human rights organizations and the governments with which they need to interact. Given the fact that the session involved ranking embassy personnel from a number of countries as well as representatives of international human rights organizations, it was edifying that the proceedings were conducted in a spirit of frankness and respect in order to facilitate dialogue, constructive engagement, and an understanding of the differing approaches to human rights.

Differing Approaches to Human Rights

In any discussion of human rights it is necessary to recognize that human rights advocacy groups and national governments prioritize human rights (e.g., freedom of speech, freedom of association, freedom of religion, freedom from want, freedom fear) as a result of their differing historical contexts and political perspectives. Depending on the recognized hierarchy of human rights in a given regime or in the focus of advocacy of a human rights–related NGO, strategic objectives will differ in discussions and negotiations.

For that reason, it is clear that the culture of peace, which has been so strongly advocated by UNESCO, the United Nations, the Interreligious and International Federation for World Peace (IIFWP), and WANGO, can best be realized if it is predicated upon the realization, first of all, of a culture of understanding. In order to realize this meta-objective, any discussant of human rights should not only articulate the human rights priorities of his or her government or advocacy group. The discussants must also make every effort to understand the genesis and the rationale of the human rights foci taken by their counterparts whom they hope to engage. One of the most common dichotomies results because of the question of whether emphasis on the fulfillment of physical needs such as food and shelter should have greater priority than freedom of speech, freedom of assembly, or freedom of self-determination.

The session shed light on cases where human dignity was grossly violated in the past. The still-fresh collective memory of such experiences explains why seemingly punitive measures have recently been taken against racial minorities through measures such as forced land reform in a country such as Zimbabwe, or through restrictions on speech that challenges the authority of the government in a place such as the People's Republic of China. The late Chairman Mao reminded his followers of the not so distant colonial days when shops did not allow entry to *Chinese or to dogs*. Governments and NGOs must engage each other, but they need to do so with an awareness of the historical conditions that have led to the evolution of their differing approaches and views of human rights.

The Case of China

With a population of approximately 1.3 billion, the government of the People's Republic of China has viewed survival as the bottom line human right. China underwent serious political and economic turmoil following the death of Chairman Mao Zedong in 1976. By 1978 it had begun a serious process of reform. The Chinese leadership has identified economic development and political stability as necessary pillars if human rights are to be expanded. China's annual income per worker reached toward $1000 last year. Within fifty years China expects to have reached a medium level of development.

China notes that its compatriots in Taiwan have experienced remarkable economic, social, and political development. In the case of Taiwan, the development was realized through a process that included forty years of martial law (beginning in 1949) before free elections and rule of law could be mainstreamed. The Taiwan model contrasts with the Soviet model where democracy was installed precipitously and resulted in the collapse of the system.

In reincorporating Hong Kong into the People's Republic of China, the government implemented the fifty-year policy of "one China, two systems." When asked why they had chosen for the "two China policy" to continue for fifty years, China's highest leadership responded that, by then, China can be expected to have implemented a democratic system.

One governmental representative from China in the session observed that, on the one hand, ongoing economic development is essential for China. However, second, he pointed out that, as the rule of law is expanded in Chinese society, it will ultimately serve as the most important guarantee of human rights. China is now the signatory of some eighteen international conventions on human rights and it has made significant progress in this arena, which should not be ignored or discounted.

At the present time there are eight political parties in China in addition to the Communist Party. Although the Communist Party remains by far the dominant political force, competition among candidates is a growing phenomenon in local government.

Religious freedom remains an issue in China. In China there are 86,000 places of worship, more than 3,000 churches, and 45 religious colleges. In the past, some religious groups have been politicized, and this has been one of the causes for concern with groups such as Falun Gong. While pillars of human rights such as food, clothing, and shelter have improved, it is nevertheless the case that in China freedom of religion and association needs to be better understood and appreciated.

Protocol for NGOs Addressing Human Rights

In the interactive session, it was noted by a representative from Zimbabwe that, in his country, the ruling party views many NGOs as having "become partisan." He argued that, instead of trying to work with the ruling Mugabe government to improve well-being and human rights, NGOs have established a pattern of aligning themselves with the opposition parties. This has resulted in a rift between NGOs and the government.

Another participant also spoke of the challenge that NGOs face of working to expand human rights without becoming tools of those who fund them. Because innumerous countries need to improve their human rights records, NGOs need to seek ways in which to work with countries as a helpful partner rather than as a hostile critic that results in them being marginalized and thus becoming outsiders to the process.

One discussant observed that countries feel more comfortable when engaging NGOs on human rights if they are not "targeted," but instead are invited to be part of a conversation that includes representatives of numerous nations whom NGOs "give the benefit of the doubt" and seek to advance the general well-being of their citizenry and recognize that the full implementation of Universal Declaration of Human Rights is part and parcel of advancing such well-being.

Conclusion

The deliberations of this session provided participants with intelligent presentations of diverse approaches to human rights. The session lent credibility to the position that, in many cases, human rights can be improved through the parties involved understanding the other's viewpoint and fostering ongoing dialogue rather than isolation. An NGO's examination of a government's human rights records should take into account not only its own hierarchy of human rights but those of the governments in question. Likewise, governments have a responsibility to understand the rationale for the views on human rights that are advocated by the NGOs with whom they engage.

The act of sincere, frank, constructive, and respectful engagement between governments and NGOs is positive. This approach, both in diplomatic and in unofficial venues, may bring better and more lasting results than confrontation and isolation have brought in the past. Countries that, in spite of complex histories and continuing economic challenges, seem committed to expanding human rights provide an especially germane context for this approach.

Part IV
NGOs and Environmental Protection

Introduction

The past century was a time of breathtaking technological and scientific advances. Since the dawn of the twentieth century, we have seen the inception of automobiles, commercial airplanes, personal computers, the Internet, the light bulb, widespread electrical power and telephone networks, and televisions. We have also seen the splitting of the atom, the identification of DNA and the human genome, cloning of animals, and the landing of humans on the moon and probes on other planets. Despite developments of a less desirable nature, such as two world wars and mass genocide, these advances, combined with such social developments such as the creation of the United Nations, gave hope to some that the new century would dawn with many of our environmental challenges well on our way to being resolved and our planet experiencing a sustainable global economy.

Alas, the new century has dawned and our environmental challenges seem more serious and profound. Whether measured in terms of loss of plant and animal species or loss of fresh water, loss of tropical forests or loss of wetlands, or increased pollution and ecosystem collapse, it is clear that few of the problems that garnered our attention in the twentieth century have been ameliorated and new problems have arisen. The trends, indeed, portend to more serious threats to our planet's future.

One promising trend, however, has been the explosion of environmental NGOs that are striving to address our environmental challenges. These NGOs are active in many ways: monitoring and investigating environmental practices; educating the public, corporation, and governments; advocating environmental legislation; promoting initiatives such as true ecotourism and debt relief in exchange for environmental protection; research activities; and purchasing and conserving tracts of land. The vast number of environmental NGOs that attended the World Summit on Sustainable Development in Johannesburg, South Africa, from August 26 to September 4, 2002, demonstrated the growth in this arena.

The papers in this section deal with the issue of NGOs and environmental protection. There is some overview of the trends of our times. These are both informative and sobering. However, in general these papers are oriented toward two particular measures for protecting the environment. One is the providing of economic incentives for individuals and communities to protect the environment via ecotourism. The importance of this approach was highlighted by the United Nations declaring 2002 the International Year of Ecotourism. The other measure discussed for protecting the environment involves the human spiritual and religious dimension and the role religious traditions have historically played with respect to the environment—both good and bad—and what current or potential role faith-based NGOs can play in conserving the environment.

One presentation that also would be appropriate for this section has been included in a latter part of the book. This presentation, which deals with environmental challenges of the Artic region and is given by Sheila Watt-Cloutier of the Inuit Circumpolar Conference, appears in Part VIII.

NGOs and Environmental Conservation

18

FREDERICK A. SWARTS

The twentieth century was a time not only of dramatic technological advances and worldwide events; it was also a time of major environmental change. Among the deleterious trends observed were collapsing fisheries, shrinking forests, an accelerating extinction of plant and animal species (the so-called Third Extinction), extensive population growth, rising global temperatures, falling freshwater tables, and declining cropland per person.

During the twentieth century, we observed 11 of the 15 most important oceanic fisheries and 70 percent of the major fish species being fully or overexploited, and more than half of the world's coral reefs dead or dying.[1] In 1900 there were no large dams—large dams being those over fifteen meters high; by the end of the century there were approximately 37,000 large dams.[2] In 1900, about 9,000 kilometers of rivers had been altered for navigation. Today, over 500,000 kilometers have been altered for navigation.

During the past century, major ecosystems, such as the Everglades, experienced a catastrophic decline both in terms of species and hydrology, leading to such sobering headlines for newspaper articles as the one titled, "Can the Everglades Be Saved?" Historically, if a forest, wetland, or river was not producing jobs and wealth, it was cut, drained, mined, or dammed.

Clearly there is a need for a comprehensive approach to our environmental problems if we are to make this new century a time of optimism and hope rather than a time of pessimism.

Dr. Frederick A. Swarts serves as assistant secretary-general of WANGO, president of the Waterland Research Institute for Water and Land Resources, and secretary-general of the World Conference on Preservation and Sustainable Development in the Pantanal.

Self-Interest and Current Environmental Approaches

A key term for understanding how environmental problems originate and how they are handled is the term "self-interest." In general, a major motivational factor for people, both individually and collectively, is according to what they perceive as their self-interest. This, of course, is reflected in their actions toward the environment.

It stands to reason that if an individual has a vested interest in preserving a particular environment for which he or she has some responsibility. Then there is a better chance that environment will be preserved. For example, if a person owns a lake and wants to fish year after year, they would want to take care of that lake. They would not want to overfish it or remove bank vegetation that may cause erosion.

Likewise, if a larger entity, such as a community, corporation, or nation, has a vested interest in sustainable development, then a greater effort will be expended in that direction. For example, if communities around the Okavango in Botswana receive substantial income from tourists coming to see the pristine nature and wild animals of that region, there is a desire to preserve that environment.

Measures designed to regulate and guide human behavior with respect to the environment generally work by taking into account self-interest.

Laws and Regulations

One such measure for protecting the environment is the instituting of legal protections, such as national, state and, local laws and regulations. By institutionalizing rules regulating behavior toward the environment, a community or nation can mold self-interest. It is in the interest of the individual or corporation to obey the laws of its community or nation; otherwise they face fines or imprisonment. In those cases where international laws are in effect, it is in the interest of a nation to obey the international law—although this aspect remains quite weak given the difficulty of imposing sanctions should a nation decide it is more in its interest to ignore the law.

While the use of environmental laws and regulations are critically important, such measures also have serious shortcomings. For one, they often lack effectiveness due to the difficulty of law enforcement. This is particularly evident in less developed countries and regions that may be especially vulnerable. For example, the Pantanal—located in western Brazil, eastern Bolivia, and northeastern Paraguay, and at sixty thousand square miles is the world's largest wetland—is protected by many environmental regulations; however, there is very poor enforcement of those regulations. Laws regulating fishing, litter, poaching, clearing of trees along rivers, and the capture of wild birds can be regularly seen violated in the Pantanal. But the difficulty of enforcement is not limited to undeveloped regions. Even in the United States it is not difficult to observe lack of law enforcement at the local level. I remember one story about a farmer who had red foxes on his property. The farmer cherished and protected the foxes. However, he also stated that had there been a law prohibiting the use of land on which red foxes reside, he would simply have killed the foxes to protect his ability to farm, and no one would be the wiser.

In addition, environmental laws and regulations often are reactionary measures to undesirable consequences that have already occurred. We are now seeing a lot of environmental regulations in the United States and worldwide protecting wetlands. However, this is after about 50 percent of the wetlands have already been destroyed worldwide, and an estimated 53 percent of the wetlands in the United States.

Furthermore, environmental regulations are at the whim of individual nations and communities, and thus sometimes leave key areas of the environment untouched. For example, most of the Amazon is in Brazil. Even if the other 190 or so countries feel it is in their self-interest that the Amazon be preserved, the river is, afterall, part of the sovereignty of Brazil, and the other countries really have no say in terms of the laws and regulations that Brazil passes and enforces. In fact, many Third World countries look at the history of industrialized nations such as the United States, which benefited from development and the use and alteration of natural resources, and feel resentful toward any foreign pressure placed on them to regulate the use of their own environment.

Environmental Education

A second measure for protecting the environment and promoting sustainable development is environmental education. Such education is generally oriented toward showing the value of environmental conservation; that is, to show why it is in the self-interest of the individual, corporation, or nation to conserve the environment. One methodology is to note the interrelatedness of nature and how its deterioration could impact these entities in substantial ways. For example, people are being educated in the loss of the ozone layer and how this can lead to increased skin cancer. People living along rivers such as the Mississippi are being taught how altering the channels has lead to increased flooding. People are being informed that killing of wolves leads to explosive growth in deer populations, and concomitant problems with deer damage to crops and increased deer/automobile collisions.

This approach has a certain effectiveness; however, it too has important limitations. While environmental education may be able to make persuasive cases for environmental conservation on the larger level, people may not see any value in terms of their own local self-interest. Preserving wetlands is a good thing, they submit, but as for the wetland on their own property, it would be much more lucrative if they could drain it for residential, commercial, or agricultural use. Communities that otherwise are concerned about the environment question the merit of preserving the spotted owl or the darter if it is going to costs their citizens' jobs and income. Generally, if jobs and wealth can be gained by draining a wetland, chopping down a forest, or damming a river, then people tend to do those things.

Furthermore, this approach is hampered by those cases where it is hard to establish a meaningful linkage between the environment and its obvious impact on the individual, community, corporation, or nation. Educating in terms of the preservation of some small and obscure species in a distant region is less persuasive than those cases whereby one can see how human impacts on the environment can boomerang to impact the individual and community.

Perhaps this has led to an effort to win hearts and minds through the creation of inaccurate and misleading linkages, such as when environmentalists in the last century strove to spur interest in preserving the Amazon by falsely claiming that the Amazon in particular and rain forests in general were the source for much of the world's oxygen. However, the Amazon, as an old-growth forest region, generally contributes little net oxygen, with much of the world's oxygen source coming from phytoplankton in the oceans. Likewise, environmental education sometimes utilizes incomplete or speculative knowledge as if conclusive in order to spur action. Such is the case with global warming, whereby the observed phenomenon of global warming sometimes is presented as decisively tied to anthropogenic sources, such as the burning of fossil fuels in our cars, homes, and factories. While a plausible and reasonable assumption, this is not an indisputably established fact and remains controversial even in the scientific community and among climatologists. This does not mean precautionary global action should be precluded; however, it remains that global warming should be presented to the public exactly according to what is known. When inaccurate (oxygen and the Amazon) or incomplete (global warming and fossil fuels) information is presented as incontrovertible truth in order to guide environmental practice, the essential confidence in environmental education and science can be weakened should contradictory information be brought to the public's attention.

Economic Incentives for Environmental Preservation

A third measure to guide human behavior in favor of environmental protection and sustainable development involves giving economic incentives for individuals, communities, and nations to care for their environment. A prominent example of this is the promotion of ecotourism by governments and communities. In its ideal conception, ecotourism is travel to natural areas that both minimizes the impact to the environment and improves the well-being of the local inhabitants, thus providing the local communities with an economic incentive to keep pristine these local areas that people are visiting. On an international level, one can note economic incentives such as the proposal to promote environmental conservation in developing countries by having industrialized countries agree to disregard a certain amount of Third World debt in exchange for preserving the environment.

Such economic incentives align with the individual, community, and national self-interest and are potentially effective. However, there are difficulties inherent in this measure also. Ecotourism, for example, has a seemingly intrinsic flaw. How can an idealized ecotour company, which pumps money back into the community and thereby provides an economic incentive for the community, compete with a nature tour company that instead maximizes its profits, even by environmentally unfriendly actions—and which therefore not only has a greater potential for profitability but can reduce its costs to the consumer and spend more on advertising its service? Also, many ecotour companies use facilities—such as car rental and office space—from outside the community visited, and even use tour guides from outside the community rather than train local guides who will later become competitors. There are few true ecotour companies, but many pseudo-ecotour companies that not only do not provide economic benefit to the local communities, but which themselves degrade the environment with their tours.

In the case of national debt reduction, such measures have not been approved on a global level. And it is not hard cash that is being offered, but the reduction of debts that would be paid in the future—this often counterbalanced by the risk to the nations of not developing natural resources that offer immediate profits.

In guiding human behavior with respect to the environment, a wide variety of laws, educational programs, and economic incentives have been extensively used, with varied effectiveness. Non-governmental organizations (NGOs) can play a key role in enhancing this effectiveness in all three areas.

For example, NGOs are able to provide an advocacy role in identifying and campaigning for needed laws and regulations. On the international level, NGOs have been at the forefront of the campaign for a treaty regulating the emission of greenhouse gases, pushing governments to support the Kyoto Treaty on climate change. Greenpeace is active in calling for governments to endorse basic principles related to corporate responsibility and accountability. Likewise, on the national level and local levels, NGOs are involved in advocating desired legal safeguards, whether they are local groups striving for protection of their own watershed area or major organizations such as the Society of Wetland Scientists addressing issues related to national wetland definitions, compensatory mitigation, restoration, and so forth.

International, national, and local NGOs also play a critical role in oversight and accountability, such as monitoring that various legal proscriptions and remedies are indeed followed. These include bringing alleged violations to the attention of public authorities or actually bringing their own lawsuits against individuals or corporations that are in violation of various legal safeguards.

Organizations such as the Nature Conservancy and Ecotropica provide protection by purchasing large tracts of land, which they can legally control and conserve.

In terms of economic incentives, many NGOs have been active in promoting and/or researching ecotourism, including the International Ecotourism Society, the Nature Conservancy, and Conservation International. NGOs played a vital role in having the United Nations declare 2002 the International Year of Ecotourism. Furthermore, NGOs have been promoting the use of national debt reduction in exchange for environmental protections.

One area where NGOs have been especially active is in terms of environmental education. A vast number of NGOs provide information on the links between human behavior and environmental impact, as seen by the thousands who were involved in the World Summit on Sustainable Development in Johannesburg, South Africa, in 2002. Some NGOs deal with a specific project or issue. For example, the Rios Vivos Coalition was originally formed to deal with the possible impact of a large-scale waterway project, the Hidrovia, on the Paraguay–Parana River system. Other NGOs have a broader focus, such as the Worldwide Fund for Nature, Conservation International, or the Worldwatch Institute, which produces excellent reports on global environmental trends.

Foundations may provide support for NGOs in many different areas of environmental protection.

Fourth Fundamental Arena: The Human Spiritual and Religious Dimension

In addition to legal protections, environmental education, and economic incentives, a fourth fundamental arena should be of significant value in guiding human behavior with respect to the environment. But it is an area that has not been extensively or effectively utilized in recent years, and indeed is often disparaged. This fourth pillar for guiding human behavior involves the human spiritual and religious dimension and the fundamental role that faith-based NGOs can play in environmental preservation.

However, not only has this role not been effectively utilized, but traditional religions in general and the Judaic-Christian and Islamic religious traditions in particular are often portrayed as hostile to the environment. Critics often advance the view that such monotheistic religions are inherently antagonistic to the environment because they view humans as being above nature in having a special relationship with the Supreme Being, leading to an exploitation of nature for personal benefit. This view was reflected, for example, during a 1999 conference on the Pantanal when a Brazilian federal attorney, who holds a key position in terms of major environmental works, passionately laid blame for the planet's woes on such a religious viewpoint.

There may be some merit in this criticism. Clearly, religion and religious text can be twisted to justify all sorts of crimes. Religion has been used to justify slavery as well as to mobilize people to fight against slavery, to justify war as well as pacifism, and so forth. And thus religion can be distorted to allow for practices that exploit the environment for material gain without regard for the needs of others, either presently or in the future.

However, the perception of religious traditions as inherently hostile to the environment is a distorted and partial view. A religious apologist could advance just the opposite position, that it is not the application of religious principles that is at fault, but rather the mis-application of religious principles and the rise of secular humanism.

A religious apologist, for example, could point to the scientific-humanistic viewpoint arising from the Enlightenment, and even the ascendancy of Darwinism, and proclaim that these views negated any lofty, special status of humans and thus allowed humans to view species as not part of a special creative act of a Supreme Being, requiring special care, but simply accidental products of chance via natural selection. Therefore, in the name of survival of the fittest, it becomes acceptable to do what one wishes with other species. Even extinction can be justified in such a manner. There is a selective advantage in removing all dangerous animals, such as rattlesnakes, vipers, and tigers. Just as some blame religion, others could blame humanism and note that the rise of environmental problems this century, and the so-called Third Extinction caused by humans, coincides with the expansion of the scientific-critical view and the rise of humanism.

Critical, Important Element

What is unquestionable is that the spiritual and religious dimension brings a critically important element and an enormous potential to solving our environmental challenges. Religion is fundamental to the human condition. And each religion has elements of faith that deal with a proper attitude toward the environment and the sanctity of nature.

For example, the Judeo-Christian tradition, while seeing humans in a unique position relative to the rest of the created world, posits humans as having a special covenant with God as stewards of nature, which is to be tended, maintained, and made fruitful. Jainism is noted for its view of *ahimsa,* meaning nonviolence toward all living beings. A Jainism text states, "One should not injure, subjugate, enslave, torture or kill any animal, living being, organism, or sentient being. This doctrine of nonviolence is immaculate, immutable, and eternal." Islam, Buddhism, Hinduism—all have sacred scripture talking about reverence for all life, and about the sanctity of nature. Shinto text admonishes humans to regard all things as your brothers and sisters. A Taoism text states: "Buy captive animals and give them freedom.... While walking be mindful of worms and ants. Be cautious with fire and do not set mountain woods or forests ablaze. Do not go into the mountain to catch birds in nets." Confucianists note that their founder would not fish with a net, and Mencius admonished people to not use nets with too fine a mesh and to limit cutting of forests.

Without religion there is really no ethical basis for caring for nature. There are environmental ethicists who attempt to construct a philosophy fundamentally based on the view that humans are just another species, neither higher nor lower than any other species. They use this beginning point to argue that ethically humans do not have any special rights over other species, and that we cannot infringe on the rights of other species. However, this philosophy runs into problems when the philosophers then try to justify eating, wearing clothing, raising livestock, and so forth. In attempting to make philosophical allowances for such actions, they end up with arguments that are quite convoluted and which do not really translate to the human condition. People do not think like that normally. However, they do think in terms of their religion in caring for nature.

Shared Principles and Precepts

Despite the variability of religions, one finds a remarkable concordance in quite a number of fundamental principles and precepts. Thus, it is not unusual that religions share common spiritual laws and precepts that are of definitive value in helping us resolve our environmental challenges.

Law of Cosmic Justice. One fundamental spiritual principle of most, if not all, religions is sometimes called the Law of Cosmic Justice or the Law of Cause and Effect. This principle holds that a person's right or wrong actions rebound to the doer in like kind, with good actions, performed with the right heart, returning benefit to the doer and accruing merit and wrong actions returning corresponding consequences and incurring penalties. In short, this law affirms that the universe is a just one, yielding over time just recompense for one's actions—"What one sows, one reaps." All major religions affirm that actions do not go unnoticed or unrewarded. Christianity, Hinduism, Islam, Buddhism, Judaism, Taoism, Sikhism, Jainism, Shinto, and so forth, recognize this principle.

This principle leads to a recognition that if one cares for nature, one will likewise reap benefit, and if one exploits the environment for pure material gain without regard for the present or future needs of others, one will receive corresponding consequences and accumulate demerit. As noted earlier, religious teachings can be distorted to allow for unsavory practices toward the environment. However, religious leaders maintain that in our conscience we know what are right actions and what are selfish and wrong actions.

Living for Others and Higher Purpose. Religions also share the spiritual precept of living for the sake of others. Thus, for example, the Golden Rule, "Whatever you wish that men would do to you, do so to them"—which is sometimes called the Silver Rule of Confucianism, "Do not do to others what you do not want them to do to you"—is found quite similarly stated in the scriptures of most if not all religions. These include Christianity, Hinduism, Buddhism, Islam, Judaism, and Jainism. In a similar vein there is a spiritual Law of Higher Purpose shared by most religions, which affirms that when human action serves a higher purpose rather than being centered on the self, it exists in harmony with the nature of the universe and thus will attract unity, prosperity, and joy.

Such an ethic of living for others and living for higher purpose naturally translates to care for the environment—for to truly care for others, it is important to have a sustainable vision of the planet, whereby the environment remains for the sake of others and for future generations.

These and other spiritual principles lead to a view conducive to caring for nature. The more that religious traditions inform their practitioners in the applicability to the environment of such spiritual laws, and inspire them to care for nature, the greater that this key fourth pillar of environmental measures becomes effective.

Spiritual Education

Through spiritual education, religious leaders and faith-based NGOs can help promote good environmental practices. Unlike "environmental education," which deals with physical consequences of our actions, "spiritual education" deals with spiritual consequences. There are two basic levels of applying spiritual law in the service of the environment.

The first level involves promotion of self-interest, but not simple self-interest, but what can be termed *enlightened self-interest*. By promoting the application of spiritual law to the environment, religious leaders and faith-based NGOs can help adherents look beyond one's gain in terms of immediate and obvious material profit to include a spiritual dimension whereby one's actions result in future material gain or in spiritual merit if his or her present actions are in accordance with spiritual law. It becomes in one's self-interest to care for the environment because we reap what we sow, and because benefit, unity, prosperity and joy result when one's actions are for the sake of others.

On a second and higher level, *religion has the power to teach its practioners to move beyond self-interest itself.* Religious leaders generally hold that to be in harmony with the Divine, our actions should spring out of a higher purpose: to live for others and to act out of love for the Supreme Being. Religions and faith-based NGOs have the capacity to systematically guide people in such a manner so as to act beyond self-interest to put others, nature, the future, and the Supreme Being before our selfish desires. That is, to do things out of the motivation of love, pure and simple, rather than to do things for what we can gain. In this way one can be willing to sacrifice oneself simply because it is the right thing to do. Most religions teach that such a heart is most in harmony with higher principles, and thus the person will benefit greatly.

Faith-based NGOs

This fourth pillar is starting to be energized more and more. For example, the International Consortium on Religion and Ecology (I-CORE), the Interfaith Center of Corporate Responsibility (ICCR), and the Association of Evangelical Relief and Development Organizations (AERDO) are examples of faith-based NGOs active in environmental protection. The United Nations, among other intergovernmental bodies, has been increasingly promoting this fourth arena as a valued component.

Truly, for a comprehensive solution to our environmental problems, it is important to activate this fourth pillar. The religious leaders, religious communities, and faith-based NGOs should take an active role in solving our environmental problems.

Religious leaders can advance a greater spiritual understanding to consider one's actions toward our environment. Then people can be motivated at the highest level to do the right thing, even when there is no law and no law enforcement, even when there is no economic incentive and little clear educational guidance about the benefit to us personally, even when no one is watching.

Even in the most educationally poor and remote areas of the world, there are religions. The leaders of faith-based NGOs can play, along with other NGOs, a most fundamental role in solving our environmental crises.

Endnotes

1. Abramovitz, J. N. (2000). "The Profound Shift Toward an Environmentally Sustainable Economy." In F. A. Swarts, editor, *The Pantanal* (St. Paul, MN: Paragon House, 2000), 245–50.
2. Ibid.

The Power and Ethics of Environmental NGOs in This Era of Earth Two

19

GARY GARDNER

I am not a specialist in ethics, and so rather than dwelling strictly on ethical questions confronting today's NGOs, I will address the context in which NGOs are operating today. This will involve three parts. The first is to discuss how unique this era in human history is. The second part will be to examine the role of NGOs in this new era; in other words, the new power that NGOs have. Finally, I will close with a few questions regarding that new power.

In terms of this era, if you were to ask somebody to look back and ask what is the most momentous event that has happened in the last one hundred years, you would get a number of answers. Landing on the moon, the dropping of the atomic bomb, the unveiling of the structure of DNA are a few of a number of things that might be considered. I would submit that it is actually the combination of many environmental and social trends that we have seen accelerating over the last century that ought to head the list. Let me go over a few of these trends.

We often hear about deforestation, and indeed the planet has lost almost half of the forested area that it had more than eight thousand years ago. But what is really interesting is that most of that loss has happened in the twentieth century. While this deforestation trend extends back thousands of years, there has been a very rapid acceleration in that deforestation just in the last hundred years.

We can talk about the ways in which we are changing the climate. No human generation before ours can talk about the capacity to change weather patterns, and we are finding that glaciers are melting on

---

Gary Gardner is director of research at the Worldwatch Institute, a nonprofit research organization devoted to the analysis of global environmental and resource issues.

many continents. We are finding that storms are more intense, flooding is more intense. Island states that are subject to obliteration by a rising sea level have banded together to organize for their cause because this is such a threat to them, all from the prospect of a changing climate.

We can talk about population changes. If you were born before 1950, you have seen more global population growth in your lifetime than the world experienced in all previous human history. Another way to say that is that those born before1950 are the first generation ever to see global population double in their lifetime. No human being before this generation could say this, and some of these people may see the global population triple in their lifetime. So population is another accelerating trend during the twentieth century.

We can talk about species loss. We always hear that there are more and more species going extinct. Let's put that in a global historical context. We live, biologists tell us, in an era of mass extinction. This is the first mass extinction since the dinosaurs went extinct 65 million years ago, only one of six mass extinctions in the history of this planet, and the only one to be caused by another species, that is, by human beings. Again, another sign that we are living in quite a unique era.

We should not forget to talk about growing poverty as well. Sometimes we focus extensively on environmental issues and forget that human beings are part of the environment which also require fair treatment. We have seen the ratio between the richest 20 percent and the poorest 20 percent of the world grow from thirty-to-one in 1960, to double that, more than sixty-to-one today. So the gap between the richest and the poorest twenty percent of the world has been growing.

I could mention many other trends, many of which we are quite familiar, from water scarcity to soil erosion to coral reef destruction. The writer Bill McKibbin has said that, "So extensive is our impact on the planet that we're essentially dealing with Earth Two," that is, a second Earth, because we have altered so many of its natural systems. That is the big-picture context in which NGOs are operating today.

A More Active Civil Society

NGOs are stepping up to many of these challenges because NGOs themselves have become much more powerful over the last century. There were only about 175 international NGOs in 1909, the first time a survey was done. Today there are about twenty-five thousand international NGOs. Many of these have come into being just in the last decade, or in the past thirty years. For example, half of all the non-governmental organizations in Europe were founded since 1990, and 70 percent of those in the United States were founded since 1970.

This is in part because of the much more active civil society that we are seeing today. We are seeing a trend toward democratization in many parts of the world, in Eastern Europe, in the former Soviet Union. We are also seeing the elimination of dictatorships in Latin America in particular, but also in parts of Asia and Africa. We are seeing a growing middle class, at least in some regions of the world, where people have the time to become active in civil society, people who are not spending all of their day worrying about their next meal or education for their children. And, very important, we see new communications technologies that are empowering civil society.

A very inspirational example of the activity of civil society and the new communication technologies was the international campaign to ban land mines, which was active during the 1990s. There was not any central office or staff associated with this movement. It was initially run, primarily by a single woman who used e-mail and later the internet, to organize NGOs around the world. She ended up rallying more than a thousand organizations in sixty countries to demand a treaty to ban land mines. That organization, the Coalition to Ban Land Mines, was started in 1993. By 1999 we had a treaty, and it was signed by 131 nations. That is indicative of the kind of power that NGOs can have, and the kind of positive impact that they can have in this very rapidly accelerating, changing world in which we live.

It is no surprise, then, that the nonprofit sector, according to a 1998 John's Hopkins University study, is a $1.1 trillion industry. It is larger than the GDP of all but seven countries in the world. So it is a very large and rapidly growing sector of society.

It is evident then that we live in an era of very rapid change, which is matched to some degree by an era of greater power of NGOs and a greater capacity of civil society to address many of these issues. But with access to power come questions of ethics. It was Lord Acton who stated, "Power tends to corrupt, and absolute power corrupts absolutely." That is no less true of NGOs or any other sector of society than it is of government or business. So as NGOs become more powerful, the ethical questions that face them become more and more important.

Three Questions

Let me very briefly address three questions about ethics and NGOs: What is our work? Who is involved in our work? And how do we carry out our work?

First, what is our work? Most of us in the NGO community do very valuable work. I do not think that most of us need to be defensive about the kinds of work to which we are dedicated. But we could ask ourselves, in the context that I laid out earlier of a very rapidly degrading planet, a planet becoming rapidly and increasingly unequal, is our work addressing those issues of our day as well as it could?

For example, at Worldwatch, where I work, we are primarily known by the general public as an environmental organization. But it is very clear to us that we need to be engaging social issues as much as environmental issues, especially the question of poverty, because of the growing inequality in the world. I think it is an example of how we are reading the signs of the times, looking at what is happening in the world and saying, "How can we still be true to our mission, but also be addressing the contemporary challenges that face us?" For example, Worldwatch, which has been around since 1974, puts out an annual publication called *The State of the World*, which looks not only at global environmental trends but also global social trends. NGO leaders might ask themselves whether there are ways in which their NGO, within the scope of work that they have set for themselves, could be better in tune with the world's problems today?

The second question then is: Who is involved in our work? Who is at the table when we are dealing either with other NGOs, or with business, or government, or with individuals? Who are we talking to? Who are we working with? Are we doing our best to ensure that all who should be represented are in fact represented? It is quite a challenge to any of us to be talking to people with whom we disagree, people who have fundamental differences with us. And I think it is important we all recognize that we live in an increasingly pluralistic world. Many, many people with many, many different views are coming together, and if we isolate ourselves and talk only to those who agree with us, we will find ourselves less effective, and less enlightened, because we learn from each other.

At Worldwatch, for example, there is no doubt that we have a definite point of view on many of the issues at which we look. But when we convene meetings, we try to bring in other points of view so that people are learning from us. We have done that recently in a meeting that we had in July when we were talking about the World Summit for Sustainable Development that was coming up in Johannesburg, and we made a real effort and were successful in getting the Bush administration to send some representatives. Not because we agreed with their positions, but more because we wanted them to hear our position, and also so that we could share ideas and learn from one another. I think, also, when we talk about who is involved in our work, it is important to remember that living in an era of rapid change often means that the people who are least powerful, the people who are poorest, are least able to adapt to the era of rapid change. We need to ask ourselves, if our work is addressing the needs of those people who are not able to adapt.

Finally, there is the question of "How do we do our work?" I think a fundamental question for us is, "Are we truthful in the work that we do?" It is wonderful that there are twenty-five thousand international NGOs working in the world today, but that makes it harder for any one of us to get money, to get attention, to have the kind of access or influence that we would like to have. That in turn increases pressure on us to appeal to some of the basest instincts, exaggerating our message, twisting the facts, ignoring counter-arguments, all in an effort to impress the public, funders, or policymakers. I think that it is a mistake if we head down that road. Certainly we want to be intelligent in crafting our messages, but truth is our best friend, and we need to be sticking to the truth of our issues. Truth will ultimately prevail.

At Worldwatch, we had a reputation for many years of being a gloom and doom organization—that is, reporting all of the worst possible facts about the environment and exaggerating the problems we face. I think that we can pretty credibly defend the work that we have done to date. But I think we also recognize that we need to be offering people hope as well. We need to be giving solutions as much as describing problems. As part of a strategic planning process we have made that one of our goals, to focus as much on solutions as we do on describing problems. An example in *The State of the World 2003* report is that we have a chapter on religion and the environment, and the role that religious groups can play in helping to create a more sustainable world.

Finally, in terms of how we do our work, we might ask ourselves if we are living what we preach. There is tremendous power in the example that we set for others, and it is often a power that we never realized. We have a silent influence on people and organizations that are watching us, and it is very important for us to be sure that we are doing exactly what we are claiming that others should be doing.

Ecotourism and the Non-Governmental Sector and Business Sector

20

MEGAN EPLER WOOD

I would like to address the issue of ecotourism and the work that I did for the past twelve years in this arena. I will also discuss the International Year of Ecotourism, which was a UN-declared year that took many by surprise. The naming of this year actually engendered quite a maelstrom of controversy. The International Ecotourism Society (TIES), of which I am founder and president, really had nothing to do with the naming of the year. But we were the largest international non-governmental organization in the world working on the issue of ecotourism, and thus we were thrown into a very extensive international discussion about the value of ecotourism as a conservation and sustainable development tool. I will discuss briefly some of that experience, and some of the results of those consultations that we did worldwide.

At the time that The International Ecotourism Society was formed, in 1990, ecotourism was a concept, but absolutely lacked principles. There had been one book, *Ecotourism: Potentials and Pitfalls*, written by Elizabeth Boo of the World Wildlife Fund, which described some of the trends. But as a business and what some call a conservation enterprise, there were no guidelines. Certainly there was not any international oversight, and thus any government, any business, or any community worldwide could say that they were taking on the task of delivering ecotourism without any entity in the world being able to ask their meaning. What ecotourism meant was wide open. Any organization could interpret ecotourism any way they wanted, and we saw an immense boom of interest in this field.

Many countries in the world, such as Costa Rica and Ecuador,

Megan Epler Wood is founder and past president of The International Ecotourism Society (TIES).

have seen double-digit growth rates per annum in their tourism businesses in the last decade, and in some cases over two decades, as in the case of Costa Rica. Growth has been so dramatic that tourism has surpassed the economic statistics of such stalwarts as bananas or sugar and many other well-known agricultural enterprises, even coffee. And tourism has skyrocketed as the enterprise of which everybody wants to be a part.

Establishing Guidelines

When we founded The International Ecotourism Society, it was a consortium of non-governmental organizations in Washington, DC. We were do-gooders, to tell you the truth, from the World Wildlife Fund, the National Audubon Society, Conservation International, and The Nature Conservancy, who decided to reach out to business because we realized that if we did not work with business, we would have no luck in setting standards. And so TIES became an international consortium of businesses and non-governmental organizations committed to work together on a professional basis to set standards for the field of ecotourism.

How did we do our work? Well, for twelve years we held a lot of meetings. I am a real veteran of all kinds of multistakeholder meetings from around the world. I often say, give me a stakeholder group and a working committee, and I will put you in a circle and record results! We would talk about issues, and as we became more sophisticated we made sure that we had the multistakeholder participatory approach to ensure that with each issue we were getting the full realm of opinion.

Granted, probably no one could ever get the full realm of opinion on anything. But we tried. We did a lot of survey work in advance. So what we would do is we would go and do surveys of businesses that are already working in ecotourism, at least that is what they claimed, and we would find out what their business practices were. That was step number one.

Then we would take it out to multistakeholder groups and say to them, "How does this fit in with your perspective of what should actually be done?" But we would not let them just discuss it without the presence of business in the room because otherwise it became a very polarized discussion as to what NGOs wanted versus what business wanted, and our goal was to get everybody to agree on what it was. I have been on every continent holding these meetings for twelve years so that we could come up with what we called "guidelines." We have publications now on all of this work that are fully available through The International Ecotourism Society. These publications are ultimately in the form of guidelines in terms of setting standards for business.

These are voluntary standards, and some people feel voluntary is inadequate. But after twelve years of work, I can tell you that it is a very important start, because if we had not gone through this process, there would be no guidelines available on this industry at all. Business would not have been involved period. And business was deeply involved in this process, and they agreed internationally through all kinds of laborious processes—which included actually involving businesses in the review of the publications before they came out as well, to make sure that they did not find these guidelines to be inhibiting business.

There are a variety of guidelines. There are guidelines for tour operators in the field of ecotourism. There are guidelines that just came out for the building of lodges, in terms of how to do this in a way that will be environmentally and socially sustainable. It is a large volume that took us five years to complete. We have just finalized guidelines for businesses working in marine and coastal areas, which is the area where more tourism businesses are located than any other place. In other words, the heavy volume of tourism is still on the coast. In almost every country, that is where the number one site is going to be.

We also do industry launches. We launched Marine Ecotourism Guidelines at the largest dive show in the world where all of the dive professionals go. We launched the lodge guidelines at the World Ecotourism Summit in Quebec in May 2002, which was the largest group of individuals coming together to discuss ecotourism.

Economic Impacts

Despite the effects of September 11, tourism is one of the fastest growing economic engines, or sectors, on the world stage. It continues to be so, and it is particularly important in certain parts of the world. Revenue generated by all forms of tourism has grown 35 percent faster than the world economy in the last thirty years. It is outstripping other forms of economic development by quite a bit. In 1999 international travel was 8 percent of all world exports, surpassing food, textiles, and chemicals.

In countries like the United States, which has a multitrillion-dollar economy, tourism is important but it does not play, percentagewise, the role that it does in the lesser-developed countries. In the lesser-developed countries, we are seeing that in nearly every such country tourism is becoming not only significant, but a priority. One of the reasons is that it is a relatively low-cost industry to enter into comparatively. A small tourism business has fairly low start-up costs, and therefore tourism as an export economy can be launched in lesser-developed countries relatively quickly. This is one of the only economic areas where developing countries are showing a trade surplus.

It is important that we grasp the economic impact of this industry, which is very little understood and very little discussed in world forums, including the environment forum in Rio, where tourism was not even discussed as an industry. At the World Summit on Sustainable Development in Johannesburg, the economics of the ecotourism industry received a few mentions, and yet it is the largest export economy in the world. It has been an ongoing battle to look at tourism as an economic and development tool.

We are seeing an incredible annual growth rate in the industry. Yet, we are seeing extremely low government investments in tourism. What does that mean in terms of sustainability? In order to make any industry sustainable, there has to be investment and infrastructure. If there are to be coal-fired plants, there have to be scrubbers. When it comes to tourism, there has to be planning. There is no other way. There also has to be a sustainable infrastructure in terms of decisions of how transportation moves individuals around.

There must be land-use planning. Where will a hotel be allowed to go? These are massive decisions that will have long-term impacts on economies around the world and on the people who live in those countries. This kind of planning is almost never done before tourism is used as an economic development tool.

What do we have? Essentially, a potentially sustainable industry that is not so for one simple reason: lack of planning. At the same time, reliance on this industry is growing dramatically. We are seeing an incredible growing reliance on tourism, especially in small island states.

Thus, what we have is a real potential recipe for disaster. We have countries becoming increasingly dependent on tourism. We have governments that by and large are not investing in making it sustainable, and we have almost no accounting for how tourism is contributing to local people's benefits. In other words, we have a rapid rush to bring in foreign investment without any accounting for how local people are getting a piece of the pie.

These are our current national policies. Most countries have national tourism organizations. They are there to attract foreign investment, usually of tourism multinationals into countries so that they, can get back cash from the tourism business. The way most countries tax systems are set up involves a tax on tourists. There is a bed tax, whereby every tourist that comes to the country pays a percentage tax on their stay. There is also in most countries a departure tax. That is, whenever you go to the airport and you depart, you pay a tax.

Has anybody ever thought about where that money is going? Well, in fact, it is not going where we might hope. It is going towards attracting foreign business visitors for investment. It is going toward economic growth, but it is not going to sustaining the landscape, environmental protection, or to sewage infrastructure. Hundreds of places in the world that have absolutely no sewage infrastructure are growing dramatically in tourism, and all of the sewage is going straight into the sea. I have personally visited dozens of these places, and they are legally permitted. These basic health standards are being ignored, and yet taxes are going toward bringing more business in rather than addressing these issues. Environmental controls at the moment are almost entirely voluntary in most countries.

If a country has a tourism minister, which most countries do, how do they account for success? They normally account for success by telling how many visitors come to their country. It is somewhat of a joke. If you were to account for the success of a textile or banana industry by how many bananas you send out of the country, or how many sweaters you send out of the country, you would be ridiculed. But this is how our tourism ministries are accounting for success. They do not talk about the economic portion of the pie that is staying with the country. That is what you need to know. So there is no accounting for what is the economics term, leakage.

This is still going on, at almost every level. I am talking about bilateral, multilateral, and I have sat in forums with the major multilaterals and most of the bilaterals. There are no guidelines and inadequate attention to equal economic opportunity for local citizens. There is inadequate investment in things like sewage treatment.

What is fundamental to bringing the economic pie home, of giving access to capital to local entrepreneurs? This is a critical issue. If local people do not have access to appropriate capital to make business, they do not make business. They work for multinationals who come in with capital. So we have a situation here, one that is totally confirmed by hundreds of stakeholder meetings around the world. We are dealing with entrepreneurs who do not have access to capital. There are no separate policies to facilitate these kinds of businesses, even though there is a tremendous demand to do so. There is little public-private cooperation, although some good examples have recently emerged. In certain countries, public-private cooperation is the key to success, so that business, communities, and governments can work together to solve this problem.

International Year of Ecotourism

When the year of ecotourism was established, understandably it was very controversial. If you think about what I just presented, there were absolutely no guidelines internationally for this kind of enterprise. So, needless to say, many people around the world, many of whom are involved in the United Nations and NGOs, immediately started protesting, "What is going on? Why are we having an International Year of Ecotourism when there are no UN guidelines for this kind of enterprise, period?"

Indigenous people became very concerned. They started to lobby right away, saying that there had been a lot of problems with tourism enterprises being built on indigenous lands without permission. Actually, in many parts of the world the indigenous people have no land rights. They do not own their own land. The best example is perhaps Kenya. It is not the only example by any means, but the Maasai are living in one of the heaviest tourism areas in the world for ecotourism. I held a large regional meeting in Kenya, with the support of the Kenyan Wildlife Service, and we looked at the situation of marginalized people on public and private land. A large majority of the people have no property rights. So if the government chose, which they often do, to give a permit to a private entrepreneur to build a hotel on indigenous land, the hotel is built and the native people have to move.

It is a controversial situation, and remains so. We have drawn an awful lot of attention to issues that no one else was paying attention to, and it has been a great work, and there is tremendous potential for further cooperation. Non-governmental organizations absolutely have a fundamental role.

The International Ecotourism Society has worked very much with business. You cannot, as NGOs, ignore business. So business, NGOs, and communities, all have to work together.

So what came out of the discourse? There was a world ecotourism summit with conclusions that are on the United Nations Environment Program site. My organization held six consultative meetings with the United Nations Environment Program in six biodiversity hot spots of the world that are also rural, that also have tremendous amounts of ecotourism. We held multistakeholder meetings and we built some recommendations.

These are very basic recommendations. One is that we have to have policies, period. In most places they do not even have policies, and there is a need for policies that are consistent with sustainable development. We have to ensure involvement and participation with all stakeholders. That was universally missing. Everywhere local people came to us and said, "Our government is bringing Hilton, but they are not talking to us."

Create objective standards. This has to be done mostly at the national level. What my organization did was set international guidelines that are very, very good. Any national government or local NGO can now access these standards. But local standards have to be set. And while voluntary guidelines are great, ultimately you have to have stronger standards. When you do not have required sewage treatment, you have got to get such regulation. The international organizations that represent big tourism and business do not want regulation.

Through UN forums, it has become clear that municipalities strongly agree. For example, the representative from Hawaii, who was in the room at a UN forum in 1999, said, "We want not only regulations, we want contribution from business towards sewage infrastructure, because our citizenry is so small compared to the number of tourists that are coming that you need to be paying a tax to help us build this kind of infrastructure we need to service tourists." Certain countries have implemented such measures. For example, in Egypt, for their Red Sea development, that is exactly what was done. The authorities told businesses that they could not build on the Red Sea unless there was enough infrastructure support.

Finally, there needs to be support for small businesses from the NGO community. For NGOs, we have to be players, we have to grease the wheel, we have to do capacity building, we have got to monitor, we have got to do research. We have to look at what these businesses are doing, and we have to report on their activities, and we have to ensure that whatever data we are using is based on research. Many people stand up in tourism forums and say they know what they are talking about, without any research backing up what they are saying at all.

Ecotourism is a field, a field that is a form of development. One had better get educated in the field if we want to speak about it. NGOs are responsible, like any other entities, for knowing what they are talking about based on research. We have to cooperate with research institutions, which include many who would be willing to tie in to the NGO community to provide those research and practical solutions.

In summary, we do see the field of ecotourism growing. Johannesburg recognized tourism and ecotourism for the first time, and we also saw ecotourism listed as one of the seven signs of progress by *National Geographic* magazine, post-Johannesburg.

We need more international cooperation, and we need development agency strategies that look at this sector, and we need community development through focused training and regional exchange. We absolutely cannot ask local communities to enter into this kind of enterprise without appropriate capacity building.

World Religions and Ecology

21

MARY EVELYN TUCKER

My own area of expertise is East Asia, and since the early 1970s, I have spent a great deal of time in the region, and in China and Japan in particular. Over these past thirty years, I have observed an enormous amount of destruction of the environment in Asia. When one begins to factor in the size of this region, and that South Asia and East Asia account for at least two-thirds of the world's people, it has been a horrific wake-up call to those of us who are particularly interested in Asian cultures, religions, and history as well as the future of sustainable life on the planet.

There is an awareness as well that science and technology, while absolutely critical to the solutions to these problems, will probably not be sufficient to make the changes that are necessary. Tapping into the resources of the human spirit as well as into the remarkable resources of culture and religion that have guided civilizations for centuries and indeed millennia, will be perhaps one of the most important nodes of change in the future. This is what I would like to address.

World religions and their sensibilities in terms of forming cultures and civilizations need to be understood within the context of the geological history of the planet as well as within the universe that contains this planet. We have been observing terrifying trends in the diminishment of life, such as the fact that we are living in the midst of a sixth extinction period. What is quite remarkable is that at the same time we are awakening to a new sensibility of the vastness of the evolution of the universe over 13 billion years.

Diminishment of all life support systems is increasing, and that has been within the past fifty to a hundred years. At the same time, we are realizing a heightened sensibility to our own possible demise.

Dr. Mary Evelyn Tucker is professor of religion at Bucknell University and with her husband, John Grim, directed a series of ten conferences on World Religions and Ecology at the Harvard University Center for the Study of World Religions from 1996–98. They are editing the volumes from the series.

"Is humanity suicidal?" Harvard biologist Ed Wilson asks. "Will we become an endangered species as we pollute our life support systems?" As director of the Missouri Botanical Garden, Peter Raven says, "We are destroying our world."

At the same time, we are awakening to a new sensibility of the profound interconnection of life, of life systems, of ecosystems, of species, and of who the human is at this moment in history. I think that is the critical sensibility that humans are awakening to right now: Both this destruction and the awesome beauty of this planet, of the evolutionary history that has carried life through for 4.6 billion years on the planet and 13 billion years of universe history.

Thus, this moment of creativity and tension is an awesome moment of opportunity for the human community to ask: "How can we assist the future of life on the planet?" It is at that level that we need to think through this issue.

World Religions and Ecology Conferences

It was with this in mind that my husband John Grim and I began to ask how can we draw on the enormous resources of the world's religions that have provided sustenance through suffering, through tragedy, through tremendous challenges for the human community. We are faced with a new kind of challenge. How can we draw on these resources of deep spiritual wellsprings in the human community? We realize that just as civilizations have been shaped by scriptures, by traditions, by rituals, by ethical practices, we need to begin to survey this splendid multiform sensibility of religions from all over the world, and also recognize that environmental ethics clearly cannot be just secular-based environmental philosophy.

Secular-based environmental philosophies have been emerging over the last several decades. We can talk all we want about intrinsic rights, utilitarian rights, and so on. But it is still not tapping into the deeper transformations that are needed. A linkage with religious sensibilities is crucial. Environmental ethics from a secular basis only have not been able to effect the larger transformations that are needed.

When my husband and I began this conference series at Harvard on World Religions and Ecology in 1996, we addressed the issue with great humility. To be honest, religions are late in coming to this issue. They have not been in the forefront of recognizing environmental destruction and loss of societies. Therefore, they need to work in conjunction with the voices of other disciplines that are working on this issue of environmental degradation. They need to be partners, not necessarily preachers, and that is a big difference, in approach.

Furthermore, we need to recognize that religions have had tremendously negative consequences in human history. We see it across the planet today in various parts of the world. We need not even mention that except to say we need to have humility, we need to recognize this dark side of religion in terms of conflict and oppression. So religions are late, religions have their dark side, but religions have this promise and potential as well.

In order to draw together scholars from all parts of the world, these Harvard conferences on world religions and ecology were international in every sense, in terms of those who attended and the groups that provided support in getting people from every continent. We tried to bring together both scholars and practitioners of these world religions along with environmentalists working in local communities. We wanted to identify the resources available from the traditions: the scriptures, the rituals, the ethical practices. In addition, we highlighted grassroots movements that illustrate this new kind of conjunction of NGOs and religious environmental cooperation.

The sense of cooperation began to give people a feeling for the weaving of worldviews toward nature (some of which are very ancient and very much implicit in cultural practices) with the ethics that can bring these ideas forward. What we have been trying to suggest is that this is a process of *retrieval*, *reevaluation*, and *reconstruction*. In other words, many religious traditions, especially indigenous traditions and many of the Asian traditions, have enormous resources concerning human-Earth relations. Part of the problem has been that religions have had a highly developed sense of human-God relations and often human-human relations, but human-Earth relations have been forgotten. We are trying to retrieve these ideas, reevaluate them in light of present circumstances, and reconstruct them into a new mixture for contemporary circumstances.

Another way to put it would be to say that the religious communities have been very good in talking about issues of homicide or suicide, but not biocide or geocide. That is the challenge that we face. In this retrieval of religious resources, there needs to be a reevaluation of what will be particularly helpful in the new human-Earth relations that will move toward a sustainable future.

The final part of retrieval and reevaluation is reconstruction. The religious communities, as they begin to formulate a more comprehensive environmental ethics, are renewing themselves. They are gaining a revitalized sense of their spiritual depth for our historic moment and for future generations. It is a mutually enhancing process that religions have always responded to changes over time. As they respond, they themselves will renew their own spiritual depths and their own ethical efficacy and moral potential.

Anthropocosmic Concerns

What we are trying to do in this project is tap into what we would call the "wellsprings of inspiration for enduring transformation." We can also put this together with a sense of both inspiration and perspiration. Religions have historically had an ability to activate people and motivate transformations in areas like social justice, civil rights, and more recently women's issues. Now the challenge is to bring to bear that sensibility to a larger ethical concern, not only for the human community, but for the human-Earth community—for other species, for life systems, and that which sustains all species.

This is the moment of the extension of moral concern out into the human community—the democratization, the NGO movement, civil society, and so forth—but also outward to the whole Earth community. This is the moment when we need to embrace, and are beginning to embrace, the Earth community in a new way, and that is what survival depends on in every possible dimension.

We could almost summarize this extension of moral concerns by saying it means we are moving from exclusively anthropocentric or human concerns to what could called *anthropocosmic* concerns. That is, to resituate ourselves within the vast rhythms of the natural world, to remember that we are cosmic beings, that we are part of a larger feeling sensibility that has sustained life for all of these centuries, and that is what the religious traditions have also helped humans to do. To embed the human community within the rhythms of nature, within harvest cycles, within hunting rituals, and so on, and to feel the sacredness of water, of air, of plant, and animal life that have sustained these communities. These are the cosmological rhythms that the religious communities have brought forward in rituals, in prayers, in celebration, in ceremonies.

The challenge then is to bring them forward in this particular moment. From the Harvard World Religions and Ecology conference, we are producing ten volumes on the world's religions, including indigenous religions. Eight of the ten are completed. This is just the beginning of retrieving these incredible wellsprings of the world's religions. We have also created a major website under the Harvard Center for the Environment: environment.harvard.edu/religion. Next is to ask how we translate this outward into other communities, into synagogues, into mosques, into churches and so on. We have completed booklets for this purpose, such as one for the United Nations Environment Program on Earth and Faith, which can be used in discussion groups. It highlights scriptures and teachings, serving as a summary of what each of the world's traditions might contribute to this ongoing discussion.

Another book we have published called, *Earth Ethics*, is available on the Harvard website. I would also like to draw attention to the Earth Charter, which I think provides an extraordinary moral basis for the type of transformations we are talking about (see www.earthcharter.org).

Let me conclude with a few examples of how I think this sense of moving from an anthropocentric to an anthroprocosmic universe is already happening around the world. One is the tree-plantings of various NGOs. The Buddhist community in Southeast Asia, especially Thailand, has been very active in ordaining trees to protect forests and so on. In the south of India, the largest Hindu temple, and one of the wealthiest in Andhra Pradesh, has been doing significant tree planting. In Zimbabwe religious communities have been united in cooperation for over ten years to plant a million trees a year. They also have developed a theology of the importance of trees. This is called Zircon, and it involves the Shona tribal peoples in the south of Zimbabwe, along with the traditional Christian churches with Dutch reformed influences. This is an amazing interreligious cooperation, which illustrates this movement toward embedding humans within these larger cosmological rhythms of nature and understanding the sacredness of trees and all of nature.

Much more remains to be done, but the religious communities in cooperation with NGOs are making a unique contribution to the larger transformations that are required to sustain life on the planet for future generations.

Sustainable Community Building

22

DONALD B. CONROY

I am pleased to be able to address the issue of sustainable development, especially as applied to sustainable community building. As we proceed into the twenty-first century, we have to be very aware that we are at a point of breakdown or breakthrough. It has become clearer and clearer that we are approaching a point of breakdown in many sectors—ecological, economical, and cultural. But we also hope that there will be a breakthrough and a new energizing shift in the consciousness of the species. We face the need to "reinvent" the human species at this point, and as we go into this era it is very important that we are able to look into a process by which we can do that.

If we in the twenty-first century have a new vision, a shift from an anthropocentric view to a more cosmic vision, we need to be able to accomplish this on a practical as well as a theoretical level. More and more, the point of breakdown is often the point of breakthrough. Religions know that. That is what crucifixion/resurrection is pointing to: death is the moment of new potential and the breakthrough point in the Christian tradition. In a regenerative cycle of the Earth itself we often see this happening.

In the new era of globalization and technology, we have the possibilities that we did not have before of doing some very fantastic things. However, technology is a two-edged sword. It can cut one way and harm us; it can cut another way and help us. So in looking at this era of globalization, which is also an era of ecodevastation, we have to be very cautious, and we have to be very circumspect. At the same time, we must be bold and charge into a new era together in a new collaborative fashion. The advances in religion and ecology have been significant, but we must speed them up.

Dr. Donald B. Conroy serves as president of the North American Conference on Religion and Ecology (NACRE), and is also chairman of the International Consortium on Religion and Ecology (I-CORE).

Collaboration

In the book *Earth at Risk: An Environmental Dialogue between Religion and Science,* that I coauthored and edited with Rodney Petersen of the Boston Theological Institute and which came out on Earth Day 2000, there was an attempt to get deeply into that dialogue. This collection of essays shows how scientists and theologians are saying science and technology cannot solve the problems alone. It also explains why religionists and theologians are acknowledging more and more that it is impossible to achieve what needs to be done unless we form a genuine partnership and a collaborative way of viewing the universe in the wonder and the glory of the last several billion years of cosmogenesis. As we experience this macroshift, which the Club of Budapest has talked about so much, we have entered into an era in which new spiritual awareness and values will be needed to advance an era of building a sustainable planetary community. In every sector of society, ethics and spirituality can no longer be the realm of religion and theology alone. This new consciousness must penetrate every sector from business and politics to agriculture, health care, and technology. This must be foremost in the discussions of new policies and new laws.

I have been working heavily on the local to global aspect with our I-CORE "Caring For Creation"™ project. In our consortium we have made a much greater effort in the last two years to involve the new technology leaders in how to bring together the collaborators, and how we are able to share the information that becomes knowledge, and the knowledge that becomes wisdom. We need to advance from raw data to knowledge, from knowledge to wisdom. In so doing we need a twofold or complimentary way of approaching things, one that involves both analytic science and a unified values-driven vision.

A decision-support-and-planning system is possible. It is possible now in new ways both on a global level, but also on bioregional and local levels, and even at a neighborhood level. The new technologies of sustainable community building work from an evolving historical context. You are able to search out the story, bring things up to date, and then project into the future, extrapolating the curves so that they might converge in a solution that is sustainable.

This takes into account the diversity that we face everywhere from the local neighborhood to the planet as a whole. But diversity can be a strength if we see paths to sustainability: paths to collaboration and in fact paths to profitability at the same time as we deal with the ethical situation. Now in "Caring For Creation,"™ which is the phrase that we use in the local-to-global process, we found that it is important to make things replicable, and to internalize the process among leaders. Whether they be local, national, or international, it is important to get patterns of success so that it is replicable. In so doing, you will have a "decision support system" and a "sustainable building process" emerging at all levels of action.

One very encouraging thing has been a dialogue with some of those who worked with the G7 and various groups on the Y2K problem. Y2K was a real problem, and could have been an absolutely devastating moment if the corrected software had not been ready. The G7, several enormously important businesses, and the military got together and really addressed that problem. They set up a strategy room, not a war room, but rather a strategy or peace room in which they could really put together all of the information, and take it from information to knowledge to use for practical solutions. As a result, there were actually very few breakdowns, although some breakdowns did occur. But it was the great example that by January 1, 2000, we were able to do something very practical and sustainable for the planet as a whole.

The events of September 11, 2001, were the opposite. We did not cooperate. We had a lot of information and data, but nothing connected. There was a lack of cooperation, a lack of urgency, a lack of a number of things. It shows that in this era of technology we can have either devastation or success. In terms of the possibilities in decision support and collaboration, we can involve a number of the global players in discussions in various fora.

New Opportunities

The dimensions of what we have to do to get together are exceedingly complex. To simplify the complexity, we have to be able to characterize and put together things in a new graphic way as well as design a metric system that can quantify a new fiscal, social, and ecological system of bottom-line accounting. It is evident in the past two years that even on the fiscal level, accounting firms have faltered. But we have to take a quantum leap and be "triple-bottom-line" accountable in our major corporations, in government, and in our personal stewardship of the Earth's resources.

When we see events such as 9/11, they shock us. But let us not be shocked into inaction or be paralyzed by fear, but rather realize this tremendous opportunity that we have in building a sustainable civilization. We can dialogue in new ways, with new success, where we can point to new models of sustainable community projects.

We have to have bioregional agendas and local agendas that coincide with these larger agendas. In regard to ecotourism, for example, I think you can get to very practical models. One group we have been in contact with is the Camaldolese monks at Big Sur on the California coast. They have worked with the Native American tribe there, with the local Buddhist center and community, and with a nearby New Age retreat house. They meet quarterly, taking turns hosting the gathering. They were able to get together and realize that the tourism interests were just about ready to pounce on prime Monterey Peninsula property. They were able to show the religious significance, the cultural significance, and sway the voters in Monterey who voted to keep out those disruptive and unsustainable interests. This success story shows the tie-in in a practical way when a local interfaith group moves on it in a significant way. But they were talking before this happened and were ready when a significant issue came up.

Building a new ecovillage is another example. We have worked with the Department of Energy and EPA on solarizing churches, mosques, and synagogues. We are able to now look at new types of sustainable technologies in building that are less devastating, and they are much better in terms of the R-factor of heating and cooling. So we are looking at practical programs like House a Family Program, a senior-based housing program, and the six phase Eco-Building Initiative. These are fiscally, socially, and environmentally sound ways of building. They also get a significant return on investment in a much more ethical way than simply putting money in the stock market.

Cultural and Religious Lag

When you go back in Western Civilization to the time of the transition in the late 1400s and early 1500s, from the manuscript era to the movable type and print era, it took the traditional church about 55 to 75 years to catch up and realize that they were no longer living in a manuscript world, but print through movable type was the new technology and cultural norm. This transition took too long to make in the Age of Discovery as navigation opened up, as the new technologies of geography and so on and new sciences opened up. Thus it is important that we understand and make use of the new technologies while remaining true to our ethical principles.

Today we cannot take that much time to start a new sustainable initiative. We cannot have the long implementation time that cultural and religious institutions have often had at times of major transition. Keeping this in mind, local action groups are necessary, and they need more and more training in capacity-building. They need leadership development. At the same time we have to work with global and national leaders. Moreover, we need to educate three generations at once. This is a big order never before done in history, but we may have the beginnings of that in the wake of recent events and as ecodevastation more and more becomes a reality.

Recently I had the opportunity to address this problem with the Institute for Global Solutions, with whom I-CORE is working. We are working on solutions that are practical in light of the Earth Charter. We were able to get Walter Cronkite and Stephen Rockefeller together for the beginnings of what may be a three-part series on PBS that will point to the ethical and technological solutions that are dovetailing. Stephen Rockefeller, who is professor emeritus of religion and philosophy at Middlebury College, has worked over the years with Maurice Strong, Mikhail Gorbachev, and others on the Earth Charter, a set of sustainable ethical principles.

I would say that the Earth Charter is a great example of the ethical and policy advances that we are now able to see on the horizon. We need to know more about them; we need to integrate them into our decision-making; we need to educate a mass public. So with this in mind, a dialogue of sustainable civilization is needed. This can be done getting your own NGO, your own faith community, or your own corporate group together to sit down with the other sectors in a new dialogue. Making use of the new communications technology and the insights of ethics and spirituality in this era of globalization is going to bring us to a point where we must break through.

This must be a regenerative era, when we can go into the powers of planetary regeneration, which may really challenge the second law of thermodynamics. This is the big question. Does the second law of thermodynamics ultimately hold, or is this a time like when Einsteinian quantum physics replaced Newtonian physics in the sense that there is a new spiritual and cosmic physical force that is possible? This is seen in the formation of the galaxies when things collapse into a black hole and then come out on the other side in a regenerative fashion. Is such power available in the practical realm that we are facing as we try to "reinvent" our species and take up the challenge of being responsible leaders in this new era?

Part V
NGOs, the Family, and International Organizations

Introduction

Article 16 of the Universal Declaration of Human Rights states, "The family is the natural and fundamental group unit of society and is entitled to protection by society and the State." One of the major policy front lines in the twenty-first century, however, centers on the issue of what actually constitutes a family and what moral and social norms are to be protected. Since the adoption of the Declaration in 1948, much has changed. The traditional concept of what constitutes a family, marriage, and the parent-child relationship is being countered by radical new conceptions. Major international and intergovernmental organizations, such as the United Nations, often reflect some of the same societal changes. Some NGOs as well as some governmental leaders consider such international organizations and their various agencies as moving in a direction inimical to the nuclear family and advancing an agenda that will actually promote family breakdown. Other NGOs not only welcome the changes but actively promote such policies in intergovernmental organizations.

The papers in this session examine current trends with respect to the family, the societal value of the traditional family, and the role of NGOs in impacting the perspective on the family on the international level and in intergovernmental organizations, with particular emphasis on the United Nations.

International Law, Social Change, and the Family

23

RICHARD G. WILKINS

The last half of the past century has manufactured more social change than perhaps any other period in world history. Modifications of social machinery are swiftly affecting all aspects of life—particularly the natural family: motherhood, fatherhood, and childhood. While there are many causes for the breathtaking speed of these modern developments, I would like to focus on one particular engine for social revolution: the unprecedented, rapid development of international law. Conferences and international conventions sponsored by the UN system are promulgating norms that alter dramatically the natural family. Whether much of this social experimentation is sound, however, is questionable. Solid empirical evidence supports the conclusion that the long-established and natural institutions of marriage, family, motherhood, fatherhood, and childhood are essential to the social health of men, women—and particularly children. Moreover, social science evidence demonstrates that as societies around the world depart from these natural norms, the family—and our children—are becoming increasingly fragile. Furthermore, and quite unfortunately, some well-intentioned international tinkering actually may be hastening the world's growing social fragility.

I. International law and national policy

In the last decade, the United Nations System has assumed a major new role: that of world policymaker. Recent conferences, including the Special Session on Children, the Second World Assembly on Ageing, and the World Summit on Sustainable Development, are influential norm-setting events.[1] Moreover, the declarations flowing from these

---

Dr. Richard Wilkins, J.D., is professor of law and director of the World Family Policy Center at Brigham Young University.

meetings are playing a growing role in shaping and solidifying the content of enforceable international law. UN conference declarations now influence not only international—but national—policy. In addition, widely adopted conventions—perhaps most notably the Convention on the Rights of the Child (or CRC)—are making rapid inroads into areas of family law that were once the sole concern of nation-states.

An extended analysis of the process of international lawmaking is beyond the scope of this paper.[2] What is important to understand, for purposes of my present remarks, is that international law matters a great deal. It matters because modern international law now deals—not only with the obligations of states—but with the rights of individuals, including children.[3]

Treaty law—beginning with the Treaty of Westphalia—began as the primary fount of international law. The importance of treaties in establishing international law (and, increasingly, domestic obligations) continues unabated. Customary international law, however, is beginning to play an increasingly important role in shaping the rights of citizens throughout the world. It once required centuries to create international customary law, because that law was developed through the uniform, consistent practice of nation-states over time.[4] More recently, however, some legal scholars have begun to argue that international customary law may be developed (at least in significant part) by the mere repetition of agreed language at UN conferences. As a leading international scholar has asserted, negotiated language "repeated by and acquiesced in by sufficient numbers with sufficient frequency, eventually attain[s] the status of law."[5] Some scholars have even argued that the negotiation of international conference agreements, such as the World Summit on Sustainable Development, to be finalized next month in Johannesburg, may create (in some instances) *instant* customary international law.[6] This argument at present is controversial. But whether or not the doctrine is sound, academic discussion of instant customary law demonstrates at a minimum that international law can be dramatically influenced by purportedly nonbinding instruments—and without the passage of much time.

This is a momentous and troubling new development. Customary law is binding upon states, often whether or not they agree with a particular customary norm.[7] As a result, even technically non-binding UN Conference Declarations—such as the recent document "A World Fit for Children"—can *become* binding if the language in those documents is repeated at future conferences, thereby crystallizing emerging rules of international law.[8]

Accordingly, individuals and groups interested in understanding the meaning of "marriage" and "family" within domestic legal systems must pay increasing attention, not only to national laws, but to international treaties, conference declarations and the ongoing review and implementation of those treaties and conference declarations.

II. International Law and the Natural Family

Until relatively recently, the concepts of "marriage," "family," and even "children's rights" were not commonly linked with the notion of "international law." Family and marital law presented issues so closely tied to unique cultural and religious norms that the international community did not undertake any real efforts to regulate marriage and family issues on an international scale.[9] Nevertheless, the Universal Declaration of Human Rights[10]—as well as other UN founding treaties—announce (or at least recognize) the importance and centrality of marriage and family to human civilization.[11] Moreover, human rights issues have become an increasingly important topic of discussion at international conferences. Because of the confluence of these two factors (that is, the existence of "family" and "marriage" language in international agreements and the growing importance of human rights rhetoric), marital and family structures have recently become the centerpiece of discussions at international conferences.[12]

As a result of this discourse, there has been a curious new development. In order to improve the social and political standing of women—a goal that is quite laudable—international law has become unusually hostile to long-standing notions of marriage, the natural family, and the rearing of children. As a consequence, marriage, motherhood, fatherhood, and childhood often have been presented as cultural and economic "problems" that demand immediate "solutions."

The "solutions" have tended to focus on two initiatives. First, and perhaps most prominently, there has been a major effort to devalue motherhood and childbearing. The second major drive has involved deconstruction of the natural family. This deconstruction proceeds in four steps: (i) assertions that religious faith is irrelevant or dangerous, (ii) attacks on parental authority, (iii) claims that there is nothing unique about the union between a man and a woman, and, finally, (iv) the submission that children should be granted broad autonomy rights. These "solutions"—to the extent they are eventually determined to be binding as treaty or customary international law—could radically restructure domestic law around the world. I will briefly discuss a few examples from each area of concern.

I start with the unyielding attempt to redefine the status of motherhood and childbearing. This effort begins with claims for abortion on demand and concludes with disparagement of maternity. A clear example of this international initiative comes from the committee charged with implementing the Convention on the Elimination of All Forms of Discrimination Against Women, or CEDAW. The CEDAW committee routinely criticizes governments for limiting abortion[13]—even though abortion is nowhere mentioned as a right in the convention itself.[14] The committee as part of this effort also labels motherhood as a mere "stereotype" that holds women back.[15] When countries have attempted to follow the admonition in the Universal Declaration of Human Rights that motherhood (and the correlative right of childbearing) deserve special protection and care (Universal Declaration of Human Rights art. 25(2)), the CEDAW Committee has complained that these efforts are "paternalistic," or—even worse—that encouraging motherhood discourages women from seeking (ostensibly more valuable) paid work. In recent reports the committee has gone so far as to tell Western European countries like Germany, Spain, and Luxembourg—countries with below-replacement birth rates and imploding populations—that their governments must do more to get women into the full-time workforce and to "eradicate stereotypical attitudes."[16] And what are such "attitudes"? The committee asserts that countries must "use the education system and electronic media to combat the traditional stereotype of women 'in the noble role of mother.'"[17] Childbearing and rearing in short are viewed as somehow "ignoble" and are discouraged despite the demographic realities facing nations and/or regions.

Once past this antinatalist philosophy, modern social theorists and their supportive non-governmental organizations turn their attentions to the deconstruction of the natural family. This deconstruction commences (as noted above) with attacks upon faith and religion. The CEDAW committee again is a good example of the approach of some within the modern international community. The committee frequently takes aim at religion and culture, expressing the view that "cultural and religious values cannot be allowed to undermine the universality of women's rights."[18] The Committee, in fact, boldly pronounced that "[i]n all countries, [one of] the most significant factors inhibiting women's ability to participate in public life have been the cultural framework of values and religious beliefs."[19] The committee concluded that "[t]rue gender equality [does] not allow for varying interpretations of obligations under international legal norms depending on internal religious rules, traditions and customs."[20] The committee, in fact, has gone so far as to instruct Muslim nations that they must reread the Holy Qur'an in ways that will better comply with modern social trends.[21] Broader condemnations of the value of religion and religious life within various cultures and the family can hardly be imagined.

After demeaning the important role of faith and religion, the international redefinition of the family continues with an obstinate refusal to recognize that parents play a vital role in child-rearing and culture-building.[22] Even though study after study shows that the weakening of parents' supervisory roles—even more surely than poverty—leads to serious dysfunctions such as crime, UN bodies often interpret international norms in ways that intrude on and weaken the parent-child relationship.[23] The Committee on the Rights of the Child, for example, views the child as a miniature adult who has rights to privacy, freedom of expression, and freedom to decide what he or she will learn, even against the parents' wishes.[24] Thus, according to some of the more extreme advocates in the international community, children must be freed from parental supervision so that they can be the masters of their own upbringing. I will discuss the consequences of this development shortly.

The step in the deconstruction of the natural family that is the most difficult to address (primarily because any reasoned discourse is almost immediately dismissed as "phobic" or "insensitive") is the modern assertion that there is nothing unique about the relationship between a man and a woman;[25] there are "various forms of the family." Paragraph 31 of the Habitat Agenda, for example, proclaims that "[i]n different cultural, political and social systems, various forms of the family exist." On one level such language is absolutely correct. The family has always included single-parent households, households involving stepchildren, and those embracing aunts, uncles, grandparents, and other intergenerational relationships. But the modern assertion is more expansive: it is nothing less than the claim that the very concepts of "family" and "marriage" have *nothing to do* with childbearing or procreation. So understood, any group can claim marital status.

The fourth approach often used to deconstruct the natural family has been adverted to above: that is, to separate the child from the family by "reinventing" the child as an "autonomous rights bearer" free (to one degree or another) from parental control, guidance, and support. One of the principal tools used to achieve this result is the Convention on the Rights of the Child, or CRC. The CRC, cited as the centerpiece for the "rights-based approach" at the recent Special Session on Children, represents an international attempt to ensure children's well-being. This is a laudable goal and one that is repeated in the preamble to the convention. The preamble emphasizes children's rights to "special care," "assistance," "protection," "safeguards," and "consideration." However, after reciting the vital special care, assistance, and protection that children must be accorded, the convention veers off in a questionable direction by granting—not protective rights for children—but autonomy rights that may harm rather than strengthen children.

III. A Critique of International Law and the Natural Family

The discussion to this point should make two points clear: (1) the international legal system is gaining considerable clout in establishing norms that, by various means (including the development of treaties and customary law), may one day become enforceable international law; and (2) some of these new norms are being used to destroy innocent life and deconstruct long-standing concepts of marriage and family. These two points in turn raise questions regarding the effect these newly articulated norms might have on global society.

A careful review of available social scientific evidence suggests that the world community should be exceptionally cautious in adopting and implementing the norms discussed above. There are legitimate grounds to question whether continued discouragement of childbearing, disparagement of religion, intrusion upon parental authority, redefinition of the traditional concept of marriage, and emphasis upon the autonomous child are in the best interests of either women, men, children, or the international community. Indeed, evidence suggests that further reinforcement of these policy initiatives many undermine social well-being, particularly for children. Instead of continuing on its present course, the international community should seriously consider reemphasizing the importance of childbearing, religion, parental authority, natural marriage, and protection—not emancipation—of our children.

A. The Need for a Positive Emphasis upon Childbearing, Motherhood, and Fatherhood

As noted above, the first step in the modern, international "solution" for the perceived problems inherent in family life has been to discourage childbearing and demean the role of parenthood—particularly the role of mother. In light of demographic realities and current social science findings, neither of these approaches appears sound at the dawn of the new millennium.

First, contrary to widespread discussion of the so-called "population explosion," the world community *needs* children—and needs them badly. Fertility rates in the entire developed world are now well below replacement levels.[26] As Dr. Nicholas Eberstadt of Harvard University has noted, "the trend [in population growth] appears to have reached a monumental turning point. For as the 21st century commences, the tempo of population growth is unmistakably in decline."[27] And, if current declines in fertility rates in the developing world continue, the entire world will soon be below replacement level fertility.[28] Indeed, the dramatic declines in population that the world will face in the next fifty to sixty years were last seen during such dark periods of history as the Black Plague.[29]

According to Dr. Eberstadt, the much-touted "population explosion" of the past century "was entirely the result of health improvements and the expansion of life expectancy. Between 1900 and 2000, life expectancy at birth at least doubled from something like 30 years to 63 years."[30] By contrast, the current rapid decline in populations within both the developed and the developing world is the result of "sustained and progressive reductions in family size due to deliberate birth control."[31] Continuation of current population policies will have dramatic—and potentially dangerous—consequences for global society.

In the words of Dr. Eberstadt:

> If the pace of global fertility decline continues for another generation—and the world consequently heads toward negative population growth—the population issues of the future won't resemble those of the recent past. In a world of long life expectancies, small families and negative population growth, the Malthusian specter will cease to be relevant to public policy....
>
> [In addition,] rapid global aging [will] have a number of ineluctable implications. For one thing, it [will] increase the salience of addressing the health care and income security needs of the elderly. In Western countries, current public programs for these purposes are coming under increasing demographic pressure, and require far-reaching overhauls to maintain financial soundness. In low-income countries, where coverage by public pension and health systems is limited, the issue of how to take care of the elderly could be all the more pressing.
>
> Rapid global aging [also raises] the question of how to educate and train the work force of the future. It is not difficult to imagine circumstances in which a majority of a country's workers were over the age of 50....
>
> Finally, prolonged sub-replacement fertility in a

> world of long life expectancy would presage a radical change in family structure.... For the first time in the human experience, there could be societies in which the only biological relatives for many people would be their ancestors. With sufficiently low fertility for just two generations, people with blood siblings and cousins would become the exception. Exactly how a society would operate under such conditions—how, for example, children would be socialized—is difficult to imagine.[32]

The continued emphasis on population control within the international community therefore appears misguided. It is time to turn our attention from continued abortion and the burdens of childbearing to the social need for responsible reproduction. As Ben J. Wattenberg noted on the March 4, 2002, editorial page of the *Wall Street Journal*, the "birth dearth" and "subsequent depopulation" should now "share the billing [with population control] and soon move center stage."

Regaining and maintaining a healthy population trend, however, will require refashioning some of the rhetoric used within the international community. Motherhood, for one, should no longer be considered an unhealthy "stereotype." While the notable advances made for women in economic, cultural, social, and political spheres should be applauded and continued, the world community should not continue to make such successes contingent upon diminishing the status of motherhood. For that matter, the importance of fatherhood should be increasingly stressed.

Recent studies emphasize the critical role dual-parenting plays if children are to become law abiding, well-socialized citizens. As one researcher noted, "The single most important factor in determining if a male will end up incarcerated later in life is...whether or not he has a father in the home."[33] The mother-child relationship is equally important. "As mothers spend less time with infants and toddlers...the boys' developing brains, and thus their behavioral systems, are affected."[34] Children without this crucial early bonding are "more likely to start out on a path of later narcissism and out-of-control behavior as [they] compensate for [the] early deprivation."[35]

Thus, the natural family—where children enjoy the protection and support of both a father and a mother—is "by far the most emotionally stable and economically secure arrangement for child rearing."[36] Furthermore, recent research indicates that—for children—nothing else compares to a solid, stable marriage between their biological parents.[37] It is well past time for the international community—and particularly the UN Conference System—to recognize these important realities.[38]

B. The Need for a Return of Religion and Faith

The world community needs to do more than recognize that children are our greatest natural resource. International fora also need—now more than ever—to pay close attention to the structure within which most children are raised: the family. The legal and social science literature of the recent past has done much to deconstruct the family. It is time to reverse that trend and do a little construction work to preserve the family. Any such construction work, moreover, will have to recognize the centrality and importance of religion in building stable marriages and families.

I do not question that there are certain practices—sometimes inaccurately justified under the rubric of religion—that demand condemnation. To the extent that such abhorrent practices as honor killings, female genital mutilation, or wife burning are purportedly required by religion, religious thought and practice must be reformed. But the modern condemnation of religion by some within the international community has gone too far. To use a well-worn English adage, in order to eliminate a few particularly egregious human rights abuses perpetrated in the name of religion, many in the international community have "thrown the baby out with the bathwater." Rather than being harmful, the great bulk of religious thought and practice reinforces familial stability and well-being.

Social science literature now demonstrates that, at least in Western societies, the family unit is rapidly disintegrating.[39] This disintegration of the family unit is having a profoundly negative impact on children. Social science data also demonstrate two nearly incontestable conclusions: (1) stable, natural marital structures provide profound benefits for men, women, and children;[40] and (2) the breakdown of stable, natural marital structures imposes significant social costs upon individuals, children, and society at large.[41] As one scholar noted, "[A]lthough of late we can witness a public rediscovery of the salutary role of the nuclear family of father, mother, and their children living together and caring for their individual and collective progress, policy elites appear neither to have fully understood that public life lies at the mercy of private life, nor do they seem to have apprehended the degree to which the [traditional] virtues and [traditional] ethos continue to be indispensable for the maintenance of both the market economy and civil society."[42]

One of the traditional virtues that has supported the nuclear family of father, mother, and children is religious belief and practice. Parents and children in intact families are much more likely to worship than are members of divorced families or stepfamilies.[43] In fact, religion and religious practice appear to play an essential role in maintaining marital and family stability. Research has demonstrated that religious devotion within the family context has a host of positive impacts. These beneficial consequences include improvements in health, education, income, virginity, marital stability, the reduction of crime and addictions, and increased mental health and general happiness—to mention but a few.[44] Thus, rather than being condemned for preventing social progress for women and men,[45] the great bulk of religion and religious practices should be encouraged for the familial—and social—stability they engender.

C. The Need for Parental Authority

There is also a need within the international community to rediscover the virtues of parental authority. Marriage as it has been conceived and practiced for centuries has marked benefits for marital partners and their offspring.[46] Indeed, a growing body of research shows that natural, heterosexual marriage has significant benefits for adults[47] and children. For example, children living with their biological parents have significant advantages in education,[48] suffer less from poverty,[49] commit fewer crimes,[50] and are better adjusted socially than children living in single-parent homes or stepparent homes.[51]

These benefits do not flow from the beneficent impact of some governmental action or bureaucracy. Research demonstrates that these benefits flow from well-functioning, two-parent households. Therefore, except in those cases where it can be shown that parents are incapable or incompetent to perform their important roles as protectors and mentors of their children, they should have full authority to make the decisions that most affect the daily lives of their children. While I have no doubt that many international proposals that interfere with (or even eliminate) parental authority are well-intentioned, I am similarly convinced that no local, national, or international agency can make decisions for children that are superior to those made by a reasonably well-functioning two-parent family. However well-intentioned, no international law—including the Convention on the Rights of the Child—should be construed so as to deprive parents of the authority to determine, on their own, what is in the best interests of their progeny.

D. The Importance of the Traditional Conception of Marriage

As noted earlier, the current international debate over marriage and family that is most difficult to address is the claim that there is nothing unique about heterosexual marital unions. Any two consenting individuals, the argument goes, should be able to lay claim to the status of "marriage." Such a claim can succeed, however, only if the international community is willing to completely separate society's vital interest in reproduction—that is, in the bearing and rearing of children[52]—from the concept of family and marriage. This severance of reproduction from what the Universal Declaration of Human Rights calls the "natural and fundamental group unit of society"[53] is fraught with profound difficulties.

Separating the concepts of marriage and family from reproduction has significant legal, sociological, moral, and philosophical consequences that have been discussed by, among others, Professors Robert George and Gerard Bradley,[54] and Hadley Arkes.[55] According to these scholars, heterosexual relationships (and in particular marital relationships) differ significantly from other possible sexual acts. Sexual relations between a man and a woman bound in marriage are "an intrinsic (or…'basic') human good."[56] This is due in large part to the fact that the natural family furthers society's profound interest in the only sexual relationship that has the biological *potential* for reproduction: union between a man and a woman. This potential procreative power is the basis for society's compelling interest in preferring heterosexual relationships over other possible sexual unions.

The long-understood institution of marriage and the family, therefore, furthers society's "very…survival."[57] The law, moreover, has never been ignorant of the vital distinction between sexual practices, proclivities, and procreation. International law for its part *must* take cognizance of the biologically obvious distinction between heterosexual unions and other possible sexual acts. International decision-making, because it affects the lives of all people, must be grounded in both principle and reason. When it comes to a worldwide definition of the family and marriage, the undeniable and well-grounded principle that has guided mankind for generations is straightforward: there is a fundamental difference between potentially procreative sexuality and nonprocreative sexuality. Thus, while Paragraph 31 of the Habitat Agenda recognizes that "various forms of the family exist," it also notes that marriage is an institution between "husband and wife."

Reproduction is the only human act for which the two genders indisputably require the other. A woman can do everything in her life without a man, except reproduce. Vice versa for a man. Thus, the sexuality that unites a man and a woman is unique in kind. This uniqueness, in fact, is the very basis of the legal, religious, historical, and metaphysical notion that "marriage" indeed joins two flesh in one.[58] As recognized by Article 16 of the Universal Declaration of Human Rights, marriage—defined as the voluntary union of a man and a woman—has been linked to procreation and the rearing of children from the dawn of time.[59] The international community will place the societal and cultural strength provided by "the natural and fundamental group unit of society"[60] in peril if it abandons this reality.[61]

E. The Dangers of the Truly Autonomous Child

The final development in international law that I wish to discuss is the novel notion that children within families are really just miniature adults, with full rights—subject to governmental, not parental oversight—to privacy, association, and speech. This notion, if taken to its logical conclusion, goes a good deal toward abolishing not only childhood itself, but the very idea of parental rights.

Prior to the adoption of the Convention on the Rights of the Child, no legal system in the world granted autonomy rights to children.[62] The convention, however, does just that. The convention, beyond question, is well-intentioned. But its sweeping and unprecedented creation of autonomy rights for children may in the long run threaten children's well-being. As Peter Neubauer has stated:

> Children who are pushed into adult experience[s] do not become precociously mature. On the contrary, they cling to childhood longer, perhaps all their lives.[63]

Two of the most potentially harmful autonomy provisions contained in the convention are the right to privacy and the right to free speech and association. CRC Article 16 states, "[N]o child shall be subjected to arbitrary or unlawful interference with his or her privacy, family, home or correspondence." Given the growing complexity of privacy laws, this sweeping grant could cause problems for parents and schools who wish to control children's access to—among other things—pornography on the Internet. By preventing "unlawful interference" with a child's "privacy," CRC Article 16 could place even the basic ability to discipline and monitor children—activities necessary for effective parenting—into serious doubt.

An even greater risk is that the CRC's language might be construed to support sexual freedom for children. Some supporters believe that CRC Article 16 grants the same right to "protections for procreation and abortion decision-making" as those that are afforded to adults.[64] Hence there will continue to be heated debates at UN conferences about granting sexual autonomy and abortion rights to children, a position that (oddly enough) is supported by the same individuals that one might expect to decry the sexual abuse of children.[65] These ideological battles, however, should not lose sight of the reality that most child development experts have long believed that "adolescent sexual activity is...unhealthy for children—emotionally, psychologically, spiritually, and physically."[66]

Article 13 of the CRC also grants children the right to "receive and impart information and ideas of all kinds, regardless of frontiers, either orally, in writing or in print, in the form of art, or through any other media of the child's choice."[67] The language of this article does little to recognize the dangers of obscenity and child pornography. Far too many supposed experts in today's world believe that pornography—and even unrestrained sexuality—are good for children.[68] Given the broadly worded language of CRC Article 13, the ability of parents and other caregivers to restrain children's access to potentially harmful sexual practices and harmful pornographic materials is in doubt.

As Professor Bruce Hafen has cogently noted, until the CRC, legal systems in the world limited "children's autonomy in the short run in order to maximize their development of actual autonomy in the long run."[69] This approach, he notes, "encourages development of the personal competence needed to produce an ongoing democratic society comprised of persons capable of autonomous and responsible action."[70] But, to "short-circuit this process by legally granting—rather than actually teaching—autonomous capacity to children ignores the realities of education and child development to the point of abandoning children to a mere illusion of real autonomy."[71]

IV. The Costs of Destabilizing the Natural Family

The international community has paid close attention to the family during the past decade. As shown above, however, whether or not that close attention has been beneficial is questionable. Throughout the world there are growing signs of distress in society. There is

> [m]uch...debate about the growing gap between rich and poor.... Analysis of social science literature demonstrates that the root cause of poverty and income disparity is linked undeniably to the presence or absence of marriage. A broken family earns less and

> experiences lower levels of educational achievement. Worse, it passes the prospect of meager incomes and family instability on to their children, making the effects inter-generational.[72]

As demonstrated above, "[R]esearch has documented that natural family structures benefit nearly every aspect of children's well-being. This includes greater educational opportunities, better emotional and physical health, less substance abuse, and lower incidences of early sexual activity for girls, and less delinquency for boys."[73] In the United States, 50 percent of children who live with a single mother live in poverty; by contrast, only 10 percent of children residing in two-parent homes live below the poverty level.[74]

But more than education, emotional health and poverty is at stake. The very safety and lives of women and children depends upon marital stability. A groundbreaking survey of scientific literature performed by Dr. David Popenoe and Dr. Barbara Dafoe Whitehead found that cohabiting, unmarried women "are more likely than married women to suffer physical and sexual abuse."[75] The consequences of cohabitation are even more serious for children. Doctors Popenoe and Whitehead conclude that:

> the most unsafe of all family environments for children is that in which the mother is living with someone other than the child's biological father. This is the environment for the majority of children in cohabiting couple households.[76]

In short, stable marital unions promote the health, safety, and social progress of women, men, and children. Unstable marital relations promote poverty, crime, abuse, and social disintegration. These realities moreover are particularly acute for women and children. While the redefinition of marriage and family—in large part—has been championed by organizations that seek the betterment of women and children, their efforts (as shown above) have not always actually improved the lives of women and children. Modern activists would do well to heed the fact that "the family as an institution exists to give legal protection to the mother-child unit and to ensure that adequate economic resources are passed from the parents to allow the children to grow up to be viable adults."[77]

IV. Conclusion

What is the import of my fairly wide-ranging discussion? I will offer a word of caution and make a plea for constructive change.

First, a word of caution. While working to improve social mobility and cultural progress, particularly for women and children, the international community would do well to begin minimizing the social costs now flowing from the modern marital and sexual revolution. As Professor Maria Sophia Aguirre has noted, "[T]he disruption of the family has had serious and high social welfare costs."[78]

Second, there is a profound need to strengthen the natural family. The deconstruction of the family has proceeded far enough. As stated earlier, it is now time for construction work.

This construction project will require the efforts of all. Indeed, the threats facing men, women, children, and the family do not face one country or culture alone. All cultures and all countries must stand together to combat the erosion of morality and the family. To do so, all nations must take their role in crafting international conference agreements very seriously. All too often, nations sign UN agreements only to "appease popular or 'politically correct' sentiment."[79] Such an approach to the negotiation and finalization of international declarations is unwise.

Virtually every UN conference addresses contentious provisions regarding the role of the natural family, childhood autonomy, and children's sexual rights. As these provisions are negotiated, the words that are used—the norms that are created—may become legally binding in the very near future. Each internationally negotiated document builds upon language used and objectives sought in preceding conferences and—as a result—forms an important link in a chain that inevitably encircles the international community.[80]

The nations of the world must carefully consider the natural family and children's rights language they incorporate into international declarations. Language may be merely a recommendation today.

But that same language may be binding tomorrow. The world community, in negotiating documents that affect the world's social ecology, must be certain that the phrases it uses, the rules it creates, and the lessons that it teaches uplift rather than degrade the world's most important resource: the world's families and their children.

Endnotes

1. Sadik, Nafis. "Reflections on the International Conference on Population and Development and the Efficacy of UN Conferences," 6 *Colorado Journal of International Environmental Law and Policy* 249, 252–53 (1995). ("More than any previous events of their kind, these conferences have fostered the mobilization and participation of civil society and the private sector in the affairs of the international community.... This process has nurtured the growth of democracy at the national level and democratized processes at the international level, increasing their transparency and accountability").

2. For an extensive discussion of the growth and impact of international law and its influence on domestic policy, *see* Ester Rasband and Richard Wilkins, *A Sacred Duty*, 111 (Bookcraft 1999).

3. See, e.g., Convention on the Rights of the Child; Rome Statute of the International Criminal Court article 25 ("The Court shall have jurisdiction over natural persons pursuant to this Statute," and such persons "shall be individually responsible and liable for punishment in accordance with this Statute").

4. Bilder, Richard B., "An Overview of International Human Rights Law," in *Guide to International Human Rights Practice*, 10 (Hurst Hannum, ed. 1992, 2nd ed.). (Customary international law is defined as a consistent practice in which states engage out of a sense of legal obligation.)

5. Higgins, "The Role of Resolutions of International Organizations in the Process of Creating Norms in the International System," quoted in Frederic L. Kirgis, Jr., *International Organizations in Their Legal Setting*, 341 (Second Ed. 1993).

6. Conference documents are viewed as significant international instruments because they are the result of consensus, following much debate and deliberation. Hannum, Hurst. "Human Rights," *in 1 United Nations Legal Order* 319 & 336, note 77 (Oscar Schachter and Christopher C. Joyner, eds. 1995); see also James C. N. Paul, "The United Nations and the Creation of an International Law of Development," 36 *Harvard International Law Journal* 307, 315 (1995) ("Because world conferences provide potential opportunities for global popular participation, expert consultations, and, sometimes, vigorous debate, they can in theory, become unique vehicles to elaborate norms [cast in the form of legal instruments] governing development.") As such, conference declarations are imbued with a strong expectation that members of the international community will abide by them. As this expectation is justified by state practice, including activities within

the UN organization, the principles of the document may—by custom—become binding upon a state. *Id.*

7. See Theodor Meron, "Human Rights and Humanitarian Norms as Customary Law 99" (1989). ("Given the rapid continued development of international human rights, the list [of customary international law norms] as now constituted is essentially open-ended.... Many other rights will be added in the course of time."); *Restatement (Third) of Foreign Relations Law of the United States,* § 702 cmt. a (1987) (noting that its "list [of customary international law norms] is not necessarily complete, and is not closed: human rights not listed in this section may have achieved the status of customary law, and some rights might achieve that status in the future"); Richard B. Lillich, "The Growing Importance of Customary International Human Rights Law," 25 *Georgia Journal of International and Comparative Law* 1, at 7 n.43 (1995/96) (reporting that in a 1996 speech, Professor Louis Henkin, Chief Report of *Restatement (Third),* indicated that "if he were drafting Section 702 today he would include as customary international law rights the right to property and freedom from gender discrimination, plus the right to personal autonomy and the right to live in a democratic society"); Beth Stephens, "Litigating Customary International Human Rights Norms," 25 *Georgia Journal of International and Comparative Law* 191, 198–99 (1995/96) (describing customary international law as a "developing concept" and predicting as likely developments "environmental protections and the right to political access [i.e., to vote] and other attributes of democracy"). Commentators have argued, for example, that customary international law includes, or will soon include, rights such as freedom of thought, free choice of employment, the right to primary education, the right to form and join trade unions, and rights relating to sexual orientation. See Curtis A. Bradley & Jack L. Goldsmith, "Customary International Law as Federal Common Law: A Critique of the Modern Position," 110 *Harvard Law Review* 815 (1997).

8. See Jiri Toman, "Quasi-Legal Standards and Guidelines for Protecting Human Rights," in *Guide to International Human Rights Practice* 192 (Hurst Hannum, ed. 1992, 2nd ed.).

9. In fact, the U.N. Charter states, "Nothing contained [herein] shall authorize the United Nations to intervene in matters which are essentially within the domestic jurisdiction of any state or shall require the Members to submit such matters to settlement under the present charter . . ." *United Nations Charter* article 2, paragraph. 7.

10. *Universal Declaration of Human Rights* article16:

    (1) Men and women of full age, without any limitation due to race, nationality or religion, have the right to marry and to found a family. They are entitled to equal rights as to marriage, during marriage and at its dissolution.

    (2) Marriage shall be entered into only with the free and full consent of the intending spouses.

    (3) The family is the natural and fundamental group unit of society and is entitled to protection by society and the State.

11. See, e.g., *International Covenant on Economic, Social and Cultural Rights* art. 10-1. (The family is entitled to "the widest possible protection and assistance"),

International Covenant on Civil and Political Rights article 23-2. ("The right of men and women of marriageable age to marry and to found a family shall be recognized").

12. See, e.g., Richard G. Wilkins, "*Bias, Error and Duplicity: Domestic Law and United Nations Conference Agreement,s*" The *World & I*, 287–305 (December 1996) (reprinted in 34 *Australia and World Affairs* 23 (Spring 1997); 35 *Australia and World Affairs* 38 (Summer 1998)) (noting the importance abortion and family structure arguments played in the negotiation of the Habitat Agenda).

13. For instance, in Mexico, where abortion is forbidden, the CEDAW committee encouraged the local and district governments to "review their legislation so that, where necessary, women are granted access to rapid and easy abortion." U.N. Doc. A/53/38/Rev.1, Part One, para. 426 (Mexico).

14. The committee now also regards abortion and lesbianism as "rights," even though such "rights" were clearly rejected by the General Assembly at Cairo and Beijing in 1994 and 1995, respectively. See, e.g., U.N. Docs. A/52/38/Rev.1, Part Two, para. 210; A/54/38/Rev.1, Part Two, para. 139; A/54/38/Rev.1, Part Two, paras. 228–29 (abortion); A/54/38/Rev.1 Part One, paras. 127–28 (lesbianism). The Committee has also recently begun treating voluntary prostitution as a "right" under CEDAW. See U.N. Doc. A/54/38/Rev.1, Part One, paras. 288–89 (China), and paras. 197–98 (Greece). This practice of inventing new "rights" raises serious questions about the committee's good faith in interpreting CEDAW and about the legitimacy of a committee of "experts" imposing these new rights on sovereign governments—when the "experts" know that these governments would never have agreed to a document expressly containing them.

15. Indeed, one of the most common "stereotypes" routinely targeted for eradication by the CEDAW committee is "motherhood." The committee recently chastised both Georgia and Belarus for overemphasizing women's role as mothers and has specifically criticized Belarus for re-instituting a national Mothers' Day. U.N. Docs. A/54/38/Rev. 1, Part Two, para. 99 (Georgia); A/55/38 Part One, paras. 359 and 361 (Belarus).

16. U.N. Docs. A/55/38 Part One, paras. 311–12 (Germany); A/54/38/Rev.1, Part Two, para. 259 (Spain); A/52/38/Rev.1, Part Two, paras. 215–17 (Luxembourg).

17. Report of the 17th Session of the Committee on the Elimination of All Forms of Discrimination against Women, U.N. Doc. A/52/38/Rev.1 (1997) art. 7, para. 65.

18. U.N. Doc. A/53/38 (Part 1) para. 282.

19. U.N. Doc. A/52/38/Rev.1 at para. 10.

20. Report of the Committee on the Elimination of All Forms of Discrimination Against Women, art 16, para. 135, U.N. Doc. A/49/38 (1994).

21. The CEDAW committee instructed Libya to alter its reading of the Qur'an with the following language:

    > ...Members felt that the interpretation of the Koran had to be reviewed in the light of the provisions of the Convention and in the light of the current social environment.... [E]fforts should be made to proceed to an interpreta-

> tion of the Shariah that was permissible and did not block the advancement of women. The Government was urged to take a leading role in its interpretation of the Shariah as a model for other Islamic countries.

U.N. Doc. A/49/38 paras. 130, 132.

22. The following objection to a U.N. Declaration by the Vatican illustrates this point. The Vatican:

> repeatedly sought to introduce the concept of parent's rights, duties and responsibilities to provide appropriate direction and guidance to their youth, in a manner consistent with their evolving capacities, a right enshrined in the most significant international documents of this century.... Despite our best joint efforts.... [the declaration] continues to fail to take into account the vital role which parents must play.... [T]here is no language currently in the draft Lisbon Declaration as regards marriage and the creation of the family.

Nunciatura Apostolica Portugal, press release, Lisbon (Aug. 12, 1998).

23. The recommendations contained in the *Report of the Youth Forum ICPD +5* illustrate this point. The report's first recommendation for action calls for "instruction" before "the end of primary school" on "sexual and reproductive health and rights." Under the heading of "Sexual & Reproductive Health, Human Rights," the Report states that:

> Comprehensive sexual education in schools should be mandatory at all levels. This should cover sexual pleasure, confidence and freedom of sexual expression and orientation.

Report of the Youth Forum ICPD +5, The Hague, Netherlands 7 (Feb. 1999).

> "Mandatory" sexual education in such matters as "sexual pleasure" and homosexuality (encompassed by required training in "freedom of sexual expression and orientation") runs counter to values of Islam and Christianity—which stress the importance of sexual chastity and forbid homosexual relationships. Qur'an 26:160–73; 1 Corinthians 6:9. Such "education," furthermore, can be expected to undermine not only the moral authority of established religion, but the primary rights of parents who (confronted by "mandatory" sexual training) will face considerable restraints in passing on their own moral codes to their children.

24. U.N. Docs. CRC/C/15 Adds. 34, 36, 40, 43, 46, 55, 61, 67, 68, 74, 76.

25. For example, the CEDAW committee criticized Kyrgyzstan for classifying lesbianism as a criminal offense. U.N. Doc. A/54/38/Rev.1 Part One, paras. 127–28 (Kyrgyzstan).

26. According to Dr. Nicholas Eberstadt:

> In all, 79 countries and territories, with 44 percent of the world's population, fit the below-replacement category. And the countries themselves are strikingly diverse in geography, culture and level of economic development.
>
> Virtually every advanced industrial democracy is on the list. In fact, 27 of the Organization for Economic Cooperation and Development's 29 mem-

> bers have total fertility rates of less than 2.1—more or less the level required for long-term population replacement. The two exceptions, by the way, are Mexico and Turkey, countries at the low end of the OECD as measured by income and education. Within the regular OECD grouping, the highest total fertility rates are the United States (2.07) and Iceland (2.04)—levels just shy of replacement. At the other end, Germany and Spain's current TFRs are just over 1.2—and Italy's is even lower.
>
> Most OECD members are in Western Europe, which had a collective TFR of 1.4 in 1998. But overall fertility levels appear to be even lower in Eastern Europe—by Census Bureau reckoning, about 1.3. Bulgaria, in fact, has the lowest fertility level ever witnessed in a modern nation not at war, with women averaging only 1.14 births in a lifetime. Were that pattern maintained indefinitely, each new generation would be half the size of the one before. In all of Europe, only remote Albania and the tiny outposts of Gibraltar and the Faeroe Islands are thought to be above-replacement enclaves—and in those cases, only barely so.
>
> Within the former USSR, fertility has fallen far below replacement since the collapse of the Soviet empire. While fertility rates in the six former Islamic Soviet republics all appear to be above the net replacement level (from Kazakhstan's projected TFR of 2.1 to Tajikistan's 3.5), the other nine states are far below replacement. In the Russian Federation, by far the most populous of the former Soviet republics, fertility is a shade over 1.3. In the next largest, Ukraine, the TFR is just over 1.3—as it is in Belarus and in the three Baltic states. With a projected TFR of 1.88, Moldova would rank as distinctly the most fertile European enclave within the former USSR today.

Nicholas Eberstadt, *World Population in the 21st Century: Last One Out Turn Off the Lights? at* http://www.worldcongress.org/gen99_speakers/gen99_eberstadt.htm ¶ 18–21 (Nov. 1999) (paper presented at the World Congress of Families II, Geneva, Switzerland) (last visited Aug. 2002).

27. *Id.* ¶ 4.

28. While noting that demographic predictions are always "a matter of educated guesswork," Dr. Eberstadt concludes it is quite likely that even the undeveloped world will face dramatic population decline within the next 50 years. *Id.* ¶ 44. As he states:

> We now know…that fertility decline can kick in swiftly in low-income settings…. [T]here are now examples of countries in which fertility levels have declined by 1.5 births per woman per decade for a full quarter of a century. In sub-Saharan Africa total fertility has been falling by 20 percent per decade, while in Latin America and the Middle East the pace is around 30 percent per decade. The comparable figure for East Asia is nearly 40 percent, thus far sustained for two and a half decades.
>
> Forget theory. It is a fact that fertility levels have fallen by three-fifths in just twenty-five years in one Arab country (Tunisia) where upwards of half of all women of childbearing ages have had no formal schooling, and by 45 percent in a sub-Saharan country (Kenya) with a dismal incidence of poverty.

> For whatever reasons, the constraints against fertility decline appear to be receding remarkably in our own time—and may possibly continue to recede in the coming century.
>
> *Id.* ¶ 47–48.

29. As Dr. Eberstadt has noted:

> The population has fallen before—in the 14th century, for example. Those earlier reductions, however, were the consequence of catastrophes; bubonic plague decimated societies across Asia, Europe and North Africa between 1333 and 1355. The 21st century population implosion, by contrast, would take place under conditions of steadily improving life expectancy and living standards.
>
> *Id.* ¶ 14.

30. *Id.* ¶ 7.

31. *Id.* ¶ 8. Dr. Eberstadt notes that:

> In historic terms, this trend is a very new phenomenon: it apparently had not occurred in any human society until about two centuries ago. France, where the trend began by the early 19th century, was the first country to experience the sustained decline. Since that beginning, the decline has spread steadily if unevenly across the planet, embracing an ever-rising fraction of the global population and depressing voluntary childbearing in the affected societies to successive record lows.
>
> *Id.* ¶ 9.

32. *Id.* ¶ 56–59.

33. See Michael Gurian in *The Good Son: Shaping the Moral Development of our Boys and Young Men* 182 (1999) (referring to research studies conducted by the University of Pennsylvania and Princeton University).

34. *Id.* 42–43.

35. *Id.*. at 43. Gurian notes that today there is a cultural strain on the early bond between both mothers and fathers. "Most boys lose their mothers not because of death but because the importance of the mother-son bond has been gradually diminishing in our culture, and thus in the home. Pressures on contemporary mothers are such that mothers can't mother their sons as they wish and need to. Similar pressures have for years frayed the father-son bond…." *Id.* at 42. Gurian also notes that "[t]he reason the question of working mothers and child care is so developmentally crucial now is that mother-child attachment itself has changed a great deal by force of culture. Our economic system forces many mothers to work far away from their babies, and the 'aunties'—the child-care workers provided by our culture—are generally so slightly paid that they don't stay around long enough to form bonds. This situation is potentially dangerous to the developing child." *Id.* at 74.

36. Berger, Bridgette, "The Social Roots of Prosperity and Liberty," *35 Society 44* (1998).

37. This research has many implications, particularly for those who are voluntarily choosing to ignore the patent benefits of marital parenting in the pursuit of indi-

vidualistic lifestyles:

> [W]hile only a couple of decades ago childbirth was sought almost exclusively by married couples in their prime childbearing years, many applicants for access to the new technologies are now single, and some are post-menopausal. Nor do these new applicants necessarily wish to establish traditional family forms. Some want their children to have only one legal parent; some want their children to have no father but two mothers; some want to establish "traditional" parental relationships by conceiving with sperm from a deceased partner.

Marsha Garrison, "Law Making for Baby Making: An Interpretive Approach to the Determination of Legal Parentage," 113 *Harvard Law Review*. 835, 839–40 (2000). Garrison also notes that

> [d]uring a 12-month period in 1986–87, there were approximately 4,000 requests from single women for artificial insemination [citation omitted]. While there are no current national data on the proportion of [artificial insemination] users who are single women, anecdotal evidence suggests that the phenomenon is increasing in frequency. For example, the director of one California sperm bank has estimated that 40% of its [artificial insemination] recipients are single lesbian women [citations omitted]. Births to unmarried mothers have also risen dramatically in recent years. In 1970, 10.7% of U.S. births were to unmarried women; by 1995, 32.2% were [citations omitted].

Id. at 839, n.9.

38. Change within the UN system may be difficult to achieve. At a recent session of the Commission for Social Development, Mr. Pino Arlacchi, Executive Director of the United Nations Office for Drug Control and Crime Prevention, concluded in his report to the Commission that "a stable, supportive family life provides a vital shield to drug abuse, particularly among minors." Nevertheless, even though Mr. Arlacchi also testified that peer pressure was one of the greatest causes of drug abuse among teenagers, the "Agreed Conclusions" drafted by the Commission for Social Development merely stated that "youth groups can also be engaged as active agents in the field of prevention of drug abuse." CSW, Agreed Conclusions for Agenda Item 3(a)(iii) para. 3 (1998). Thus, rather than assisting parents in alleviating drug use, the method actually advocated by the UN's Executive Director of the Office for Drug Control, the Commission on Social Development mobilized "peer groups"—the very forces that the Executive Director feared when it came to increased drug abuse.

39. See, e.g., David Popenoe in "Family Caps," 33 *Society* 25, (1996):

> That substantial family disintegration has occurred in the United States in recent decades is now widely recognized. Here are some of the key statistics: From 1960 to 1990 the divorce rate in the United States doubled or tripled (depending upon how one calculates the rate); the percentage of families headed by a single parent tripled, growing from 9 percent to 27 percent; the percentage of out of wedlock births increased from 5 percent of all births to 30 percent; and the percentage of children living apart from their biological fathers more than doubled, growing from 17 percent to 36 percent. It is

very much in the public interest for the government to prevent such family disintegration—to promote marriage and the two-parent family and to try to limit single-parent families and out of wedlock births.

40. See, e.g., Steven L. Nock, *Marriage in Men's Lives* 11 (1998); Linda J. Waite, "Does Marriage Matter?," 32 *Demography* 483, 494 (1995).

41. See Dr. Maria Sophia Aguirre, "Family, Economics, and the Information Society: How Are They Affecting Each Other?" *at* http://www.worldcongress.org/gen99_speakers/gen99_aguirere.htm (Nov. 1999) (paper presented at the World Congress of Families II, Geneva, Switzerland) (last visited Aug. 1, 2002).

42. Berger, Brigette, "The Social Roots of Prosperity and Liberty," 35 *Society* 44 (1998).

43. Myers, Scott M. "An Interactive Model of Religiosity Inheritance: The Importance of Family Context," 61 *American Sociological Review*, 858–66 (1996).

44. Patrick F. Fagan, "Why Religion Matters: The Impact of Religious Practice on Social Stability," The Heritage Foundation, *Backgrounder*, No. 1064, Jan. 25, 1996, available at http://www.heritage.org/library/categories/family/bg1064.html (last visited Aug. 2002).

45. *See supra*, notes 18–21.

46. *See* Steven L. Nock, *Marriage in Men's Lives* 11 (1998). "Married people are generally healthier; they live longer, earn more, have better mental health and better sex lives, and are happier than their unmarried counterparts. Furthermore, married individuals have lower rates of suicide, fatal accidents, acute and chronic illnesses, alcoholism, and depression than other people." *Id.* at 3.

47. Marriage is the ultimate social bond that can be formed between a man and woman because

    > [b]y their marriages, husbands and wives accept an obligation to be faithful, to give and receive help in times of sickness, and to endure hardships. Not everyone will be able to remain true to such vows. However, it is more difficult for a married than for an unmarried person to break such promises *because* they are part of our laws, religions, and definitions of morality. Others have taken identical vows throughout history. Collectively, society enforces these ideals both formally and informally. Nothing can be said about any other type of intimate relationship between two adults.

    Id. at 4.

    > It should come as little surprise, then, that this ancient social union has particular (and unique) social value. This unique social value, moreover, does not flow from some natural selection process in which healthy, strong, bright, and charismatic people are the most likely to marry and, therefore, the most likely to benefit from the union. "Married people do not simply *appear* to be better off than unmarried people; rather, marriage changes people in ways that *produce* such benefits." *See id.* at 3 (emphasis in original) (citing R. H. Coombs, "Marital Status and Personal Well-Being: A Literature Review," 40 *Family Relations* 97–102 (1991)); *see also* Walter R. Gove et al.,

"The Effect of Marriage on the Well-Being of Adults," 11 *Journal of Family Issues* 4, 25 (1990) ("[T]he evidence suggests that [the link between individual benefits and marriage] is not primarily due to particularly competent and healthy persons being more likely to marry and stay married but instead is primarily due to the effect of the marital relationship on individuals").

48. Studies consistently show that children in an intact natural family are significantly less likely to drop out of high school than children in a one-parent family. *See* Linda J. Waite, "Does Marriage Matter?" 32 *Demography* 483, 494 (1995). In some studies, the likelihood of dropping out more than doubles for children in single-parent households. *See id.* at 494. Important, Waite notes that the statistics regarding the likelihood of dropping out of school for children of single-parent households "take into account differences in a number of characteristics that affect educational attainment," thus accentuating the accuracy of the statistics' indications. Children of nontraditional families are also more likely to have lower grades and other measures of academic achievement. *See* Paul R. Amato, "Children of Divorce in the 1990s: An update of the Amato and Keith (1991) Meta-Analysis" 15 *Journal of Family Psychology*, 355–70 (2001); *See also* William H. Jeynes, "The Effects of Several of the Most Common Family Structures on the Academic Achievement of Eighth Graders," 30 *Marriage and Family Review* 73–97 (2001). Finally, children of divorced parents are more likely to have lower occupational status and earnings and have increased rates of unemployment. *See generally* Catherine E. Ross & John Mirowsky, "Parental Divorce, Life-Course Disruption, and Adult Depression," 61 *Journal of Marriage and the Family* (1999).

49. Studies show that children raised outside marriage are more likely to be raised in poor economic conditions. *See* Waite, note 48 above, at 494. Even after controlling for race and family backgrounds, children raised outside of marriage suffer not only from economic deprivations, but also from a lack of parental attention and from high rates of residential relocation, all of which can work to disadvantage the child's development. *See* Pamela J. Smock, et al., "The Effect of Marriage and Divorce on Women's Economic Well-Being," 64 *American Sociological Review*, 794–812 (1999); *See also* Teresa A. Mauldin, "Women Men and the Economic Consequences of Divorce: Evidence from Canadian Longitudinal Data," 30 *Canadian Review of Sociology and Anthropology*, 205 (1990)(finding that the presence of two parents potentially means more parental supervision and more parental time helping with homework).

50. *See supra* notes 33–35. Adolescents with married parents are least likely to use marijuana, cocaine, or smoke cigarettes. Patrick Fagan, et al., *The Positive Effects of Marriage: A Book of Charts*, at 35–36, 38 (The Heritage Foundation, 2002). Children with nontraditional family structures are twice as likely to use marijuana or cocaine and are 30 percent more likely to have experimented with cigarettes than children with two biological parents. *Id.*

51. "[C]hildren of divorce do not accept monitoring or supervision from live-in parents nearly as much as they do from married parents." Sanford M. Dornbusch, et al., "Single Parenthood," 33 *Society* 30 (1996). Young women from single-parent households are more likely to give birth out of wedlock, and young adults are more likely both to be out of school and the labor force. *See* Waite *supra*, note 47 above,

at 494. Furthermore, "children who spend part of their childhood in a single-parent family…report significantly lower-quality relationships with their parents as adults and have less frequent contact with them." *Id.* at 495 (citing D. N. Lye, et al., "Childhood Living Arrangements and Adult Children's Relations with Their Parents," 32 *Demography*, 261–80 (1995)). Children of fragmented or divorced families are also more likely to commit suicide and have higher risks of obtaining mental illnesses. *See* William J. Doherty et al., *Why Marriage Matters: Twenty One Conclusions from the Social Sciences*, 14–15 (Center for the American Experiment Coalition for Marriage, Family and Couples Education Institute for American Values 2002)(stating that high rates of family fragmentation are associated with an increased risk of suicide among both adults and adolescents. In the last half-century, suicide rates among teens and young adults have tripled. The single "most explanatory variable," according to one new study (David M. Cutler, et al., "Explaining the Rise in Youth Suicide, Working Paper," 7713 (Cambridge, MA: National Bureau of Economic Research)) (2000), "is the increased share of youths living in homes with a divorced parent." The effect, note the researchers, "is large," explaining as much as two-thirds of the increase in youth suicides over time.

52. *Skinner v. Oklahoma*, 316 U.S. 535, 541 (1942).

53. *Universal Declaration of Human Rights* art. 16(3).

54. Robert P. George & Gerard P. Bradley, "Marriage and the Liberal Imagination," 84 *Georgia Law Journal*. 301 (1995).

55. Hadley Arkes, "Questions of Principle, Not Predictions: A Reply to Macedo," 84 *Georgia Law Journal*. 321 (1995).

56. George & Bradley, *supra* note 55, at 301–2.

57. *Skinner v. Oklahoma*, 316 U.S. 535, 541 (1942).

58. Robert P. George, "Public Reason and Political Conflict: Abortion and Homosexuality," 106 *Yale Law Journal* 2475, 2497 (1997) ("Professor Bradley and I [Robert George] defend an alternative conception of marriage—one which we believe to be reflected in traditional American and British marriage law, especially in the law governing consummation of marriage. We argue that marriage is a one-flesh (i.e., bodily, as well as emotional, dispositional, and spiritual) union of a male and a female spouse consummated and actualized by sexual acts that are reproductive in type. Such acts consummate and, we maintain, actualize the intrinsic good of marriage whether or not reproduction is desired by the spouses in any particular marital act, or is even possible for them in a particular act or at all.").

59. *Universal Declarations of Human Rights* art. 16:

    (1) Men and women of full age, without any limitation due to race, nationality or religion, have the right to marry and to found a family. They are entitled to equal rights as to marriage, during marriage and at its dissolution.

    (2) Marriage shall be entered into only with the free and full consent of the intending spouses.

    (3) The family is the natural and fundamental group unit of society and is entitled to protection by society and the State.

60. *Id.* at art. 16(3).

61. Before attempts are made to legitimize or sanction same-sex unions, careful attention needs to be paid to the facts surrounding homosexual behavior and lifestyles. A significant body of current research suggests that according homosexual unions the same status accorded traditional marriage could be risky, indeed. Homosexual behavior increases the likelihood of psychiatric, mental, and emotional disorders. Sandforte et. al., "Same-sex Sexual Behavior and Psychiatric Disorders Findings from the Netherlands Mental Health Survey and Incidence Survey," 58 *Archives of General Psychiatry*, 10, 85–91 (2001)(Youth are four times more likely to suffer major depression, almost three times as likely to suffer generalized anxiety disorder, nearly four times as likely to experience conduct disorder, four times as likely to commit suicide, five times as likely to have nicotine dependence, six times as likely to suffer multiple disorders, and over six times as likely to have attempted suicide. Additionally, this research originates in the Netherlands where homosexuality is much more mainstream and accepted.). Beyond mere emotional and mental disorders, epidemiologists estimate that one out of two men who have sex with men will eventually become HIV positive. Hessol et. al., "Incidence and Prevalence of HIV Infection among Homosexual and Bisexual Men, 1978–1988 ," National Library of Medicine AIDSLINE MED/00002789 (1989). This result is sad, yet predictable, given that a 1991 study of homosexual men in New York City revealed that the average number of lifetime sexual partners was 308, while the mean number of partners stands at a staggering 755. Meyer-Balburg et. al., "Sexual Risk Behavior, Sexual Functioning and HIV-Disease Progression in Gay Men," 28 *Journal of Sex Research*, 1, 3–27 (1991) (he "average" figure differs from the "mean" as follows: the "average" takes the total number of men in the study and "averages" the number of partners for *all* the men in the study; the "mean" figure reveals the number of sexual partners of the gay man precisely "in the middle" of the study—that is, the man who had the number of partners halfway between the lowest number of partners and the highest number of partners). Finally, the most alarming and troubling aspect accompanying the gay lifestyle is the prevalence of physical and emotional abuse. Susan C. Turnell, "A Descriptive Analysis of Same-Sex Relationship Violence for a Diverse Sample," 13 *Journal of Family Violence,* 281 (2000) (finding that 44% of gay men report having experienced physical violence in their relationships; 135 report sexual violence, and 83% report emotional abuse. Among lesbians: 55% acknowledge having experienced physical violence, 14% report sexual abuse and 84% report emotional abuse); *See also,* U.S. Department of Justice Study, *Citizen Magazine*, (January 2000) (reporting that the U.S. Justice Study found an epidemic of violence between homosexuals: an annual average of 13,740 male victims of violence by homosexual partners and 16,900 victims by lesbian partners. By contrast, the most recent numbers—1999—for "hate crimes" based on sexual orientation totaled 1,558 victims).

62. *See* Bruce C. Hafen & Jonathan O. Hafen, "Abandoning Children to Their Autonomy," 37 *Harvard International Law Journal*449, 459 (1996) (quoting the drafters of the CRC as creating, for children, "the 'totally new right' of individual personality" independent of parental control).

63. Quoted in *Children Without Childhood*, by Marie Winn, 1981, ch. 13. Available at http://www.bartleby.com/66/87/41387.html (last visited Apr. 2002).

64. Robert E. Shepherd, "Civil Rights of the Child," *Children's Rights in America* 143 (1990).

65. *See, e.g.,* Professor Anne Hendershoot, "The paradox of the postmodern pedophile," *The San Diego Union*, April 26, 2002 (Union Tribune Publishing Company) (noting that the coming publication of *Harmful to Minors: The Perils of Protecting Children from Sex* by the University of Minnesota Press promises a "a radical, refreshing and long overdue reassessment of how we think and act about children's and teens' sexuality." In published interviews on the University of Minnesota's website, author Judith Levine decries the fact that there are people "pushing a conservative religious agenda that would deny minors access to sexual expression" and adds that "[w]e do have to protect children from real dangers.... But that doesn't mean protecting some fantasy of their sexual innocence").

66. Henry J. Redd, et al., "Cntraception and Adolescents: A Dissent, 21 *Child & Family* 105, 106 (Nov. 2, 1990).

67. *Convention on the Rights of the Child* art. 13(1).

68. *See* Hendershoot *supra* note 65.

69. Hafen et. al., *supra* note 62, at 491.

70. *Id.*

71. *Id.*

72. Patrick F. Fagan, "How Broken Families Rob Children of Their Chances for Future Prosperity," The Heritage Foundation, *Backgrounder*, No. 1283, June 11, 1999, available at http://www.heritage.org/library/backgrounder/bg1283.html (last visited Aug. 2002).

73. Craig H. Hart, Ph.D., "Combating the Myth that Parents Don't Matter," *at* http://www.worldcongress.org/gen99_speakers/gen99_hart.htm (Nov. 1999) (paper presented at the World Congress of Families II, Geneva, Switzerland) (last visited Aug. 2002).

74. *Id.*

75. Dr. David Popenoe and Dr. Barbara Dafoe Whitehead, "Should We Live Together? What Young Adults Need to Know about Cohabitation Before Marriage," at 7 (The National Marriage Project, Rutgers University 1999).

76. *Id.* at 8.

77. Aguirre, *supra* note 41.

78. *Id.*

79. Neil H. Afran, "International Human Rights Law in the Twenty First Century: Effective Municipal Implementation or Plan to Platitudes," 18 *Fordham International Law Journal* 1756, 1758 (1995).

80. *See* Sadik, *supra* note 1, at 252.

NGOs and the Assault on the American Family

24

SERIAH L. REIN

I would like to thank the World Association of NGOs for their kind invitation to me to address concerns that are mutually shared and of critical importance if we are to preserve the institution of the family—the most precious of all human institutions.

It is through the stability and protection within the family that our youth are taught the wisdom of the parents—wisdom that will help guide them into making wise choices, which will bless them throughout their lives.

Is the primacy of intact families merely a *sentimental* relic of the past that is no longer practical, given our modern philosophy of individual rights to explore our individual personas? If it feels good, just do it? How relevant *is* the family?

Consider Professor Sorokin of Harvard, who after studying the genesis and fall of every civilization that existed throughout two thousand years of recorded history, made the following conclusion: When a civilization no longer sought to preserve and protect the primacy of the family—no longer held it in high regard—it spelled the beginning of the destruction of that civilization—*without exception*. If we do not learn from history, then we are surely on a disastrous course to repeat it.

Many NGO leaders who are in the forefront of working on behalf of the family have not been lulled into complacency that all is well since the Berlin Wall fell, which to many spelled the fall of communism. Communism and socialism are two destructive philosophies that continue to be active behind the scenes, imposing "government knows best" policies upon the families of the world. The forced sterilization of the women of Peru is merely one glaring example of direct governmental interference into family matters. Thanks to US pro-

---

Dr. Seriah L. Rein is chairman of the Council on the American Family.

family organizations exposing this horrible burden upon Peruvian women, sterilization has now dropped in Peru by 68 percent.

Cultural Battle in the United States

Even in the United States, there is a strong contest being waged between those policymakers who are bent on imposing socialism through the welfare state and those who seek to preserve our constitutional republic by recognition of the individual freedom embodied in the Constitution of the US and our Declaration of Independence—the right to life, liberty, and the pursuit of happiness. Today the social engineers have distorted the right to life to be a right only for those children whom they deem acceptable—there is no room for the unborn, the disabled, or the poor children—only if they are supposedly *wanted.* The big criterion continues to be whether the child is *wanted.* Professor Singer at Princeton University has gone so far as to say parents should have the right to kill their child within the first month of birth if in their judgment it is best. I would ask Prof. Singer *best for whom? And what of the child's rights?* I am here to tell you that every child is wanted—by someone. And every child is loved by the Creator from whom every child is sent into the world. The Council on the American Family works diligently to retain the sanctity of life and the dignity of the family in the national and international arenas. Our form of government allows us to do this largely unhampered.

Our forefathers and the European philosophers who admired this young nation made it abundantly clear in their writings that our form of government could work *only as long as the people remained righteous.* Because we are a world leader, our perceived moral standards become a world model. Likewise, what immorality we may tolerate and export to other nations in the form of social programs becomes perceived—whether accurately or not—as the American standard. This false perception threatens to sublimate almost a century of American goodwill.

The enormous sacrifices Americans have historically made in the cause of helping less fortunate nations is sublimated—whether it be to feed the hungry, build homes for the poor, train in modern technology, or bestow generous funding to rebuild, as General MacArthur did for the Japanese people, our former enemy. Our willingness to send our boys into harm's way to help restore freedom itself has turned the tide in one conflict after another. This perception of the US exporting *immorality* also gives illegitimate, lame excuses to the likes of delusional terrorists to destroy America. We add fuel to this delusional mind-set when all that can be seen exported by the mass media are the Madonnas, Howard Sterns, and Britney Spears, the US movies that glorify sexual licentiousness, and certain government policies implemented by an elite few—policies such as condoning forced sterilization, forced abortion, and disrespect for the culture of other nations.

What is not promoted, and what the media seldom advertises to the world at large, are the millions of Americans who have deep religious faith, who pray daily, go to their houses of worship on Sunday or Saturday, work hard throughout the week, yet make time to serve their fellow man in a host of volunteer services and who dip into their pockets generously to help the less fortunate—men and women who live out their faith on a daily basis. To this extent the popular media has done a grave injustice to America, and its impact has been felt on a global scale. Blatantly biased and poorly documented studies conducted by Marxist professors at liberal universities seek to tarnish America's global image, which only continues to compound the problem. These professors are imparting their contempt for America to the next generation who sit as a captive audience in their classrooms.

In the midst of this cultural battle for the mind and souls of the next generation, the terrorist attacks on the World Trade Center and the Pentagon took place. Of course the social engineers immediately seized upon this attack to suggest that America somehow had it coming to her for not spreading her wealth generously enough. This warped philosophy explains the statements made by university students and academia that reasoned America might look to itself for inviting this attack. A reality check is in order. A murderous attack upon innocent civilians is never justified and is a criminal act. That it was done to a nation with whom war had not even been declared renders the act brutal to its core. Period. That message has to be clear and uncompromising.

When you hear such America-loathing statements, it would

be helpful to remember that when the Berlin Wall fell, the Marxists fled Europe, and many are currently holed up teaching their distorted views of the human condition in our most prestigious American universities. They are dinosaurs of another age, but they are reaching our youth with an atheistic philosophy. As President Lincoln said, "The philosophy of the schoolroom of one generation will be the philosophy of government in the next."

Our right as free citizens to pursue liberty was understood by America's founding fathers to be within a moral framework. Liberty today has been interpreted by our mass media, arts, and entertainment to mean license—license to do whatever "feels" right. Feelings alone are no indicator of what is right! You may not feel like arising at 5:45 A.M. to accomplish an important goal—but you do it…because it is part of the self-discipline we are wired by our Creator to be capable of exercising. Each of us make choices daily between the desires of the flesh, human temptations, versus self—comfort vs. hardship—on every level of our lives. There is nothing new under the sun, for it is a fact of life since Adam and Eve. Yet the social engineers would have us believe that we cannot control the baser human impulses—and our children are being taught that these baser human impulses should be satisfied in order to remain psychologically and physically healthy. Let us now consider how this plays out in the international arena and what you can do as an NGO to sustain the identity and cohesiveness of the nuclear family.

International Treaty Language

In my capacity as special assistant to Mrs. La Haye of Concerned Women for America, I worked diligently to enlighten the delegates at the UN Fourth World Conference on Women in Beijing, China, that the platform for action was woefully neglectful in including language reflecting the importance of the family staying together; in other words, language preserving parents' rights for the education and upbringing of their own children, language respecting two genders, modesty, the sexuality of young women, and the sanctity of human life. Furthermore, the attempt to insert language that seriously compromised the stability of the family was repeatedly pushed at this world conference.

It was pointed out to the delegates that the platform for action in their language was appreciably different wording from the English version, and thus they were not alerted to the real dangers to the family. The attempts to insert dangerous language likewise were evident in Istanbul, Cairo, and Beijing +5.

The importance of international treaties containing language that is supportive of the family is foundational to the preservation of the nuclear family, because this language is adopted in one nation-state after another, verbatim. I have repeatedly seen the exact language trickle down into state policies and into the local schools of not only America, but local schools and government agencies throughout the world—policies that rip at the heart of parents who are striving to raise up and train moral children, striving to spend as much time with them as possible, to love them, to teach them, guide them through the mine fields of life. The drive to separate children from their parents for as many hours as possible is persistent. We call it "womb to the tomb" government interference. We wrestle with imposition of this same language on the Governor's Advisory Council on Adolescent Pregnancy and the Governor's AIDS Advisory Council, on which I serve.

Language that sounded perfectly reasonable on first reading has had double-meanings—and even the most intelligent NGOs and delegates to the United Nations have been fooled—until further documentation clarified the reality. When soft and euphemistic terms are used, it is difficult to detect threats to the nuclear family. It is my goal to make you more alert to their true meaning. Many delegates who were initially fooled have been apprised of the real meanings and in turn rendered a valuable service to their country by opposing such language. Time does not allow a full slate, but we shall take on some of the majors terms.

Family planning. This innocent-sounding euphemism has come to mean imposing forced, dangerous, and unhealthy contraceptive procedures (and on young girls, often without parental knowledge or consent), resulting in serious disability and even death in young women. It has also involved forced abortion and sterilization of women. Dr. Margaret Ogala of Kenya complained to me that her patients were dying for lack of simple medications while the family planning clinic across the street was well stocked with family planning contraceptives, condoms, medications, and so forth.

A full day could be spent discussing the devastating consequences to the family exacted by this policy alone. The world at large is aware of China's inhumane family planning policy—killing the extra child even after born—yet international pressure is not brought to bear for this human rights violation. Eating fetuses has now become a delicacy in China. God will not be mocked, however. There is some poetic justice in that there are now so many boy babies who have grown into young men, who now have a serious problem. So few women were allowed to live that the men are hard pressed to find a wife. The *New York Times* and the *Washington Times* have quoted successful businessmen who would settle for any woman.

Gender. Generally, people would say there are two genders: male and female. The delegate representing Guatamala was a testimony to honesty and integrity. She called for gender to be defined—since it appeared over eight hundred times in the "Platform for Action" document. She was mocked for her request. The delegate from the Netherlands at the time said she lacked a sense of proportionality in her request. She graciously stood her ground. In the ensuing weeks we finally uncovered the fact that wherever the word gender appeared in this document, it would be interpreted to mean not male and female exclusively, but instead male, female, bisexual, homosexual, or transsexual—five categories. Gender was explained as a "social construct" rather than a biological construct. In other words, we are to believe that we are not born male or female, but our environment and life experience may cause us to be heterosexual during one season of our life, but homosexual in another, bisexual in another. This deconstruction of gender is now rampant teaching in major universities. These same policies were attempted at the Cairo conference, the Istanbul conference, and again at Beijing +5, held at the United Nations headquarters in New York City. There will be no letup until the social engineers get what they want. You are the watchdogs overseeing the "family stability" gate to see that this does not happen.

Sustainable development. This is another term that bears watching. We are called to be good stewards of what we use on our planet. Conservation and care for the environment are part and parcel of that stewardship. The environmental movement has now been hijacked by those who would undermine what is best about America. The social engineers have slipped in one more element. There is a big difference between "responsible" development and "sustainable" development. Sustainable development for some means eliminating those people that are a threat to having enough food and water for the remaining population. It is a call for draconian measures to enforce population control. How to do it? Have everyone agree to the importance of "sustainable development" and implement the other euphemism "family planning" to implement it? One can now see how critical it is to have the terms defined.

Population Control

You may wonder, How then do you control an exploding population? The CATO Institute and the Heritage Foundation have done extensive research into this perceived crisis and have already reported their findings. We are actually not in crisis regarding a population explosion—not in the United States and not in the world as a whole. We are approaching a population crisis, however, for we are barely replacing ourselves currently, and have a serious birth dearth in a number of countries already, which seriously threatens their economies. The social implications are enormous.

What makes the difference in a country's ability to truly sustain itself is allowing people the freedom to exercise their entrepreneurial spirit—to create, invent, work, to be able to save and reap the benefits of one's own labor. To share the rewards of one's labor with someone who will not work is anathema to human nature. It diminishes the enthusiasm of the industrious if they are not allowed to benefit from the fruits of their intelligence, creativity, and labor. Look at the difference between North and South Korea. Look at how Hong Kong thrived economically throughout all the years it remained separate from communist China.

Compare Japan's success to China's financial stature. Communist China's economy is being sustained only by massive infusions of money from outside sources in loans and building projects to improve what was a woefully backward infrastructure. The appearance of Beijing is already changing drastically, but it is not the result of the success of communism. Having spoken at length with the ordinary Chinese citizen on the street, there are many who have so long been under oppression they are conditioned to need a "model" by which they can follow proscribed behavior in so many situations. The heart of the average Chinese citizen is a gentle one. We need to pray for the people of China. This one-child policy is ripping at their very souls. This is the same policy, by the way, that has been applauded by the "family planning" advocates.

Barriers to Implementation

This is another term filled with double-meaning. Whenever you see that expression, read the full text carefully. It frequently refers to parents. Parents are the barriers—parents are getting in the way—parents make it difficult for the family planners to get to their children. Parents object to the dispensation of condoms to their young children as the wrong message to send their children. Most parents teach their children social virtue and purity, which includes refraining from sexual activity until marriage. Handing them a condom would suggest an expectation that they will not obey their parents—and will not remain sexually pure. Sexual promiscuity is antithetical to the strongly held religious beliefs of most parents, these same beliefs and values they strive to inculcate into their children.

Ironically, the notion that condoms will protect our youth from disease or pregnancy is a terribly misguided one. The unreliability and ineffectiveness of condoms has already been widely documented.

Another barrier to implementation of family planning may be the delegate. Frequently we see a delegate whom we have educated concerning the truth contained within a proposed document or treaty. If this delegate persists in representing the truth, he or she is then replaced with another delegate at the next UN convention—a delegate more receptive to the "family planning" philosophy.

Another barrier may be the minister of health who feels the policies do not square with the values being taught to the citizenry of his country. Suddenly this minister finds coercion being used. This is frequently through US programs of assistance—like USAID. Countries are desperate for this aid for food, medical supplies, and so forth, but there are strings attached. You must accept the family planning program also. If the minister still fails to comply, pressure is put on the nation to replace him.

Does not this cultural imperialism build resentment? A learned physician from Iran who was very involved in the political affairs of his country informed me that this was the very policy that compromised the Shah of Iran, who was subsequently deposed and replaced by the Ayatollah Khomeini. According to the physician, the Shah's countrymen were furious with him for accepting the family planning policies exported by those "blue-eyed devils" in the United States. They insisted on a leader who would be faithful to the moral values taught in the Koran. Do you see how the United States, with a long history of humanitarianism, can be regarded by another nation when we export immorality? The United States continues to be by far the most generous nation in the world, helping nations all over the globe. Yet this immoral policy compromised us and even contributed to the eventual downfall of the Shah.

This issue of family planning is a battle that will continue to be waged within our borders and internationally.

Family under Assault

Today the family finds itself assaulted by an increasing number of educational, medical, and professional groups that no longer seek to preserve the primacy of the nuclear family. This is reflected in current position statements. For example, consider the remarks made in the *Bulletin of the American Psychological Association,* suggesting that an adult having sexual relations with a child may not necessarily be harmful. Dr. Laura Schlessinger and Dr. Judith Reisman were quick to put the APA on the defensive, and the public outcry caused the APA to backpedal on their initial position. Be aware. The push for adult-child sex is real and insistent. The family as we know it is very much at risk today, not because parents are not capable of raising their children, but because of the plethora of toxic influences that compete with parents for the souls of their own children.

As chairman of the Council on the American Family, I can assure you that most Americans believe in such radical notions as the sanctity of human life, fidelity within marriage, sex with one individual within a mutually monogamous relationship we call marriage, and regard marriage as a sacred covenant between one man and one woman. How then, while most Americans believe in these fundamental values, do most of our media outlets report a far different perspective on these basic American institutions, further fueled by interviews from the most liberal sources, rather than those conservative sources that reflect that part of America that has kept her strong and a beacon of freedom to the world? Time and again organizations like NARAL (National Abortion and Reproductive Rights Action League) and NOW (National Organization of Women) are sought out for the interview rather than one of the many pro-family organizations that represent the much larger mainstream of thought and that have a wealth of research to further document the validity of their positions.

Two Competing Worldviews

The reason for such a disconnect between reality and what is reported as such is one's worldview. There are two competing worldviews that all of mankind struggles with. One worldview sees man as the measure of all things, not God as the measure of all things. Many of our youth are being taught by social engineers who have invaded our classrooms that they have what are described as "sexual rights." Giving into anything the flesh wants is rationalized, and nihilism reigns in the hopeless pursuit of self-esteem. It is the worldview that has no rules except what is expedient to man. It is the worldview whereby we are evolved from primordial slime from a cacaphonation of atoms that over time finally came together.

According to the Darwinian theory of natural selection, time, lots of time, is supposed to take care of all those gaps in the fossil record. Darwin himself stated that his theory would stand or fall on the future discovery of transitional forms. However, the passage of time has revealed no transitional forms, in spite of an explosion of fossil discoveries since Darwin. This is confirmed by Ph.D.'s in all the science disciplines. Yet our schoolchildren continue to be taught that evolution by chance natural selection is a fact.

What is the lesson for our children? We are merely animals, and therefore animal behavior is not to be considered surprising. If you believe this thinking is not dangerous, consider that when a gang of young men were apprehended at a New York public swimming pool for gang-raping a girl (whirlpooling), their response was that they were just doing what they were programmed as higher-order thinking animals to do—they were merely attempting to satisfy their natural urges. Their claim was pure evolutionary thinking. There was no shame, no remorse! How far off course can this type of thinking lead?

Consider that Jeffrey Dahmer, the mass murderer, had the same philosophy! His crimes made international news. He lured gay men to his apartment where he tortured, decapitated, and even cannibalized them. It cannot be described in this paper the further degrading practices he carried on while his victims were alive and even after they died. After a TV program on which I appeared, his father, Vernon, a stable, congenial college professor, told me that his son did not start out that way. Vernon learned something during his conversation with his son after Jeffrey's imprisonment. Jeffrey revealed the following: "Dad, it began when I learned about Darwinian evolution. When I learned that there was no God, and no more rules, that man can make his own rules, I was free of any concerns of accountability—punishment. It was like being given the green light to follow my *animal* [italics mine] instincts. I was allowed to make my own rules, and change them to fit the circumstance." Man allowed to make his own rules can put society into chaos.

The truth is we are NOT evolved by random chance from animals, but we are divinely created by a loving and Holy Creator. We have souls, we think. This is the second worldview. Marriage was created by the Creator as the foundational society unit in which our progeny, our children, are taught how to conduct themselves in a civil society—how to be able to discern right from wrong. We are also the only of God's creation that can pray, only Homo sapiens, of all creation, is created in the Creator's image and likeness. You are unique, for you were designed to be loved by your Creator and to follow His moral principles.

Is it not enough that Stalin, Marx, Lenin, and even Hitler embraced Darwinian evolution as the rationale for their solutions to the social and political debates of the day—resulting in millions upon millions of their own countrymen being slaughtered? Our youth today are being bombarded by this worldview in an unprecedented way.

Kinsey Study

Darwin presented the theory, but it could not be put into practice behaviorally until the publishing in 1948 of Alfred Kinsey's *Sexual Behavior in the Human Male,* in which Kinsey's research normalized sexual deviancy. It was Judith Reisman, the Ph.D. researcher, who discovered how fraudulent Kinsey's so-called "research" actually was. She presented her findings at the Fifth World Conference on Sexuality in Jerusalem in 1981. Subsequently, Dr. Reisman was appointed by the US Department of Justice as a full research professor and principal investigator to conduct, at American University, an $800,000 grant study to investigate Kinsey's role in child sexual abuse. Dr. Reisman testified of this fraud before US congressional committees and the Department of Justice regarding Kinsey's poor sampling methods, and how this false data was used to change some of the basic tenets of medicine, education, law, and public policy, not to mention the arts and the media.

Here is only one example: Kinsey falsely claimed that 95 out of 100 American men are normally involved in one or more illicit sexual activities. Therefore, the conclusion of behavioral scientists, judges, and lawmakers was: "If this is so, then there are contradictions in our laws regarding sexual behavior and marriage, and there is a pressing need for revision to accommodate the most recent science [i.e. Kinsey]. If we do not change the laws, most of our American men would have to be arrested."

Does one wonder what factors came into play to cause one man to become eventually so self-destructive and destructive to the very fabric of our society? This was a highly intelligent man, but he also came to believe he could make his own rules. Upon graduation from Bowdoin, Kinsey was so impressed with Darwin that he quoted Darwin in his commencement address. He then studied at the Bussey Institution, then a hotbed of Darwinism. By age 26, Kinsey was a strong atheist, according to his colleague and coresearcher Wardell Pomeroy. Kinsey became one of the scholarly eugenicists of pre–World War II, and his most recent biographer writes of Kinsey's "terrifying" call for mass sterilization of "lower level" Americans and his breeding plan for the better classes (James Jones, *Kinsey: A Private/Public Life*).

Dr. Reisman has since documented all her findings in her seminal work, *Kinsey: Crimes and Consequence*, which is now available for purchase through Council on the American Family (CAF).

Our CAF team researched the paper trail of how the laws were changed to fit—to accommodate—Kinsey's false research findings. His research claimed to expose the real sexual habits of mainstream America. This was when he was supposedly interviewing the average American male, back in the 1940s, when most of America's virile young men had gone off to war—the same period during which there was emphasis on the importance of the family at home, and certainly a period of far greater modesty than today. Where did Kinsey find all these available men when so many of our best and brightest were off to war? Dr. Reisman discovered the answer: the majority of his subjects were not average American men and women at all, but disproportionately included pedophiles, prostitutes, and other kinds of sexual deviants and sexual predators. Kinsey misrepresented as "married" common-law relationships of one year, which could include prostitutes if they had been with their pimp for at least a year. He classified "college-age men," but the men were not college men—many were prisoners who were simply college-age! Naturally, asking highly personal questions regarding human sexuality of the criminal and sexually deviant will result in bad data.

Yet Kinsey and his disciples took that false "research data" and traveled from one state to another, calling for committees to be set up for one purpose: to see if the laws regarding human sexuality were consistent with the latest "scientific" research. The result? The laws that protected families, women, and children from sexual predators were washed away with the introduction of the Model Penal Code in the 1970s. In one fell swoop it wiped away four hundred years of English common law—laws which had served Western Civilization well.

At the same time the US Supreme Court was deciding on *Roe v. Wade,* Mary Calderone of SIECUS (Sexuality Information and Education Council of the US) and Planned Parenthood called upon Kinsey to provide helpful data to persuade the judges. He did—by providing bad data from poor sampling again in stating that "between one-fifth and one-fourth of the white married American women interviewed in their sample had had at least one induced abortion. Three-quarters of them reported no unfavorable consequences. Most did not regret the experience." He further stated that "90 percent of all illegal abortions are done by physicians," implying that family physicians *commonly aborted* the unwanted babies of massive numbers of single women and respectable wives. It was the Kinsey data that finally tipped the scales in favor of the justices ushering in *Roe v. Wade.* Justice Blackmun, writing for the majority, cited the ALI-MPC (American Law Institute–Model Penal Code), based wholly on Kinsey "research," three times!

Leading Cultural Indicators

All the problems concerning sexuality in the United States that Kinsey categorically predicted would disappear if we removed guilt and gave free reign to our sexuality have instead shot through the roof—as evidenced by all the leading cultural indicators. We had more divorces, not less; more sexually transmitted diseases, not less; more women were thrown into poverty as a result of no-fault divorce; and more youth were becoming violent and confrontational. Domestic violence is climbing alarmingly.

Consider why we did not have riots and violence during the Great Depression in the United States. Why did those who had lost everything not express their rage through violence? Why were there so few murders during such times of terrible loss? That generation understood moral restraint—especially in the face of trials and temptation. The sixties generation was taught no boundaries. The free love of the sixties did not just happen in America; it was the natural outcome of the dissolution of important moral laws—laws that called for self-restraint, self-discipline—moral laws that ensured stability in our society. Kinsey predicted a utopia with full sexual expression—but that was before AIDS and the human papilloma virus.

It was Kinsey who for the first time ever stressed that early sexual satisfaction was age-appropriate and an important childhood goal. Nothing could be more damaging to our concept of the needs of our youth. Children are absolutely not sexual from birth, yet our comprehensive sex-ed courses in the public schools are based on this false and dangerous assumption; even some religious texts repeat this lie. Our children are taught in sex-education their *sexual rights* "in spite of the Victorian attitudes of their parents...who mean well....but really don't understand their need."

The main purveyors of sex education materials to our schools is SIECUS—the Sexuality Information and Education Council of the US. SIECUS also produces journals, research studies, training materials for health professionals, and sample classroom curricula. It was launched in 1964 at the Kinsey Institute, no less. SIECUS's cofounder and president was none other than Mary Calderone, past medical director of Planned Parenthood. The primary goal of SIECUS, she said, is to provide society with a very broad and deep awareness of the *vital importance of infant and childhood sexuality.*[1] Is the linkage clear? Is it understood why it has been so difficult for parents to purge their local schools of this offensive material? Why it has been so difficult to curb the family planning activity in many other countries? It is a very, very lucrative business and it fulfills the goal of "sustainable development" and the Darwinian philosophy of more of the fit and less of the unfit.

Destructive Consequences

What has been the result of this practice, and why should what happens in America affect the stability of the world community? By distracting our children with their sexuality and with entertainment, there is little time to focus on matters of more lasting significance: a classical education, creativity, development of intellectual curiosity, interaction and accountability to and from the family; in essence, preparation for leadership.

Preparing for future responsibilities is significant as part of the maturation process, and youth throughout the world are not fulfilling their potential. Squandering this creative energy into sexual preoccupation and sexual license has had destructive cultural consequences: skyrocketing rates of out-of-wedlock pregnancies, skyrocketing rates of abortions amongst our youth, an entire demographic group of single mothers raising children without a father—no father to teach about love, valor, responsibility, or human virtue. No one has been telling these children that condoms provide absolutely no protection against human papilloma virus (HPV), a major cause of cervical cancer in women. Our children bought the Kinsey lie and are paying a very high price.

Albert Einstein Medical School did a two-year study of the coeds of a major American university. By their sophomore year, 60 percent were infected with HPV—most unaware—rendering them dangerous carriers. If not detected through the study, HPV has the potential to be a silent killer: ravaging the young bodies of the future generation with this insidious disease.

I would like to bring attention to a US federal government study released in July 2001 titled "Scientific Evidence on Condom Effectiveness for Sexually Transmitted Disease Prevention." It was issued by the US Department of Health and Human Services, the National Institute of Health, the Center for Disease Control and Prevention, the Food and Drug Administration, and the US Agency for International Development—the major agencies dealing with health in the US government. It should be noted that these agencies were uncomfortable with the results of their study and therefore unwilling to originally release the report until public pressure was brought to bear.

What did this report reveal? What was the fuss about that there should be such reluctance to release it to the public? The result of this report confirmed what the pro-family community had been warning of all along: There is little to no conclusive proof that condoms protect against the vast majority of STDs. This study showed only an 85 percent risk reduction in HIV transmission (or a 15 percent risk of getting AIDS), and no clinical proof of effectiveness in preventing gonorrhea in women and only a 50 percent reduction in men, no clinical proof of condom effectiveness for chlamydia, trichomoniasis, chancroid, syphilis, herpes, or human papilloma virus (HPV). These health agencies informed us that currently 45 million Americans are already infected with herpes, 20 million with HPV alone. They predict 650,000 new cases of gonorrhea each year. Think of the human cost of these diseases and the cost to society in providing hospitalization, nursing care, rehabilitation surgery, or medication to ease the pain of impending death. Reflect for a moment on the plethora of derailed plans and broken dreams.

Through international family planning agencies, of which Planned Parenthood plays a significant role, the United States and Canada have been the main purveyors of this toxic form of education to the youth, especially young children and young mothers. The European Union has also played a significant role. Common sense must prevail again. We have a serious medical emergency on our hands. It is reassuring to know that President Bush has already taken concrete steps in international funding policies in order to help curb such abuses.

I would also like to note that throughout the 1970s, 1980s, and 1990s many NGOs in America have diligently worked to preserve what is best about America. We are not all wedded to careers alone, as the popular media would have you believe. I shall never forget the delegate from Sudan who was so shocked to learn that I, an American woman, was there in Beijing because I loved my family and loved my children. She wept and embraced me with surprise and relief when I told her that I was there to help preserve a woman's right to raise a family if she wishes, a right to keep the government from imposing draconian and unhealthy birth control procedures upon her healthy body.

Future Work

There is much work remaining, however. It is important that you ascertain what the policies are in your country so that you might play a significant role in curbing abuses against the family, particularly against women and children.

Take note of the success in Uganda, if you would seek to make inroads in decreasing STDs and AIDS in your country. One new element was introduced into Uganda, abstinence education. Here is what Edith G. Ssempaia, Ugandan ambassador to the United States, said in a February 16, 2001, letter: "We believe that the abstinence campaign in Uganda has had a significant impact on HIV infection, which has declined by 50% between 1992 and 2000, and the decline has been most marked in the 15–24 age bracket."

This is the best news—the news of hope. Bringing down AIDS, divorce, poverty, and STDs is not dependent on money alone—it can result by simply a change in behavior! It is the direct result of teaching our youth that they *are* capable of self-restraint, of waiting for God's best.

Stability of our families is a prerequisite to stability in the community. Parents are in a privileged and unique role to not only teach their children, but to *hold them accountable for their behavior*. To that end, each one of us, regardless of our title, our position of power and influence, has a primary responsibility to nurture and cherish our spouse and raise our children, secure in our love for them and self-disciplined over ourr feelings and impulses. We are, after all is said and done, ultimately responsible for the education and raising of our own children—grooming them to make a meaningful contribution to our society upon adulthood—a process that must begin early and continue through adolescence, and without government imposing practices that are opposed to your religious values.

I pray that men and women use wisdom and courage to equip themselves with documentation and truth in order to impact these realities in their areas of influence. Strong nations that have moral virtue contribute to the creation of greater global stability. I encourage leaders to stand strong in fighting evil with good, to stand in the gap for the most innocent, and to speak the truth in love to those who have compromised moral values. If is for each of us to remain informed and to do our part in bringing about restoration of social virtue and purity.

Endnotes

1. *Obstetrical Gynecological News*, December 1, 1980, p. 10.

Part VI
NGOs and the Media

Introduction

The media, whether print, broadcast, or electronic, is an extraordinarily powerful force for informing, molding perceptions, and initiating change—particularly in this day of twenty-four-hour news networks and internet publications. Two of the papers in this section deal with the role of this "fourth estate" in fostering a culture of responsibility in civil society. The basic question explored was: "What can the media do, or do more of, in encouraging and promoting the development of a culture of responsibility?" Other questions include: "Should various publics be given greater access to media in expressing responsibility options and in shaping the national and social dialogue?" and "Should greater critiques of NGOs be encouraged?"

The other two papers in this section deal with practical recommendations for NGOs in learning to deal with the media and successfully garnering media attention to advance their missions.

A Responsible Media and NGOs

25

PHILLIP V. SANCHEZ

I will be addressing the media's role in the development of a "culture of responsibility."

Although we in the media are still pained by the terrorist attacks of last year, we know that the world simply needs to move along and that we simply need to move with it. It is hard to forget those images. Some say that most of us will never forget them—neither the victims nor the perpetrators. You and I know that for a long time there will be much talk about causes and about consequences. And there will be much for the media to ponder.

Now, however, at this juncture, America is hearing the drums of war. Of war. These are not the best of times. We all know that we are still beset by images of a monstrous tragedy. We are not ready for another.

Sometimes we journalists find ourselves challenged more than we would like to be challenged. But we are a curious bunch, and we constantly hunger for news—good or bad. Often we are accused of looking only for the bad news, or at least the most sensational news. This is not necessarily true. It should *not* be true.

Out of practical necessity, we journalists look for news in all of the everyday occurrences of man and beast. Our professional responsibility is to bring this news onto our pages and screens, all of the news, good or bad. Unfortunately, too often the news is not good.

Moral and Ethical Standards

As professionals we are constrained to operate within moral and ethical standards and guidelines. And we try to do this without stepping out of line, without stepping on too many toes. As you can well imagine, this is never easy to do. Because of this we often find ourselves tiptoeing through the daisies, fearful of stepping on a bumblebee.

Ambassador Phillip V. Sanchez, former US ambassador to Honduras and Colombia, is publisher of the hemispheric, Spanish-language newspaper *Tiempos del Mundo*, vice president of the *Washington Times*, and publisher of *Noticias del Mundo*.

I am confident, however, that my colleagues will agree that we modern-day journalists, at our best, have a certain curiosity. A certain itch. An itch that leads us to try to shine light in new areas. An itch that makes us want to show that the world is a better place than many people realize. Can we do this? I believe we can. I believe we can, but we must be willing to explore new ground. With or without the bumblebees.

Let me give you an example. At a recent World Media Conference in Washington, DC, a group of media professionals from all over the world found ourselves exploring the topics of religion and spirituality. Now then, for those of us more accustomed to writing about wars, hurricanes, and political scandals, this was admittedly new ground. Why religion and spirituality? some asked. Why not religion and spirituality? the majority answered. The fact is that we soon realized what we knew all along: no facet of modern-day life should be exempted from our national dialogue.

Ironically, at the opening of that media conference it was a man of religion who gave us our welcome. He is admired friend, Dr. Chun Hwan Kwak, chairman of the Interreligious and International Federation for World Peace. Dr. Kwak, a well-known man of the cloth, looked at our room full of professional journalists and was not a bit nervous. He looked us all in the eye and told us in very clear and forceful terms, that "religion can be a force for good or for evil. Which side prevails should concern all of us a great deal." Another speaker, also an admired friend, Dr. Frank Kaufmann, did something similar. He told us that the long-term solutions to the issues we were considering had to involve the world's religions, since they did, after all, "underpin the world's major cultures."

Another well-known journalist, my admired friend from my California days, Dr. Muazzam Gill, did a good job of summing it all up. He told us, "Maybe it's time we journalists talked about religion." Now ladies and gentlemen, that was new material for some of us. I know that daily deadlines give us journalists very little room for innovation. But once in a while it does us good to step back and try to imagine the really big picture. I believe there is room in our profession for journalists who want to help mold the world of tomorrow. For journalists of today who can have a hand in fostering a culture of responsibility in civil society.

NGOs and the Media

At the WANGO annual conference our conveners were told to join hands and minds, to probe and dig into the question: "What can the media do, or do more of, in encouraging and promoting the development of a culture of responsibility?" Other questions include: "Should various publics be given greater access to media in expressing responsibility options and in shaping the national and social dialogue?" and, finally, "Should greater critiques of non-governmental organizations be encouraged?"

Ah, yes, the non-governmental organizations. The NGOs. You did not hear much about them during the twenty-eight years I spent in government. They were around, of course, but too many of them concentrated almost exclusively on local causes and small movements. Anytime a big movement was afoot, a big government program seemed to be right around the corner. For too many of us, big government seemed to have all the answers. Not so, many of us learned. Big government did not have most of the answers. What it did have was most of the money.

NGOs have come a long, long way. And we in the media need to recognize this. We need to take advantage of this fact. Those modern media outlets that truly aspire to create a better world beyond 9/11 have at hand a marvelous resource. An invaluable ally. And it is *not* governmental. It is in fact the non-governmental organization: the NGO.

Just two years ago United Nations secretary-general Kofi Annan said this about NGOs: "Whether your main activity is helping set policy at the global level, or working directly to help people; whether you work primarily in the developed world or the developing world; whether your concern is the advancement of women or education, human rights, humanitarian assistance or health—NGOs have shown, time and again, a courage, a character and a vision that we must all admire."

Too many of us in the media are badly accustomed to looking at NGOs as merely news sources. And only sporadic news sources at that. Too many of us write about NGOs only when there is a scandal in their funding practices, when they fight with one another over turf or clients, and, of course when they die a sudden death.

Yes, we do occasionally publicize the good works of the NGOs, but too often we cover only those NGOs that have money with which to hire professional PR people. The smaller ones—the ones with limited funding—too often go unheralded. That is unfortunate because the losers are really the media. Think about it. Any newspaper, any electronic news medium worth its salt, is committed to the betterment of our society. Logically, that commitment is better served by amassing the most effective arsenal possible. And NGOs should be an important part of that arsenal.

For many of us activist journalists or journalist activists, the modern-day growth of NGOs constitutes a blessing. The strength brought to them by the World Association of NGOs gives us all a new reason to look ahead with some measure of optimism as we face the post-9/11 world.

WANGO

WANGO by definition is a worldwide organization. This is how it works: WANGO's members bring together non-governmental organizations from all over the modern world in the cause of advancing peace and well-being, and WANGO provides the mechanism and support needed for NGOs to share, inspire, and multiply their contributions. All of this effort has the goal of solving as many of humanity's basic problems as possible.

WANGO assists its member organizations in accomplishing their tasks relative to creating a better society and world: economically, socially, environmentally, politically, and morally. With its global network of NGOs, WANGO has become an international leader in fostering a culture of responsibility.

The media now need to do more. Every newspaper, every TV network, every radio station ought to have a file called "WANGO." We should have an ongoing dialogue with each NGO in our service area. We should invite them periodically to editorial board meetings, and we should open our pages even more to publicizing outstanding examples of exemplary public service of both programs and individuals.

During 2000 and 2001, WANGO conducted or cosponsored

conferences and seminars in over 150 nations. WANGO Annual Conference 2002, then, is one of many. I am glad to participate in such an event, and I am sure all NGO leaders are, too.

A Critique of NGO-Media Relations

26

JOHN O'SULLIVAN

In terms of the media, I am a little less sympathetic to the role of NGOs, and if I have one single point to make, it is that relations between the media and NGOs are far too close and sympathetic. Rather, a certain amount of adversary relationship might profitably be injected into that relationship.

I suggest that NGOs are, in general, pressing upon a half-open door. The media is already on the side of many NGOs before they have ever sent them a press release, rung them at four o'clock in the afternoon, or done any of the things that one might do in terms of media relations, whether experienced or inexperienced.

Afghanistan

I will give you an example. When the Americans were beginning their campaign in Afghanistan in 2002—a campaign that included bombing and helping the Northern Alliance in the civil war—there were a series of widely reported statements to the international media from NGOs that were delivering food aid to Afghanistan. A great number of these, if not all of them, appealed to the Americans not to continue with the war, maintaining that if they did so the result would be widespread, massive starvation in Afghanistan. Because of their role as humanitarian NGOs concerned with food aid, their warnings were given very considerable credence. These warnings were not simply expressions of humanitarian positions, though they were that, but were also political acts because they made it more difficult for the American government to pursue its policy.

Now you may think that's a good or a bad thing; I leave that

John O'Sullivan is editor-in-chief of United Press International (UPI) and editor-at-large of *National Review*.

to you. But that it was a political act is scarcely deniable. When the war continued and ended rather quickly, the condition of the Afghan people in terms of the food they got and starvation was in fact materially improved. It turned out that the major reason for the starvation in Afghanistan was not American intervention. It was the continuation of an oppressive government, which hoarded food for its own supporters and kept it from the people. It was the overthrow of that government that enabled food to be distributed more quickly throughout and for starvation to be ameliorated more quickly.

I do not remember any of the spokesmen for the NGOs who were responsible for the warnings subsequently apologizing for their warnings. I do not remember their being even questioned about their erroneous warnings. I do not remember any media holding them to account.

Two-headed Organizations

There is a reason for this. NGOs in the modern world—and this is not true of all NGOs obviously, but NGOs in general—are two-headed organizations. On the one hand they generally have some kind of humanitarian purpose, such as Amnesty International, which is involved in the assistance of political prisoners, Oxfam, which is involved in the relief of famine, CAFOD, which is working to tackle the causes of poverty, and so forth.

On the other hand they often adopt specifically political stances. Amnesty International, for example, has been conducting for some years a campaign to eradicate the death penalty. Again, you may think that an excellent thing. But it is not simply a humanitarian objective, because there are large numbers of people in the world, probably a majority actually, who think the death penalty is a legitimate response to crimes like murder. Yet Amnesty International is not regarded as a political movement; it is regarded as a humanitarian one.

In viewing these organizations, the media is often relatively uncritical. They tend to treat NGOs entirely in terms of their own representations of themselves. They rarely are unsympathetic to them. They rarely hold them to account. Indeed, Greenpeace is an example of an NGO that has been able to get a good press even when acting illegally. In fact, Greenpeace has turned lawbreaking over the years into a publicity tactic, and yet it is generally treated, compared to say corporate oil companies, as the good guy in these kind of struggles.

Three Tasks

Now what should the media do in terms of NGOs? It seems to me that the media has three tasks. First, the media should report. It should simply tell you what is happening. Therefore, when it reports on NGOs, it should report the statements that they make, it should report the work they do, and it also should report the views and attitudes of their critics. Incidentally, if they do that, in the main that will yield coverage that is favorable to NGOs, not because the coverage is biased, but because the NGO is engaged in alleviating famine, and so forth. NGOs doing good will get good press, and that is right and proper.

The second task of media is more difficult, and that is to analyze the role of NGOs and see what their effects are. Clearly it is not always the case that humanitarian aims have humanitarian outcomes, and painful though it may sometimes be, we have an obligation in the media to actually point out the effects of people's interventions. In the Afghan case, of course, had the advice of those humanitarian NGOs been heeded, it is very likely that many more people would have died.

Third, the media has to put things into some sort of understandable context. Years ago, John Bert, the recent director general of the BBC, said that the walls in the media are what he called a "bias against understanding." In other words, news stories just came at you *rat-a-tat,* like the bullets from a machine gun, without the reader or the viewer being given the context that would enable him to make sense of the latest story. I think that this is largely true, but also very hard to remedy, because once you start putting things in context you have to guard against the bias of the person who is giving it contextual analysis and contextual explanations. But the context here is, I think, very plain.

NGO Revolution

There is at the moment a very important revolution in world politics going on. The NGO revolution is possibly the biggest change in world politics since the defeat of the Soviet Union and the end of the Cold

War. There are any number of NGOs in the world. NGOs have an influence not only in their own countries, but also particularly in countries of the Third World. In terms of resources, the larger international NGOs often rival the governments themselves and are often given resources by international organizations or by Western governments, making them capable of influencing the politics of the Third World. While I was at a conference of the Claymore Group in London a few years ago, the representatives of the African governments there, and of the Asian and West Indian governments, were quite hostile to some environmental NGOs, which they regarded as intervening impermissibly in their domestic politics.

The latest development in the NGO revolution is the argument of Kofi Annan and others that because transnational organizations like the United Nations and its agencies do not have an elector to report to, then the next best democratic thing would be to report to a kind of international civil society of NGOs. Well, that sounds very nice, but the fact is that the NGOs themselves are not democratic organizations. They may be internally democratic, but they are not responsible or accountable to voters as governments are, and they therefore cannot play that role. If NGOs are to become, or style themselves as, the world electorate to which UN agencies are accountable, they are in fact making an antidemocratic claim, which I hope the media will examine very critically.

It is often said that there is a natural adversary relationship between government and the media, and that is true. There also ought to be a natural adversary relationship between the media and NGOs, and I am afraid that at the moment it is a far too cozy relationship, and that we deserve to be giving NGOs a much harder time.

Getting Media Coverage for Your NGO

27

MELISSA HOPKINS

I am going to address how NGO leaders can set up their own media relations campaign or, if they have already got one in progress, provide some advice and insight on how to have a better media relations campaign.

I do come from a unique perspective in the sense that I still do media relations for the *Washington Times* newspaper. Thus, on a day-to-day basis, not only am I pitching stories and information to the other media about the *Washington Times*, but I am constantly being pitched by other media relations and public relations professionals about their stories so hopefully I can get their stories into the *Washington Times*.

Having a good media relations strategy for any organization is becoming increasingly important because getting good media coverage is getting more difficult—it is definitely getting more competitive—and what good is it with all of the work that you are trying to do to make the world a better place if no one knows about it? When I talk about the media, I address two categories, paid media and earned media. Paid media, of course, is your TV advertising, your newspaper advertising, and radio commercials. It is buying time and space to get your message out. Earned media is press coverage that is earned, not bought. Earned media is the media covering your story because of your newsworthiness or your compelling message. You have earned a place in the information marketplace because someone else thought it was important to tell your story.

Why is the media important for your organization? It not only gives your efforts exposure, but it also gives it credibility. By having a third party, the media, tell your story, it adds credibility to what you are trying to do.

Melissa Hopkins is President of The Hopkins Group, Inc., a communications company based in northern Virginia.

Proactive Media Campaign

How do you get more earned media coverage? First, you have got to set up and maintain an ongoing, proactive media relations campaign that includes writing press releases, opinion editorials, and broadcast advisories, holding press conferences, participating in editorial boards, giving radio and television interviews, producing radio actualities and video news releases, and hosting events such as panel discussions to give your organization more visibility.

When you begin your media relations campaign, you really need to know your media. You need to know who you want to contact and why. There is a difference between the *Nation* magazine and *National Review* magazine. There is a difference in how you may pitch a story to the news desk of the *New York Times*, and how you may approach the editorial board at the *Washington Times*. You do not want to change who you are or change your message, but your approach may be a bit different.

Not only do you need to know your media, you need to know your media well. Identify and target some key reporters whom you think can help you on an ongoing basis, who cover your issues specifically. Know who they are, know what they have written, know their history, and follow them closely on a day-to-day basis if you can. Once you identify them, give them a call, introduce yourself, and tell them what you do. Be brief, be concise, to the point, and educational, but ask them a few questions. Do you prefer fax? Do you prefer e-mail contact? Do you prefer a phone call? Do you prefer an e-mail followed up by a phone call?

Take very specific notes, because the easier you make it for the reporter to cover your story intact, the more likely they will do so. Also, ask them how they like to cover their events. Some reporters like to actually go to an event and cover it themselves. Some reporters like to look at studies and pull some things, and others want to have a direct interview with your executive director or an expert within your organization.

Press Release

You also need to understand the news cycle. Do not call and pitch a story to a newspaper reporter at four o'clock in the afternoon. It sounds kind of obvious, but I cannot tell you how often that happens. Do not call a news producer thirty minutes before the news goes on the air. It will just hurt your credibility as a news source for them in the future.

What if you have a big press release or a press conference scheduled? You have thought a lot about it, you have set this date to have it happen, but a major news event happens: an earthquake, a major political scandal, or, God forbid, another September 11. Reschedule, because your news will get buried.

Do not limit yourself to approaching the media with just your information. On your press release list make sure you include think tanks, elected officials, diplomats, other leaders in your industry, agencies, commissions, oversight committees, anyone who can help you leverage your message. I was talking to a reporter the other day who wrote about a study from an NGO. The NGO had not contacted him, but he was contacted by an ambassador who saw a study by this NGO, and he ended up writing about it. So do not limit yourself to the media when making contacts.

Another thing to think about is if you see someone, such as an ambassador, talking about something that you do or that is related to your organization or industry, send out a quick broadcast advisory reminding them that you have had a study done on this issue, and they can go to the website or wherever to research it. Just send a quick note to the media.

Getting the Media's Attention

How do you get the media's attention? When dealing directly with the media, you have to know what you want to say. You have to be very brief and very concise, find the news hook, and be educational, but really know what you want to say ahead of time. A reporter, especially in newspapers or television, will get a press release and decide *just by looking at the headline and the subheadline* whether to read the rest of that release. Then in that first paragraph, generally, a reporter is going to decide whether or not to show interest in that issue. So you need to have the who, what, where, when, why, and the main lead in that first paragraph to bring the reporter into the rest of the release. Overall, the release should be catchy, educational, and brief.

Oftentimes your news by itself may not be enough to get the media's attention. So tie it into other relevant and timely information, especially those working on international relations. Unfortunately, in the United States, we do not get a huge readership or audience just on international relations–related material alone. But if you can somehow tie it in to something that directly affects Americans, you are going to get a lot more attention. September 11 is a perfect example. Before then most people couldn't even place Afghanistan on the map. But now, because of the events, a lot of people know much more about Afghanistan, and not only about the war, but about the region's culture, religion, and so forth.

When you are contacting the media, remember to persuade and not dictate. They do not need a whole diatribe about who you are and what you are doing. You do not need to prove to them that you are incredibly smart, and well educated, and very knowledgeable on this issue. Know what you want to say, be concise, and be brief. Most important, tell the truth. Nothing will hurt your relationship with the media more than trying to deceive them or trying to prove or say more than you actually know.

Over time you will build relationships with certain reporters, and I am sure you will get comfortable with them. Just as a word of caution: you may go off the record or go "on background." Just be careful. Always act as if you are "on record." You can provide information and a background, but do not ever say anything you really do not want the media to know and get out to the public.

If you don't get media coverage right away, do not fret. If you have a good ongoing media relations campaign, you are informational, you are concise, and the reporter tends to ask some questions but does not write about it, they are putting it in the back of their minds and you may very well become a source for them in the future.

Partly because the news cycle has twenty-four-hour cable television, news in general has become a lot more competitive, and a lot of times reporters and editors are rushed to give a story, or give an account of the story without a lot of time to process the information, and a lot of times they are just not given the information. Whenever you see something that is not true or not quite right or just blatantly slanted politically, give the editor or reporter a call directly. Be brief, be concise, but make your argument.

When I first began working at the *Washington Times*, I noticed that many other media organizations were taking our stories and giving themselves credit for breaking a story. Not because they were mean-spirited, it was just that they were not aware of some of the things we were doing, because we did not have a very proactive media relations campaign. For example, there was a story some years ago out of the Clinton administration about a program they created called Citizenship USA, which was a speeding-up of the process for immigrants to become legal residents in this country. Many media organizations wrote their stories right out of the press release from the White House, reflecting that this was such a wonderful program. But one of our reporters wrote a story saying in fact that many thought it was a political ploy by the Clinton White House to speed up the immigration process so these new voters would vote Democratic in the next election.

National Review also wrote about this story, and was critical in the same way that we were. I had to point out to them that the *Washington Times* actually broke this story first, and they were kind to acknowledge that. That story alone about the immigration process ended up getting attributions all over the place just because of that clarification. Thus, if you see something specific that is not quite right, go right to the source and even ask for a correction or a clarification, but stick to the facts.

Media Relations

Building Personal Relationships with the Media

28

JAMES WEIDMAN

Many of my colleagues at the Heritage Foundation and other conservative organizations spend a lot of time complaining about the media, because it is hard to sell conservative ideas to an overwhelmingly liberal media. They will complain at conferences, or on the phone, or at bar stools late at night that the journalists are biased and will not give them a fair shake. They will even try to hound editors into covering stories that may be important to them, but are not news.

Ideas and stories cannot be browbeaten, whined, or nagged into the newspapers or onto the airways. The only way is by working with the media and marketing stories and ideas to them. The key word here is "with." There is not much point wasting time bemoaning how bad the media are and the fact that they will not reshape their world to accommodate yours. Your job is to figure out how you can fit your ideas into their world, into their stories, and into their minds.

How do you go about marketing your ideas? To do it effectively, the most important thing is to get to know the reporters that you are dealing with, the editors who will be writing the opinion pages or who edit the op-ed pages. Get to know the bookers and producers at the radio and television shows that you want to have your people on. Though it is simple enough, it takes time.

Planning Strategically

Since it is not necessary to meet everyone—every reporter, producer, and booker—you first need to have a strategic plan as to what you are going to accomplish. Figure out who you need to reach, which outlets

---

James Weidman is director of public relations for the Heritage Foundation. This address is developed from an interactive training session involving audience participation. The questions from the audience have been removed to preserve the flow of the presentation.

will carry your message; and then look within those organizations and find the right people who can help get your message out.

In the United States, typically everyone wants to get their story into the *New York Times* and the *Washington Post*. One must first consider if that is really necessary. It does not mean you would ignore these prominent newspapers, but it is important to point out that members of Congress read just as closely the hometown papers in the districts that elected them and that they report back to.

If you are working legislatively, and there is particular legislation you are interested in, then research who chairs that committee, who are the movers and shakers, and who are the swing votes that you need to bring to your side. Figure out which back home media are important to them and work on those media people. Get to know them. Who hosts the top talk shows back in Des Moines, for example. Get to know the producers there; tell them what is important. Cultivate the weekly community newspapers and do not think that they are second-class. Some of the world's best reporters have come from there. They are very good allies for you to have.

Consider who on a newspaper staff you need to get to know. Do you need to know the editorial page editors, or at least the editorial writers that cover the topic in which you are interested? Do you need to know the political writers or the bureau reporters? Or do you need to know the beat reporters? You probably do not need to know them all, but you are going to need to know a couple of them at least.

Figure out who you need to communicate your story to, and then do that. You cannot expect them to listen to you unless you make a conscious effort to get their attention and make a sincere effort to gain their confidence and respect. If you do not make a special effort to introduce yourself to the media—to those people who logically should be interested in your story—then they are unlikely to come to you on their own. There are hundreds of other people out there to whom they can go, and some of them are making an effort to get to know them. And that is where they will go.

It is highly important to look at the culture of the newspaper that you are dealing with, too. What is their editorial voice? Is it youth-oriented, is it trendy, is it very cerebral? The more you can remold the language in your press releases and your editorial pages to match what they are putting out, the more you have helped them accept what you are presenting. If it is fact-based, give them lots of facts in your editorials.

Competing Trends

There are two competing trends in the media world now. On the one hand, there are consolidations occurring in the United States and as a result there are hardly any two-newspaper towns left anymore, whereas it used to be common. Even the weeklies increasingly are parts of large chains, and those chains are being bought up by the dailies—even the large dailies. At the same time there is an information revolution out there. There are satellite channels, cable channels, and other sources offering more outlets for you to work. Not all outlets will access the audience you need; therefore, be aware of alternative routes to get your message out.

You can use leverage to your advantage. If you are printed up in what is a relatively small paper or a regional paper, you can use it as your third-party credibility and endorsement of what you are saying. It contains the facts on your side and it is been printed up. If you bring that to Washington or New York, it can have a big effect because the media tend to feed off of each other. And if you get a story covered in one outlet, whether it is radio, TV, or other media, you can take that, duplicate it, and send it out. Spread the word out. News sources will cover it if you get it to them quickly enough so that it is not just a one-day story. Therefore, where you have success in one place, turn it around, because the media does not want to be too far behind on a legitimate story.

Reaching Out

At the Heritage Foundation, which is a public policy research organization, we have a media relations staff of ten people, of which three work full-time only meeting and getting to know reporters and pitching their story. We have another three people who are writers, and they are also responsible for getting to know reporters. We do a lot of opinion writing for the op-ed pages of newspapers and are expected to get to know the editors, because it is easier to pick up the phone and give a push to a piece with someone you know rather than a total stranger. However, everyone in media relations is expected to be reaching out to the media constantly through phone calls, e-mails, letters, personal notes, and most important of all—face-to-face meetings. Every day, everyone on the staff expects to have at least one meal with a reporter.

Since it is important to go to where the media are, we often go on the road to keep in touch with the media outside of Washington, DC. An example of this is Mr. Hugh Newton, who retired last year, but who worked for 25 years in public relations for Heritage, specializing in working with the opinion media: editorial page editors, editorial writers, op-ed page editors, and syndicated columnists. Opinion media is important, especially if you have a hostile newspaper that you need to be published in. You can pitch their op-ed page editors, or go the circuitous route through the syndicated columnists who may be favorable to your position.

That was Hugh's world for twenty-five years. He read the same trade journals that they read. He went to the same conferences that those people attended, and at every opportunity he would add a personal touch that let them know that he valued them as individuals. He would send to an editor material that he came across that would be helpful for an editorial even if it had nothing to do with an issue that our organization was involved in. He knew what interested this guy, and if something came across his desk that he thought would be helpful, he sent it on.

For twenty-five years he was on the road for three to five days every month meeting with opinion journalists, getting to know them, getting to know their spouses, finding out what truly interested them. He would visit Minneapolis and Chicago in the dead of winter—and winters are unbearable there. He would go to Miami or Houston in the midst of their unbearable summers, so that the people understood he was there to meet them. He was not there on a junket. It was not just an excuse for him to get in some skiing or something like that. He wanted to meet these people and really care about them.

The Information Gatekeepers

Media relations is mostly an exercise in building personal relationships with the media, with the reporters, the editors, and the producers who are "the information gatekeepers" to our ultimate audiences—whether they are lawmakers, diplomats, financial supporters, or the general public. This personal approach, which is embodied by two men who have been with the Heritage Foundation for twenty-five years, Hugh Newton and Herb Berkowitz, has paid huge dividends. Over the course of these years it has also paid huge dividends for the media world in general. It is largely through their efforts that this country now has an op-ed page in most daily newspapers. This page opposite the editorial page that makes room for opposing views did not exist twenty-five years ago. It now does, largely because Hugh and Herb made the rounds arguing that many readers do not share all the same viewpoints of the editors—who risk turning off readers by their singular approach. They encouraged the newspapers to make room for differing views, and ultimately the op-ed page was born. Now, all organizations can take advantage of these pages.

It pays dividends in your personal life, as well. You will find that some of your very best friends become the people you have met as reporters. You may not agree with them on one single topic of interest to your organization, but you realize they are wonderful people and they start to realize that you are, too, and it makes them more receptive to your message. Media relations is a wonderful job to be in if you want to lead a full and rewarding life, because it is all about meeting people and selling ideas that you think make a difference.

If you have a personality conflict with a media person, find someone else—hopefully within your organization—to bring your message. Sometimes you might find someone in another organization who can be better at bringing that message around. If you go back to my central thesis, which is effective media relations is all about personal relationships, when you have a bad personal relationship then the whole construction falls apart for that particular media. If you know that, find someone who can work with you, or else write it off and move on. Moving on to Plan B may not be nearly as desirable, but a poor Plan B is much better than a totally unworkable Plan A.

Eliminate NGO-speak

Depending on your audience, you have to be able to converse in the language of the people with whom you are dealing. Typically that is more than one audience. If you are active legislatively, you need to know the legislative process. You need to know the language that they use. But when you are dealing with the media, you need to know who their audience is, too.

It is so easy to get wrapped up in the world of NGOs and affiliated like-minded groups you are working with on a daily basis back home that you think you do not have time to deal with the language of popular culture. Pop culture is the coin of communication wherever you are. What are the kids that you are dealing with watching on TV? What music and lyrics do they listen to? You need to know this so you can relate to them and speak to them on their own terms.

The absolute best way to get the attention, the confidence, and respect of newspeople—and that is what you have to do—is through a combination of this kind of personal contact and by becoming a source of interesting material for them, material that is timely, fact-based, intelligently prepared, accurate, and essentially useful. Some NGOs do this extremely well; others do not.

I am a stranger to the world of NGOs by and large, but recognizing my ignorance, I asked a friend who is an editor at a news service what major problems he encountered in dealing with NGOs. The first thing my friend recommended was that when it came to news releases and telephone pitches, eliminate what he called "NGO-speak," which is also "UN-speak." By that he meant, do not use acronyms or jargon when you are talking with a reporter. This is totally annoying to reporters and others who are not part of the NGO world. Most reporters do not know what NGO stands for even if you say, "It is a non-governmental organization."

Imagine how reporters feel when they get a news release or a phone call dedicated to the topic of UNFPRQ21. Mentally they have hung up as soon as that is out of your mouth. They do not know what it is, and when it is presented like that, they do not *want* to know. It is alien to their life. Speaking in acronyms and jargons is not just an NGO problem, it is the same problem doctors have, engineers have, and economists as well. It is an insular world where you meet with others who speak that same language. It is all part of the mystification process that makes you part of an elite mystery, but also keeps you a secret from the rest of the world. You need to remember that a reporter's job is to communicate news or opinion to regular people, to someone sitting on a bar stool. Therefore, your job in media relations is to figure out why UNFPRQ21 matters to someone on a bar stool, and then you communicate that without ever mentioning the acronym. If you communicate in simple everyday language to the reporter, you will get that, "Ah ha, I know what you are talking about, and I see why it is important."

What Interests the Media?

A second and related complaint was that communications from NGOs tend to be far too self-referential in an almost circular logic. A phone call from an organization announcing a new initiative by NGOs forming "some special coalition to complete a certain task to bring certain results" is not of interest to most news media since it is insular, self-promoting, and self-aggrandizing. What the media wants is the facts: to know what the problem is and what specifically you want to do about it. Before you get to that point, you should consider why this problem matters to the general public or to the guy on the bar stool for whom they are writing.

Generally speaking, what interests the media? Tension. Conflict. Blood. Tell them what an argument is about, what is at stake, and who the players are on both sides. Their job is to present both sides. If there is a meaningful fight going on, and if something important is at stake, reporters will be interested in it if you explain to them *why* it is interesting.

The media love numbers, and they love lists. Though technical research studies are fine—as long as they are translated into everyday English—the media will also go along with the "soft numbers" of polls and surveys. Therefore you may find the media being receptive if you do a survey on a topic that is of interest to you, at least tangentially, and you conduct it in a responsible fashion (credibility is everything here), and you are not asking loaded questions in the survey, or preselecting the respondents, and you get large enough numbers. Also it is helpful if you partner with someone who already brings credibility on that issue—either a professional polling organization or even with a newspaper or television station. That takes a little pitching, but sometimes you can do that. Thus, if you can provide the media with the authority of an issue, then they do not have to go looking for the facts. The benefit of this is that your organization is giving it to them and you are regarded as an authority on the issue.

To the extent that you find a poll that generates interest, you might want to consider doing it on a regular basis so that you can track trends—which fascinates the media. For example, is opinion going in this direction or that direction? Once you have identified a trend, that becomes news; then if you can provide a spokesman to analyze that trend describing what is driving it, what the dangers of that trend are, and what the promise of that trend is, you can get their attention.

When you are pitching a story, you need to keep things concise until you hear the reporter engage and say, "Yeah, you've got me. Tell me more." So when you are calling up to pitch a story, know what you are going to say in advance and have it honed down to approximately ten seconds. That way if you have not reached the reporter directly, you can leave a very polished engaging pitch on the line and move on.

Refining your message is all part of how you communicate in your press releases, how you communicate verbally when you are pitching a story. It all needs to be thought out in advance. Do not just wing it or hope to carry the day by the passion or length of your presentation. Getting their attention and keeping it short is what does it.

Humanize Your Ideas

It is important when you are putting out press releases to tell a story. Humanize your ideas. Start with a real-world example of an individual rather than with rhetoric and hyperbole. Use case histories and try to present people and events that embody the very point you are trying to make. It is the old journalism school thing: show, do not tell. If you start with that, it is much easier to engage the mind and imagination of the reader. And, of course, your first reader on a press release is the reporter.

Always tell the truth. Do not exaggerate. If you do not know the answer to a question, tell them you do not know but you will find out and you will get back to them. And then get back to them. Do not make a promise you are not going to keep with them.

The final word is feed the media. Literally feed them something that they are going to find tasty. You have got to read their newspaper to see how these people write, then feed them the story that you know is going to appeal to them. Literally, you need to feed them as well. Take them out to lunch, take them to dinner, or buy them a drink. It is how you get to know people and how they get to know you. Who pays for meals? The protocol is if you invite a reporter out, you offer to pay. If the reporter insists on paying, you let the reporter pay. Many news outlets in the United States have a policy that you cannot buy meals for their staff.

Mutual Learning Process

When you are with a cause-oriented organization, it is important that reporters learn that you are a person and not just a strident voice—that you have a sense of humor, that you have kids, that there is life beyond your cause. Otherwise they just have this caricature of you in their mind of how you are and of how your organization is. Learning that reporters are regular people—interesting and wonderful—is all part of the mutual learning process that helps lead to respect and trust, so important in media relations.

Incidentally, the best type of market research you can do for your organization is to call up or take a reporter to lunch and ask him or her, "What are we doing wrong? What are we doing right? How can I do a better job of helping you do your job?" It is important to remember it is up to you to fit your world into theirs, not complain that they are not changing to fit your world.

Government-controlled Media

If you are doing media relations in a country where the media is owned and controlled by the government, you must remember that he who owns the print and the press owns that thing. Recognizing this point, you have to determine what your purpose is. For example, if your purpose is to train youth, you have to decide whether to work with the government or even to inform them. You may decide to forget about going with the government-owned press and deciding to go with alternative media. However, in a small organization, the alternative might mean flyers stuck on car windows and up on shop windows advertising your project. If you do not want to deal with government-controlled media in this situation, you have a harder path to go. If there are things you can do to work with them, if you can find common ground that is not going to violate your principles, then work toward that common ground.

One approach would be to have a joint press conference with a representative from the government, especially if they have money going into a project or are making a facility available. Also, remember that reporters in this controlled media are restricted by state controls, they know the stories they write have to meet certain requirements or they will never be printed. To the extent you can give them what they need—a package deal, not just what they need straight from your organization—you have solved the problem for him and the information goes out.

Another resource well-worth the time invested is having a good website that serves as a great reference for reporters or anyone else interested in one's organization. These are invaluable tools for NGOs and a great way to really get your message out.

Part VII
Resources for NGOs

Introduction

With the advent of globalization and advances in information technologies has come a shift toward an enhanced role for NGOs in impacting global policies and providing much-needed services. NGOs are more numerous, vocal, diversified, and influential. Their flexibility, technical expertise, connections to the grass roots, passion, and commitment have allowed them to become major players in addressing issues of serious concern. Indeed, in many cases they have become more capable than governments and the free market in responding to certain needs. For example, NGOs now deliver more worldwide development assistance than the entire UN system, excluding the World Bank and the International Monetary Fund.

No matter how lofty the founding vision of an NGO, however, it is just a noisy chime without resources. The papers in this section deal with practical matters relative to three key resources for NGOs: finances, networking, and strategic planning.

Introduction

Fundraising and Getting Grants

29

THERESA RUDACILLE

I work with an organization in Washington, DC, called the Empowerment Resource Network. It is our goal to help nonprofit, non-governmental organizations do good in the community. To assist this, we provide training and courses for free to non-governmental organizations. The topic I am going to address here is how to get money for projects and operational costs.

Every organization needs money. But in order to get money, before we can even start to address how to ask for money and where to get it, we have to talk about your organization, because people do not just hand out money. Ted Turner is not going to walk up to your door with a briefcase full of a million dollars. Your organization has to have certain things in line, legal and otherwise.

Before we start, we need to talk about your organization, what it is and what it does. For those of you whose organizations are not located in the United States, it is even more important to be able to articulate why people in this country should care. Why should potential sources of funds care about what is going on in Uzbekistan? And for organizations that are in this country, why should a donor care about who you are?

Mission Statement

You cannot ask for money unless you can articulate a mission. A mission statement is essentially a task and a purpose. The mission of the International Committee of the Red Cross (ICRC) is to protect the

---

Theresa Rudacille is director of development for the US-based Empowerment Resource Network. This address is developed from an interactive training session involving audience participation and handouts. The questions from the audience have been removed to preserve the flow of the presentation. Additional information has been added for IRS recognition of foreign charities at the end of the transcript.

lives and dignity of victims of war and internal violence and to provide them with assistance; to direct and coordinate the international relief activities conducted by the International Red Cross and Red Crescent movement in situations of conflict; and to prevent suffering by promoting and strengthening humanitarian law and universal humanitarian principles. That is all they need to articulate their mission. Similarly, the mission of the International Federation of Red Cross and Red Crescent Societies is to inspire, facilitate, and promote all humanitarian activities carried out by its member national societies to improve the situation of the most vulnerable people, and to direct and coordinate international assistance of the movement to victims of natural and technological disasters, to refugees, and in health emergencies. These are well-defined mission statements, clearly delineating the task and purposes of the organizations.

If you as an organization do not have a clear, simple mission statement, then you need to start right there to develop one.

US Recognition as a Charity

In order to be recognized as a charity in the United States and receive tax deductible money, such as grants, you have to be registered and recognized by the Internal Revenue Service (IRS). Foreign nonprofits also should get recognition as a 501(c)(3) charity by the IRS. The process for foreign NGOs is the same as for nonprofits based here in the United States. Foundations such as the Ford Foundation or Rockefeller Foundation, for instance, have to be very careful to check where their money is going, especially with concerns about terrorism and NGOs affiliated with terrorism.

Essentially, the United States government has to recognize an organization as being legitimate and as doing something charitable before it will give corporations or individuals tax credit for giving money to that organization. Foundations in the United States give large amounts of money only to legitimate organizations that are registered and recognized. Foreign corporations can be located outside of the United States, but have to be registered and recognized by the IRS *(see additional information at the end of the paper).*

For example, the donor needs the IRS to know that your organization is legitimate, that is not a front for a government organization or a front for a terrorist organization such as al-Qaeda. Money given directly to a government is not tax deductible for a donor. Likewise, the US government, at a US Treasury website, www.ustreas.gov/terrorism.html, lists organizations to which contributions are prohibited by executive order as a result of being designated organizations connected with terrorist groups or supporting them. In essence, your relationship with the IRS is for the sake of the donor.

This is in reference to receiving funds from a US foundation. It is another situation if the foundation is located in your country. For example, if your NGO is located in India, you can seek grants directly from the Ford Foundation in India, through their own offices, and not have to register with the US government. This means those assets in the Ford Foundation in India are Indian assets, and you are working through the Indian government in terms of those grants.

The issue is the dollar going across borders. If your organization is only looking for resources, such as "We want doctors to come and serve our children," or "We want teachers to come to our country and teach," it still holds that if you are recognized as legitimate by the IRS, it makes it easier to get that kind of resource. The process for recognition is to apply for a 501(c)(3) tax-exempt status from the IRS.

Programs and Budget

It is important to understand that most people, corporations, governments, foundations, and individual owners give to very specific programs, not general organizations. Once your nonprofit is considered a legitimate organization, has a correct legal structure, and is recognized by the IRS, the next important process that your organization has to do before you ask for money is to plan and articulate what it is that is going to be achieved. What are your programs? If you are writing a literacy program for youth, how many people are involved? What towns or villages are you visiting? How many children are going to be affected? How much is it going to cost? What do you do?

It all has to be written down on paper. There are a lot of organizations that try and raise money saying, "We're going to eliminate x, y, z. We are going to eliminate AIDS in Uganda."

"Great! How are you going to do it?"

"Through a public education campaign. Through medical research. Through direct treatment of patients."

"Are you doing abstinence sex education? What do you do?"

So everything that you visualize has to be broken down into programs and budgeted as a program. It is important before people give you money, not only that you are legitimate, but that you can show that other people are providing you either money or resources, as well.

Let us say that your organization works with the Pew Foundation in education and literacy programs. If you have people who are volunteering their time as instructors, or there is a company that is giving you the books, those resources can show on the budget. You may have what is called "in-kind contributions," everything but money: volunteers, materials, a place where you can operate. You may have half of your total budget in donated resources and not money. So now if you are asking the Ford Foundation to give you $1 million, you are asking them to give $1 million toward a $3 million project. Thus, the donor is not the only one providing support, but recognizes that you have other resources and support.

What are those "in-kind contributions"? There are organizations in the United States that will give computer equipment for projects. They are dedicated to giving computer equipment to underdeveloped countries. That is all they do. They will put a value on that computer equipment and that will show on your budget. If you are operating out of somebody's office, they are giving you office space. That office space is worth something. That would be in your budget.

The number one asset that is overlooked is volunteer labors. Volunteers here in the United States are recognized, depending on what they do, at the market rate for their work. When your organization gets a person to volunteer to do computer work, secretarial work, and so forth, that can be valued at eight or nine dollars an hour, depending on what they are doing, and all of that counts in the budget.

Ethics and Governance

I have not yet addressed where to get money or how to ask for money because you cannot do that until you identify what you do, what the programs are, and how much it costs. Another big issue for the non-profit, non-governmental organizational world is ethics and legal/governance rules for organizations.

In the United States, for a nonprofit corporation to exist legally, it is owned by a group of people who run the organization. If you are a director on the board of directors of a nonprofit organization, normally you do not receive financial compensation, but rather are seen as a person who can either get money for the organization (either directly, by giving money yourself, or indirectly, such as lending your name or finding donors) or provide expertise to the organization. By the same token, if you are a director, you may not be involved with the everyday activities of the organization; there is a paid staff. In the United States, that is one of the checks and balances in place for nonprofit governance. The officers are held responsible to the board, which determines responsibilities and compensation for the officers, while the board itself is generally composed of dedicated individuals who are not compensated and are overseeing the welfare of the non-profit organization and its activities.

If your organization in another country has a different structure, you have to be clear to articulate how it is established. How do you make sure that the guy who owns the organization is not taking all the money and going to Paris? It is an issue of accountability and checks and balances. Usually you also have a board of advisers and someone other than your officers who handles your books to make sure that the person in charge cannot use the money without anybody else knowing about it. In some countries the owners may be the officers, and they do everything—get the money, do the work, spend the money, and so forth. In the United States there are certain safeguards designed to make sure that an organization listed as a nonprofit with the government has an acceptable system of checks and balances.

If your organization is of the type where the person in charge ultimately runs the organization, make sure that there is someone else to take care of the money. For organizations in the United States, there are generally accepted accounting practices, such as an audit every year, a third-party review by the board of finances, checks signed by two individuals, and so forth.

Four Sources of Money

So we have our mission. We have our plan. We have our budget. We have a good ethical and legal structure. Why are people going to give your organization money to do what it does? Because it is their passion. They are believers. In the fundraising world, your best source for money and resources are people who think like you do, who believe like you believe—individuals, donors, and foundations.

Governments and corporations are another story. Governments are not compassionate. Governments do not believe things like people do. People in government can be very compassionate, but governments are political and make political decisions. Corporations on the other hand are driven by dollars. Corporations can say wonderful things, "Your organization is doing great work," but generally unless it means something to their bottom line, do not ask them. Most people think that the Coca-Cola Foundation is a wonderful international organization that does good. And it does good. But they get something in return for doing good in a country, such as exposure.

There are really four different sources of money. (1) First, there are government grants. In the United States there is a lot of money here. Included in this category are grants from governmental organizations and departments and intergovernmental grants. The United Nations, for example, is always looking for partners. The French government, the German government likewise provide grants. You just have to hit them where they have an interest. (2) Second, there are charitable foundations. There are many charitable foundations in the United States who are willing to provide grants worldwide. (3) Third, there are individuals, people who may or may not have a foundation, but they can write you a check. Those are the people who believe, and who will give you a personal check. (4) Fourth, there are also sources of income are not donations, but rather compensation for offering a service for which governments and organizations are willing to pay.

For this fourth category, your organization essentially becomes a hired contractor to do its mission. For example, your organization can contract and become a partner with the United Nations, or partner with some of the world's relief organizations, if you have contacts on the ground in a neighborhood, city, or country where they wish to provide help. The American Red Cross or the International Red Cross do not know who and which neighborhoods need to be helped. You do! So in looking at whom you can go to for help in terms of donations or resources, look at whom you serve. Look at the other organizations that might need that service. You should know who the International Red Cross representative is. They should know who you are and what you do. Your organization may deal with illiteracy or helping women get jobs. If something happens in your country and you have got contacts or hundreds of women across the country, the Red Cross would want to know that.

Partnering resources and getting resources from other organizations is about building relationships, even building relationships with other organizations that sometimes you may think are your competition.

The United States has a World Relief Organization. It is based in Washington, DC, and they are always looking for partners. So one of the first things you could do is to find out who your representative is in the United Nations and their contact information. Because they are a nonprofit and are interested in helping with world relief, or different programs currently going on in your country or region, your would like to form a working relationship with them.

Niche

One of the hardest things in developing a nonprofit organization involves critically assessing your task and your vision. It is hard in the beginning to take a step back and say, "Who else is doing this work and what is the difference between what they do and what we do?" Because if somebody else is already doing the work, and doing it well, does your organization even need to exist? Maybe you should just work for them. That is a hard question! But it is one of the first questions that major donors are going to ask you. Why fund you? Who else does this?

You have a unique niche if you can quantify and identify exactly whom you serve and why you are the only ones who can do it. Or why you are the only ones who can do it in this country, or this state. Or why you are the only ones who work with girls ages fourteen to twenty when another program works with younger girls or older women. Identify your niche. Check out your competition, the organizations that do similar things. Who are they? What do they do? How do they do it? They may be able to help define who you are and what your niche is. "They do this, but they do not do that, and here is an area where we are the best!"

For example, you may assist underprivileged children who otherwise might not go to school. They fall below the radar screen of other organizations that offer scholarship funds. Nobody knows that they are here. You identify who you are and what you do and why you deserve funding. It helps the donor know why to give to your organization versus somebody else.

The Donors

Have we talked about getting money yet? No. You cannot get money until you do these fundamental tasks. It may be painful, but you have to do it. Really, getting the money after doing all of this is just asking. People say yes or people say no. They say, "Not now" or "Not this." They will not do this or not do that. Just ask.

A lot of how you ask for money depends on whom you are asking. Donors who are business-oriented—a business corporation, a business owner—generally think in terms of the bottom line—profits. If I am a philanthropist, however, I do not care what the bottom line is. I want to do good. How you phrase what you do and why you do it will be different according to each audience. Corporations are business minded. Governments need a political reason for giving. You cannot ignore that. If it is a United States government program, then they will publish exactly what they are doing and why they are doing it, and instructions for applying. They have you execute the government's vision.

The most popular granting source in the United States is foundations. Foundations give a lot of money. Here in the United States, a foundation is a legal entity designed to give away money. That is their purpose; that is why they exist, to give away money. They have to give away a certain percentage of their assets every year. Some foundations are designed to do this forever. Some foundations are designed to give away their money and then to go away. Foundations exist here in the United States just for this.

How do you locate foundations that give away grants for your type of organization? One of the best sources is The Foundation Center, a nonprofit organization that has a database of grantmakers and grants. It also publishes directories of grantmaking foundations, according to various categories, as well as fundraising guides. The Foundation Center identifies foundations by what their name is, where they are located, their phone number, who is on their board of directors, their amount of giving per year, what their limitations in giving are, who they have given to, their application process, and numerous other helpful details. If you do not have access to one of their five libraries or two hundred collections, where you can peruse the materials for free, you can visit their website at www.fdncenter.org. The Foundation Center also offers free electronic newsletters. Some of their services are fee-based. You also can query online. A lot of libraries in the United States and most major university libraries also have copies of the directories. Another source for information on foundations is the Empowerment Resource Network, for which I work.

There is a foundation somewhere in the United States that funds just about anything you can imagine. It is important to know the foundation and what they support. There are organizations that give internationally. There are organizations that only give to Australia. So you have to look at each foundation, what they are interested in, what their limitations are in terms of giving, and if their giving program fits your organization. If it looks like that foundation is a believer in what you do, then they are a potential donor. Potential! Not a prospective one yet, but a potential one.

Some foundations give large amounts of money, including millions and millions of dollars at one time, and some smaller family foundation are willing to give $500 to $10,000. The key is the fit between your organization and the foundation.

How do you use your affiliation with WANGO to help you with foundations? Every foundation is managed by a board of directors. Those boards of directors are people, and people know people. Every time I research a foundation, I look to see who is on the board of directors. Because I may recognize a name, or my board of directors might recognize a name, or someone we know through our affiliation with WANGO may know somebody who can help us get into a foundation.

Asking for Money

The process of asking for and getting money is based on relationships, first and foremost. It is all about relationship! This is why foundation fundraising is different from government fundraising—because bureaucrats just do not know how to carry on relationships with normal people! For foundations, look at the board, look and see what they do, and often you can also call the foundation and they will send you an annual report, if it is not on their website.

Many larger foundations that fund internationally have websites. They tell you what they believe. They tell you what programs they fund. They may even list who they funded and how much. Looking at this information helps you decide, does my program match what they fund? How do you know how much money to request? You take a look at who they funded and how much they gave out. That will show you a range of how much they give. McReynolds gives out an average of $25,000 to $50,000 in grants to organizations. You know that by looking at their annual report. An annual report will also list everyone on the board of directors, so you do not have to do that research.

And they will also tell you *exactly* how to write the grant. Do not pay for a course in grant-writing. Let me repeat that: Do not pay for a course in grant-writing. The Foundation Center website has an online course to teach you, which takes fifteen minutes. If you can read, you can write a grant. You do not need to invest hundreds of dollars to attend a grant-writing course.

A foundation's guidelines will outline the essentials that must be in the proposal, and you need to just read it and follow it. It may say the proposal is limited to five single spaced pages, have a left hand margin of one inch, a right hand margin of one inch, and submit only one copy. It may state that the first paragraph is the mission, the second paragraph is how much money you want. Each foundation is different, and they identify their particular specifications.

Every time a foundation prints up grant guidelines, the first thing that grant reviewers look for is a reason to throw yours out according to those guidelines. If they ask for 20 pages and you send 30—poof! You are out! If they ask for a cover page signed by your executive director and you do not have it—poof! You are out! So the first thing is to follow the guidelines. Send them only what they ask for, no more than what they ask for. But send everything they ask for.

I always have my husband, who knows nothing about what I do, read my grant to make sure it makes sense. Have somebody read your grant. If your subject and your verbs do not agree, this can be spotted. If there is a language difference, ask a university student or professor to look at your grant. They often will do it for free.

The other things that will kick out a grant: you are asking for too much. Your outcomes are unrealisitic. "I'm going to cure poverty in Uganda." "Well, it is not happening. Good luck! But I'm not giving you $25,000 on that project."

Before I send the foundation grant out, I always call the foundation first and talk to somebody. "Hi, my name is…" Call and tell them who you are. Ask to talk to a program officer or somebody involved in reviewing your type of grant proposal: "I'm thinking of applying for a grant for this kind of project. Would you consider it?" If they say, "No," do not waste your time writing the grant. But this is your opportunity to talk to somebody. "We're thinking of doing this. You have funded similar projects in Africa before. This is a good project." Even if they are not going to consider your grant, you may get some very good information about your program from somebody who has funded things where you are. Is it realistic? How was our budget? Can we do this?

Once you have gotten to the point where you know, yes or no, they will or will not look at your grant proposal, then you can start putting together all that information we talked about in the first twenty minutes: who you are, what you do, what your plans are, what your budget is on paper, and all presented in a form that they require.

Donations from Individuals

Foundations are not the number one donor, at least in the United States; individuals are. *PLEASE NOTE: Donations by individuals and businesses in the United States are NOT tax deductible if the money is being given to a foreign NGO.* This does not mean that donors will not support you; it means that you must officially notify them that their contribution is not tax deductible, even if you have an IRS 501(c)(3) letter. For foundations and trusts, the tax deductibility of the grant is not an issue. For individuals who have a passion for what you do, they may not care that their donation is not tax deductible, either. The key is to find people who believe in what you do.

In order to reach individuals in the United States, one needs certification (the 501(c)(3) letter) by the IRS. Depending on how you solicit individuals, whether it is a mass mailing, whether it is a special event, whether you are sending e-mail or sending out letters, you need this certification to be considered a legitimate nonprofit organization.

If your organization is located in the United States and you send for or go out and ask for money, you need a solicitation license from your state. The secretary of state who handles your corporation is the one who gets you the solicitation license. It may run $50 a year if you are under $50,000 and $500 a year if your annual budget is larger. Each state has its own rules and fees for soliciting the general public in their state. The solicitation letter is needed when you are approaching the general public (mass mailing to a large list of donors).

You do not need a solicitation license to apply for grants. A solicitation license protects the general public. Whether you are doing direct mail, whereby you are mailing requests for funds throughout the Untied States, or if you are having a special event to which the public is invited, a solicitation license is required to protect the general public. What that means is that if you call me on the phone like the telemarketers do, I can call the secretary of state and verify that you are a legitimate organization and I can give you money. The need for a solicitation license from each state in which you solicit the general public is one reason we DO NOT encourage you to use direct mail or telemarketing to raise money. Targeting businesses and individuals that you have taken the time to develop relationships with is more effective in the long run and prevents you from having to comply with public solicitation rules.

In the US we use the licensing process to protect the general public. If you do decide to solicit on a broad scale in a particular state or region, you do need to comply with each state's solicitation license rules. Being a 501(c)(3) organization is not the same thing as being certified for soliciting funds. The tax-exempt status involves the federal government. The certification for soliciting funds involves the state government. If you are soliciting in the state of Georgia, the government of Georgia wants a little of your money also.

It is another issue if an individual gives your organization money because you have a personal relationship. Anybody can give you money. The IRS may not count the donation as tax-deductible, but that is a problem for the donor, not the recipient organization. Note again that *your 501(c)(3) status does not make donations from individuals and businesses tax deductible if you are a foreign NGO. The 501(c)(3) makes you a qualified organization for foundation, trust, and government grants.* That is why I am saying it is important to register with the IRS, in order to make your donor's life easier. The solicitation license is needed for approaching the general public. If there is a personal relationship, it is assumed that the donor has checked up and verified the organization or individual to whom they are giving a donation, so a solicitation license is not needed in that case.

Partnering with other organizations in soliciting the general public is another option. For example, if your organization is working through churches or congregations, you can partner with them and use *their* letterhead, or their shield. Since the solicitation is only going to a closed group of people and the people who are on that list, the church or the congregation has legitimized your organization. In other words, if you are sending a solicitation to the general public in the city of Washington, DC, you need a license. If you have an agreement with an association, and you want to solicit everyone in that association, you do not need a general solicitation license.

Finding Individual Donors

How do you find individuals who believe what you believe? Conferences. Everybody attending a major international conference, like WANGO Annual Conference 2002, has probably met one person who could either write a check to them or knows somebody who could write a check, because they are sympathetic to what you are doing. Those business cards that everyone gives you, keep those! And if you have a good conversation with somebody, they may know an organization or a person who could support you.

Business leaders are another source. People who own businesses have money. Look into your professional trade journals for leaders who have an interest in or connection to the work you do. If you are from another country, which individuals have come from your country and succeeded in the United States? What about ethnic associations? Most of the money that funds the conflict in Northern Ireland comes from the United States, because some people in this country who have made money who are sympathetic and are sending it to their home country

Look at trade association publications like *Who's Who in American Business*, or the *Standard and Poors* index. Or do your search on the internet. The best search engine is google.com. Type in a person's name. Type in "Lebanon," for example, or type in your country. Look at the people who are affiliated with your area. Look for individuals who have come to the United States who are successful. If you are a U.S.-based organization, look for people who have given to organizations like yours. If you are a policy organization that works on AIDS research, look up other policy organizations that do AIDS research and see who gave them money, because their donors could be your donors. There is no rule that says people have a limited amount of money and can give to only one organization.

Corporations

Corporations right now are not giving away as much money as they used to. Again, corporations give money when it is to their benefit, unless they are a family-owned corporation or business where the owner's vision is still implemented. Chick-fil-A was started by a man in Georgia. Chick-fil-As across the United States are closed on Sunday, because Sunday is church day. Chick-fil-A's corporate giving program supports religious organizations because of who owns the corporation.

Wal-Mart is another case. The Walton family drives their corporate vision and their corporate funding. The man who founded Home Depot believes in entrepreneurism and microeconomics and will support funding to start up businesses in developing countries.

You can read *Business Week* and similar publications for the corporate CEO's philosophy. That is how you find a corporation that can support what you do. Also look at who has manufacturing plants and business headquarters located where you are. Home Depot was founded in Atlanta, so most of the corporate giving is done there, in Georgia. If you have a corporate headquarters located where you are, chances are you have got a better chance of getting money than somebody who lives someplace else.

If you live outside of the United States, look for companies that have a plant there or that want to be there, because they may give money to curry favor with the foreign government to ease the tracks for them. Coca-Cola and Pepsi, Philip Morris—even though they are cigarettes, they also own Kraft foods—are candidates, as is any organization that is international, such as international trucking and shipping agencies. Another industry that people often do not like to get involved with is beer, wine, and alcohol corporations, but they give money away. That may raise an issue with some people about what money they are willing to take and what money they are not willing to take. Here in the United States, some conservative and religious organizations do not take money from Target, because Target is owned by Dayton Hudson, and Dayton Hudson supports Planned Parenthood and abortion groups. That is a decision that is up to your organization to make. There is no right or wrong answer, as long as the decision was properly discussed. Remember: somebody giving you money means that they are buying into your agenda, not you buying into their agenda; they do not influence what you do.

If, on the other hand, a donor gives your organization money to do something specific that is not your organization's mission, that has nothing to do with your purpose and goals, do you take the money? Probably not. There are times when you have to know when to say no. It is a decision that everyone has to make.

Associations

Another broad group of donors that often is overlooked are associations. Associations are not private enterprise; they are non-governmental. They are nonprofits. A lot of them can be professional associations. The Bar Association, an association of lawyers in the United States, gives money for juvenile crime projects, which is related to what they do. The Farm Bureau in most countries, or the national farm bureau, will give money that supports agriculture, family farms, and such programs.

Search for foreign associations that are looking to have an impact and do a service project. Associations have the same sort of philosophical need to do good in a lot of cases. The National Education Association (NEA) in the United States has a firm belief in certain education principles, and sends money or teachers overseas when it is to their benefit. The American Medical Association and Doctors Without Borders are examples of organizations that use volunteers around the world to help with medical care, immunizations, and so forth. Different associations may not give money to your organization, but they may give you resources or partner with you on a specific project.

There is not a general directory for associations worldwide, although the Yearbook of International Organizations lists international associations. There is also a national directory of associations in the United States. Since associations are nonprofit organizations, you can examine directories of associations on the regional or local levels. You can also use the national database of nonprofit organizations provided by GuideStar (www.guidestar.com). Guide lists over 850,000 nonprofit organizations in the United States, and their database can be searched by zip code and city, among other categories.

Major Donors and Government Grants

We have discussed foundations, individuals, corporations, and associations. There are two other categories of donors.

One category is the major donor. Those are individuals, and a lot of the time celebrities, who can write substantial checks. Major donors usually give less than $100,000, but can sit down and write you a check for at least $1,000—just pull out the checkbook and write it. They may not be major money for your organization, but these are the people you can call in an emergency and say, "I need $5,000" and they can write you a check. To find those people, it is a matter of looking at all those other resources mentioned and finding them one at a time. Your major donors are your true believers. They are the people who you eventually want to put on your board of directors, that you want to make part of your group. They are the people you can rely on for emergency funding.

Finally, there are government grants. I personally do not write government grants simply because a lot of the time they are politically driven. It is not that they really care, but rather they are politically driven. You cannot count on government grants. You may get it this year, but not the next year. Does that mean that you should not go for them? Of course not. Government grants are just another source of funds.

All United States government grants are announced in the Federal Register, which is a website that announces every day what grants are available. There are also individual government agencies, such as HUD (Department of Housing and Urban Development), the Department of Labor, and Department of Education, which have discretionary funds to give out on their own. Those are generally the ones that non-governmental organizations can get the easiest since, for a lot of them, you do not have to be an approved federal contractor and you also are working with a special office and can develop a relationship with the people.

Government grants are usually contract-driven, meaning they want specific services for specific groups for a specific purpose. So you are essentially executing the contract rather than really taking money and doing your mission. Internationally, most major government grants are routed through bodies such as the American Red Cross, the United Nations, the World Relief Organization, or other major organizations. Very seldom does any U.S. government grant of significant magnitude go to a local, small NGO in a foreign country. This means that for organizations not located in the United States, your best way to get into that government-granting system of the United States is to make good friends and build relationships with those major organizations in your country, or via local offices in your country.

One resource that you do have in your countries is the United States embassies. You can call them and make inquiries and get referrals.

Communications

In fundraising, if you ask for money or resources, "No" does not always mean no; it does not always mean forever. It can mean not now, not this, not this much, not you. Seek after people. If it looks like they should be funding you, send them your newsletter. Send them your annual report. Let them know what you are doing.

If you ask the Ford Foundation to fund a project and they turn you down, you get the money from someplace else, you do the project, and then send a report on that project back to the Ford Foundation: "Thank you for considering our request. We were eventually able to get the funds from x, y and z. This is what we were able to do with it." Those donors stay in that realm until they tell you, "Do not call us again." Make them tell you this before you stop. I have had only one person say, "Don't call me again. We're going out of business." So send them your newsletter. Invite them to things. If you are having a dinner, or you are doing a tour of the facility, invite potential donors. Build a relationship with them. Invite government officials. Government officials run political campaigns and can be some of your best publicity—and it's free.

Ethical Guidelines

There is a big movement worldwide for professional fundraisers. Here in the United States the Association of Fundraising Professionals (www.afpnet.org) is at the forefront of this movement. They have come up with a statement of principles to guide charities called *The Accountable Non-profit Organization*, as well as a *Code of Ethical Principles and Standards of Professional Practice* for fundraisers, and a *Donor Bill of Rights*. The Maryland Association of Non-Profit Organizations also puts out *Standards for Excellence*, which is an ethics and accountability code for the nonprofit sector. These are important principles that nonprofits should follow in daily practice.

Additional Information on IRS Recognition of Tax-Exempt Status

As mentioned in the paper, foreign NGOs are encouraged to apply for recognition of tax-exempt status by the US Internal Revenue Service (better known as a 501(c)(3) letter). The following information guides you through the process of applying.

Please note: This recognition by the IRS qualifies you as a charitable organization in the United States. For foundation and trust grants, it makes you a qualifying organization. For individuals and businesses, a donation to you is *not tax deductible* because the money is being sent to a foreign charity. Only contributions used in the US are considered tax deductible.

The IRS maintains a website where the application process is outlined (www.irs.gov). Click on the section for "Charities and Non-Profits" found in the left-hand column. Then click on the "Application Process." This portion of the website will guide you through the application process for recognition by the US Internal Revenue Service. All publications and forms can be downloaded from this site. All forms must be completed in English. If you are submitting copies of documents (constitution, bylaws, or other documents), they must be notarized by a legal official. The original documents may be in a native language, but an exact translation of each document must also be provided.

1. Download Publication 557, the complete instructions for the application process.
2. Download Form SS-4. This form is an application for an Employer Identification Number. Even foreign NGOs need this number because it becomes your tax identification number. On the website and in the instructions, they have you fax the form to Ogden, Utah. Foreign NGOs can call a special IRS office in Philadelphia that handles organizations located outside of the US at (215)516-3990 for assistance in completing the form. The form must then be faxed to that office in Philadelphia at (215)516-3990. You must obtain the Employer Identification Number before completing your IRS 501 (c)(3) application.
3. Download Form 1023, the application for recognition of tax-exempt status. The instructions are outlined in the Pub 557 and within the 1023 form. It is on this form that the organization explains exactly what they do and how they do it. The form requires that the organization provide a copy of the "organizing document." That is the official form or document that created your NGO. It might be a government application, a constitu-

tion, or other official form. It should be submitted in its original format along with an English translation of the document. Organizations are also asked to provide a document that describes *how* the organization operates. Here in the United States we refer to them as organizational bylaws. Again, an original copy should be submitted along with a translation if needed.

4. Download Form 8718. The United States charges an administrative fee to process each application. This form certifies the payment of this fee. The forms 1023 and 8718, and the fee payment in US dollars are sent to the address in Covington, Kentucky, listed on the Form 8718.

For each of these steps there is help available on the IRS website or by calling the toll-free number listed on each form. For general information you can call 1-800-876-1715. If they cannot answer your question, they will refer you to the appropriate office. Make sure you tell them if you are a charity located outside of the United States.

Strategic Management of NGOs

30

MARGARET E. HAYES

While recognizing that you come from different countries, from different cultures, with different realities in your countries, what I share with you is relevant across the board because it has to do with strategic management of your NGO—not just management, but *strategic* management. That is the operative word.

In the *Encyclopedia Columbia University*, my alma mater's encyclopedia dictionary, you will see the word "strategy" defined as follows:

> *1 a (1):* the science and art of employing the political, economic, psychological, and military forces of a nation, or group of nations, to afford the maximum support to adopt policies in peace or war *(2):* the science and art or military command exercised to meet the enemy in combat under advantageous conditions *1 b:* a variety of or the instance of the use of strategy *2 a:* a careful plan or method; a clever stratagem *2 b:* the art of devising or employing plans or stratagems toward a goal.

There are synonyms offered for this word, and those synonyms are "strategic tactics, logistics: an aspect of military science." Going from strategy to the word strategic, this word is defined as,

> *1:* relating to or marked by strategy *2 a:* necessary or important in the initiation, conduct, or completion of a strategic plan *2 b:* required for the conduct of war

---

Dr. Margaret E. Hayes is president and CEO of MEH Associates. This paper is developed from an interactive, training session involving audience participation and handouts. The questions from the audience have been removed to preserve the flow of the presentation.

> *2 c:* of great importance within the integrated whole or to a planned effect *3:* designed or trained to strike an enemy at the sources of the military, economic, or political power.

What is the common thread that you hear in those definitions? One word, a three-letter word: War. War, military, strategic command, combat, military command. These are all terms that connotate aggression, fighting, the exercising of warlike power. Now we ourselves are not warlike people. We are peaceful people. We are people who are gathered together to see how we can address the world's issues in peaceful terms. We do not define ourselves in those terms of war. Ours is a quest for unity, brotherhood, sisterhood, and global solidarity. In other words, we make love, not war.

So what do we do? How does this apply to us as managers of peaceful organizations that pursue peace to achieve our goals? It reminds me of a story of a man sitting on a park bench, whittling away on his piece of wood. A reporter comes up to him, and the reporter says, "Excuse me sir, you do not seem to notice, but you know there's been a terrible riot in this community. A lot of destruction and killing, and people died, and people say it is because of ignorance and apathy." The man looked up from his whittling, and looked at the reporter and said, "I do not know and I do not care." We do not want to be like this man, ignorant and apathetic. So how does war apply to us and how do we use war to effect what we do?

I submit that because of our knowledge regarding today's problems, and because we do care, we must wage war. We must wage war against hunger, war against poverty, war against poor health care, lack of democracy, oppression, slavery, mutilation, terrorism, weapons of mass destruction, just to name a few. We must wage war against the devastating outcomes of imperfect human beings, when they engage in negative behavior against innocent people. We must wage war in our own special way. So in order to effectively wage war, we must have strong NGOs with a well-planned and clearly defined mission, and a strategically developed management plan.

Basically, what I do in my business is provide technical assistance—management design, fundraising, grant-writing, and so forth—to nonprofit organizations and in particular to faith-based organizations. I originally got involved with the faith-based community after the pastor at my church sent me to our state's capital, Trenton, to respond to an invitation that our church had received from the governor of the state of New Jersey, Christine Whitman. The purpose of that gathering was to announce the initiation of a social service program involved in giving faith-based funds to faith-based organizations. When I got there, and I listened, I noticed that there was a lot of patting each other on the back and congratulating each other over this program. I pointed out, however, that in this discussion nothing had been stated regarding technical assistance for those faith-based organizations who have never had, or used, government money before. Those organizations did not know how to use it, did not know how to manage it, did not know how to financially put in place a mechanism for dealing with it, and so without technical assistance they would be built up for failure. At that point I was invited to Trenton to address this topic, and I became a consultant to the governor's faith-based initiative, working with churches who were applying for state government money at that time, evaluating where they were in terms of their capability and capacity for accepting this money and utilizing it efficiently, effectively, and successfully.

Six Paths to Strategic Management

Eleanor Roosevelt stated: "Somewhere along the line of development we discover what we really are and then we make our real decision for which we are responsible." The title of "Culture of Responsibility" in the theme of WANGO Annual Conference 2002 is certainly appropriate since we want to be responsible as NGOs leaders.

Whatever your mission is, you must succeed. And if you are, in your estimation, succeeding, there is always something else you can do to improve and get better. In this respect I would like to address the Six Paths to Strategic Management.

The first path is *Evaluate the Non-Governmental Organization.* It is important to evaluate clearly: determine the strengths and weaknesses of your organization and your management team. Be honest. The management team may be nice, you love them, they are faithful, they are loyal—but do they have the skills to tackle a particular project?

The second path is *Community Resources*. You have to identify community resources, assess the value to the organization, and decide when and where to use them. Whether they're your local banks, your local funding sources, your government funding sources, your corporate funding sources, your community funding sources, or other organizations that may be useful to you at some point, identify them.

The third path is *Management Style*. Determine the best leadership style needed to reach your goal. Do you need to be autocratic? Sometimes it works, sometimes people need to be led to where they need to be. But then you need to know when to let go and let them do what they have to do. Do you need to be democratic? Sometimes you have a group of know-it-alls, credentialed people at the table, and so you need to think about your approach. It is not good being autocratic with people who see themselves as bringing something to the table.

The fourth path is *Develop Your Strong Suit*. Determine the management/leadership competencies, and develop or recruit those important individuals to assist in reaching your goal. If you assess that on your boards you need a legal person or a certified public accountant to help you understand the management of the books and the management of your agency, do that. Identify those people. Do not get your sister because she knows you so well, or your cousin because she used to work for senator so-and-so. Get people who have something to bring to the table and can help you in your goals.

The fifth path is *Individual Interests and Goals*. Ascertain the interests, values, and goals of each individual member of the organization. I have worked with some organizations and they have had problems with their staff, and it is because some of the staff is just there.

One executive director of an organization told me that she had groomed this woman employee and put up with this woman's nonsense, her late coming to work, and so forth. This woman was supposed to have a driver's license in her employment, but did not have one when she got the job. However, because she was good at certain tasks, they kept her. They continually asked her to get the driver's license, and she said, "Oh I will. I have to do this. My baby's sick. My this, my that." They kept after her and after her. Then finally the executive director said, "If you do not have your driver's license within thirty days, we'll have to let you go." That was the force and motivator to get her moving; she did get the driver's license. She came in and told the executive director, "I have my driver's license." Then two days later she told the executive director that she was leaving for another job.

As managers, you have to hire the right people for the right job, and you need to have procedures in place and stick to them. Having established procedures is only fair for everyone, and you have got to stick to them or you will have turnover of staff. Staff members are not necessarily in the organization for the same reasons you are. You should have some understanding of what they have bought into when they came into your organization.

The sixth path to strategic management is *Personal and Professional Growth*. Plan for development. Plan for your own development, for personal and professional growth, and then you benefit your organization and yourself.

Coming to conferences like the WANGO Annual Conference is wonderful, because you can go back renewed, and you can go back helping your organization to develop. What you have experienced is real, so be critical of it, listen to it. I listened to some discussions at the annual conference, and I heard too much of some NGOs wanting to get involved in the Iraqi crisis in a political way that is not true to their mission. I do not think that is a good thing for NGOs to do at this point. There are other things that they can do in terms of the crisis that would still be true to their mission. So we have got to be very careful of what we apply, be critical of what we hear, and understand whether it applies to us or not.

Know Your Community

The nature of non-governmental organizations today requires a great deal of attention to external forces. Learning about the community your organization serves within the context of the world in which we live is essential to effective management and delivery of service.

A lot of people do not know their community. I have been working with some of the largest nonprofits in the greater northern

New Jersey area and some of the faith-based organizations of the largest churches in Newark. Some of them do not know, for example, that City National Bank has a housing program that can teach people how to maintain and care for homes and help them get mortgages. They do not know that the Urban League has a computer training program that is free in their communities, and that they can direct their clients there if their organization does not have its own computer-training program—a service their organization can take credit for, in that they are providing assistance to their clients.

You need to know what is going on in your community. What is going on at city hall that would affect you? What is going on at the town seats of government, and in the county seats of government, and then the state and federal seats of government? Find out who are your representatives, your ambassadors, your congresspersons—find out who they are, and let them know you. Know your community.

Do a data-gathering checklist. The next big key to knowing something is knowing where to find it. Where do you find certain things? Reading about a community is a good thing to do, but often the information is old and out of date by the time it reaches your desk. The only way to be sure of knowing what is happening now, this very day, is to gather the information yourself. In the United States each city has a master plan, a city plan. It is good to look at it before you embark on some project for which you cannot get support.

I had a client in the city of East Orange who wanted to develop a senior citizen assisted-living home. We went to the city planning office and obtained the comprehensive city plan, and what we observed was that the lowest priority of the city of East Orange was a senior citizen assisted-living residence. In their view, they had enough of them and did not plan to accommodate another. This does not mean that you abandon the plan, since you can find another city that will accommodate what you want to do. But you have got to know your community and gather your data.

In doing this you might ask, "How can I uncover resources that I do not know about?" How can the information I gather best support my organization and maximize my ability to achieve the organization's goals?" In order to determine the strengths, weaknesses, opportunities, and threats inherit in your organization's community, the following entities are recommended as resources:

- *The Client or Stakeholder Community.* By this, I mean anyone in the community who stands to benefit from what you do. Who stands to benefit? The business community may benefit. If I am doing job training, for example, then I am preparing people to go in and be hired. Perhaps the educational community, the government community, the church community, people who are purchasers, or women's groups will benefit from what you do. List all who stand to benefit from what you do.
- *The Organizations within the Community.*
- *Same-Purpose Organizations.* Know who are the same-purposed organizations in your community, so you are not competing. Get to know them, get to talk to them, collaborate with them. There are many times that you might collaborate on an issue that comes out of the political arena that is going to affect both of you, or many of same types of organizations are in your community. When I was executive director of Jobs for Youth, I knew all the youth function organizations in the city of New York. We met frequently, and when the issue came down from Washington that the federal government was eliminating summer jobs, we mobilized quickly and began to turn that around, because we knew the devastating effect it would have on the city. This could happen because we had been meeting prior to this event and we knew each other. Know who your like organizations are and approach them, so that they will understand that there is no competition here, that you are all in the same boat and can work together on issues of mutual concern.
- *Government Institutions.* It is important to know your government institutions—local, county, state, and federal. For example, if you are involved in housing, you have to know who approves permits and zoning, and so forth. Meet these officials and shake their hands and say who you are. You are important, and they need to know who you are and what you are doing, and how you are serving the community.

- *The Media.* Know the media. Get to know the editorial board of your local paper. Look on the editorial page and see who they are, and call and get an appointment. They will then tell you to whom on that editorial board you should send your stories, and address your stories to that individual. If you send your stories to Joe Jones and Joe Jones does sports, it is going to be tossed. Or if you send it to the person who does the woman's column and it is about an issue of machinery that is needed by farmers, it is not going to get published just because you are friendly with the woman who does the woman's column.

  Find out when is the best time and manner to send information. Ask, "How do you like information to be sent to you? E-mail? Do you want me to phone you? Do you want me to e-mail you with a follow-up phone call? Do you want me to send it as a hard copy in the mail? How is it best for me to reach you with my message?"

  It is also important to remember that news is time sensitive. Never give a reporter in the United States a news story at four o'clock because the paper is going to press and it is too late. The media person will discover you are not savvy when you do things like that. Find out from your contact what is the critical time to send news releases to the paper. Get those news releases in so they know what you are doing at all times and make friends with the media.

- *The Political Climate.* It is important to know the political climate. zcertain projects that you get involved with might be controversial. You may think you are doing a good thing, but if it is too politically controversial, then you can hold back and examine it carefully, and not impulsively advance something that may not be good for your organization.

- *The Economic Climate.* Know the economic climate. Know what you can ask for, what you cannot ask for, and what you can expect. In the United States at the present time, people are quite concerned with the stock market, and where their pension funds are going, and the shrinking of their savings and retirement benefits. They are concerned about their companies going out of business because some executive is pocketing the money, and now it is being found out. These are all factors to consider. Know the economic climate.

- *The Social Climate*. Know the social climate. Know how people feel. I happened to sit at a table at a conference and I realized that I was in George W. Bush country. I realized that this was not the place to air my views about certain things because I did not want to offend these people, they had the right to their viewpoints, and I had invited myself there. So you have to understand the social climate, and be careful and cautious.

The Organization's Action Plan

Laurence Peter said, "If you don't know where you're going, you will probably end up somewhere else."

An organization's action plan is just what it says. You need to have one. Strategic goal-setting and action planning is a process that can be broken down into fairly simple steps. There is nothing magical or complex about "how to do it." The following seven steps can serve as a guide:

1. Assess the organizational and management reality to get an accurate picture of the internal strengths of the environment.
2. Determine what needs to be done and what the organization can realistically do about it.
3. Decide what to do by using criteria that will facilitate decision-making.
4. Determine what the management team needs to learn or develop in order to implement the decision.
5. Establish an action plan, which outlines each step, an activity that will produce the results desired. Determine the people who need to be involved, the resources that are required, and the time they will need. For each action plan, have an optional plan.
6. Test the plans against reality. Make adjustments as necessary.
7. Supplement your plan, focusing on "first things first" and "one at a time." Never lose sight of why you are doing something.

How to Develop a Planning Chart

By now the organization has been assessed along with the community, the environment, and management. Meaningful goals should now be set and a determination of the competencies needed to achieve them. Now is the time to set down what actually needs to be done and who is going to do it. On the planning chart you will want to do the following:

1. List all of the steps you will have to take to reach your goal.
2. Examine each step and state what specific activities need to occur to accomplish it.
3. Look at the activities. Who, besides yourself, needs to be involved in each activity?
4. How, specifically, do you plan to involve these people?
5. What kind of support or resources will they—or you—need to accomplish the activities?
6. When, realistically, do you see the completion of each activity? Be sure to allow plenty of time—if anything, overestimate.
7. Having examined each activity, go back and project completion dates for each of the steps. Again, it is best to overestimate.
8. Once the chart is completed, spend some time looking it over and ask the following questions:
    - Does it look realistic?
    - Do the activities really lead to the accomplishment of each step?
    - Will the steps achieve the goal?
    - Do the steps provide benchmarks for adjustments?
    - Have we budgeted enough resources?
    - Is there sufficient delegation of responsibility to everyone involved?
    - Does each person have the resources needed to complete each task?

It is important to see things on paper, written down, so you can correct them and go back to them. These points above will tell you what the planning chart should provide when you do it correctly.

Reality Testing

Between the plan and the accomplishment lies reality. Once you have completed the planning chart, there has to be some reality testing. We have the plan. It is all laid out: date, place, who is going to do it, the outcomes, and so forth. What are the chances that the plan can actually be carried out?

The following questions should be asked to help you examine your goal and action plan against the face of reality.

- Where will the organization be with regard to its goal six months from now?
- Where will the organization be with regards to its goal six weeks from now?
- Where will management be with regard to its goal next week?
- Review the activities the staff performs during the course of a normal week. How will this be changed to accommodate the activities outline in the activity plan?
- If members of your staff are involved in the activities listed in the plan, do they have the experience, abilities, and motivation to carry them out? If not, what can be done to help them?
- Review the personal life goals of each staff member. How compatible is each individual's personal goal to the chosen goal of the organization? What needs to be done to make them more complementary?

Do a little reality testing and ask yourself some of these questions about your organization and write your answers down. Then you can see what you can change or eliminate. Based on these questions, you will know whether you are ready or not to do what you have set out to do.

Action Plan Chart

Julian Huxley stated, "It is because of the devotion or sacrifice of individuals that causes become of value."

You should prepare an action planning chart that lists the steps to be taken, and for each of these steps, the activities to be undertaken, who is involved in the activities, how they are involved, what support/ resources are needed, when the activity will be completed, and when the step will be completed. This makes you think things through and see it on a design and a graph. Producing such a chart provides an opportunity for the goals to be restated in final form and for the action plan steps to be summarized. This will present a graphic picture of what needs to be accomplished and how it will be done.

To complete the chart, you begin by stating the goal at the top. Then fill in each step for the action plan, including dates when each action plan step will be accomplished. Under "resources," write in whatever resources you have available to carry out the plan. These include people, organizations, financial means, personal competencies, and current information.

You can do a Plan A and a Plan B, and complete the chart. If you do not want to do a Plan B, you just do Plan A.

When the chart is complete, it should be placed in a prominent place for everyone to see. It represents what everyone has pledged to achieve. Keeping sight of the goals makes the work more meaningful.

However, do not think of this as the only and final goal. Life is going to be full of struggles and achievements.

Networking

31

KAREN M. WOODS

Networking is basically about relationships. None of us really live in this world alone, and God in his wisdom did not give any of us all that we need. Scriptures of various faiths are very clear about the fact that we are intended for a relationship with our Creator, and we are intended for a relationship with one another. What that seems to mean is, if I do not have what I need, I have got to find someone who does. Thus, networking is developing the relationships you need to get done what you believe you have been called to do.

There are several areas to consider: What do you need to have in place before you start; what attitude should you have—are you ready to network; what tools will you need to network effectively; and how to handle general problems that arise and those specific to the developing world.

Although my experience has been in the United States, I have tried to see the challenges that exist in the Third World particularly, and try and focus on some general concepts that can be useful, or concepts that can be modified to fit contexts other than in the United States.

Vision and Your Mission Statement

Whatever program you have, or whatever movement that you joined, or whatever NGO you felt motivated to begin, or whatever desire you had to work with other people and contribute your skills to that organization and its mission—whatever the reason—it all began with a vision. Vision could be described as something that wakes you up at night and will not let you go back to sleep, when your mind races and you end up getting up and working. A vision is something that motivates you; it drives you. In your mind you have a picture of how things can work, though you may not be sure how you are going to put it together or how it will

---

Karen M. Woods is executive director for The Empowerment Network (TEN).

work, but you just know that it can. That is your vision.

Envisioning what you want to do is your macrosolution. This is the big picture. But how you break that picture down into digestible, workable pieces is your mission statement. A mission statement is simply a concise statement of a task, and a purpose for the organization that is going to accomplish that task.

From the standpoint of beginning an NGO, you need a mission statement that is clear and that everyone can understand. If you already are part of an existing NGO and you already have a mission statement, ask yourself "How good is it?" Perhaps you should rethink your mission statement. An excellent little paperback book, *The Path,* says that your mission statement should be one sentence long, one that anyone can understand and one that you could recite when someone is holding a gun to your head.

Organizational Infrastructure

The first decision regarding your organizational infrastructure is naming an executive director, or chief operating officer, or whatever title is culturally appropriate in your situation. It is the person responsible for moving the organization forward, the one who gets things done.

The next requisite is your board of directors, preferably a working board. If, for example, your organization plans to host a banquet fundraiser once a year, it helps to have a caterer on your board or someone with restaurant management experience. The point of having a caterer in that case is to have an insider who is knowledgeable of what facilities are available for an anticipated five hundred guests, for instance. They will know what kind of meal is appropriate and the way it should be set up. It is an efficient way to go about what you do so that you have quality input for your organization based on who your board members are.

It is great to have people who are passionate about what you do, but you need to be very critical about what that person has to offer in addition to their passion. It may be writing skills, it may be political connections, it may be a close relationship to already established people whom you want to serve, such as a pastor, or an organization that already has a relationship in the community. Choose a board that can help you get where you need to go.

Accountability

In terms of fiscal management, you need to have a system. Though financial practices may vary from country to country, you need to know what they are. The advantage to the Internal Revenue Service (IRS) in the United States is that the information is online. You know what they expect of you and who to call. That may not be true in developing countries, especially in areas where you have to be very mindful of political people raiding what you have.

Look at what the rules are, look at the fiscal reality of your circumstances, and then have a system. What you are looking for is accountability. Now, accountability is not only from the standpoint of your credibility, but also when you are raising resources for your work. These resources can be in-kind services, access to other things that exist in your country; or especially financial support from organizations, corporations, and foundations in the United States. Whichever kind of support you are seeking, you have to be accountable.

In-kind donations include things like food, clothing, vehicles, or other tangible goods. For example, one program in Africa gives computer training to young people, since farming and agriculture is very limited, and training young people in these agricultural skills and careers is kind of a dead end for many of them. But if there is not money to buy the computers, they might find a corporation or a connection in the United States that would give them the computers.

In-kind donations can also include services. That means you do not have to learn how to do strategic planning since there are a lot of business types—no matter what country you are in—who know how to do that. They would not have a successful business if they had not done some very specific and targeted strategic planning. That corporation can be approached and asked if it will give you a couple of hours of that planner's time for three months, to come and work with you and your board to outline your strategic plan. There is an advantage when you ask someone from outside the organization to come in and help you, because that person can ask difficult questions that you need to be able to answer. This provides an opportunity to explain your work to someone who is hearing it for the first time. Having a system in place that fits reality and knowing the rules, is fiscal management. Maybe in some ways you have to work around those rules, but find someone who knows how to do that and can help you do it, and then have a system of accountability.

Your Strategic Plan

The next foundational step is creating a *strategic* plan. Your strategic plan is going to include your major goals. You have to have a plan, e.g., What to do first, what to do next, what do I do third, and how all these things relate. You need to understand your major goals, and for each goal you must have an objective. What is it that I want to accomplish? The strategies and tactics you use are simply ways to do that.

For example, there is a serious problem with cholera and also a serious problem of children not being vaccinated. There is also a serious health problem of women not receiving prenatal care. One must then ask whether those are interrelated. What are we going to do? Are we going to start with the vaccinations? How do we do that? Are we going to partner since we do not have the resources in our country? What other countries might be able to help us? All of those things have to do with the question, "How am I going to do what I need to do?"

Objectives, strategies, and tactics are ways to accomplish your goals, or get where you want to be. Sometimes the reality is that some of those strategies may include politics when it involves policy matters. For some people in the world this is a dangerous reality, and so you have to be very aware of what strategies and tactics it will take to get your job done.

An example of a major goal would be to improve the health of mothers and children in the Comoros Islands. An objective could be prenatal care, elimination of cholera, and giving vaccinations. Your strategies and tactics would be how you accomplish that, such as using preschools to connect with vaccinations.

Set a Target

How do you know that you are getting to where you are supposed to go? In the United States we do research, and some corporations do nothing except evaluation. But if you have an NGO that is just getting started, and what you are going to do is at a very elementary level, at least have in the back of your mind the question of, "How do I know that I'm getting where I need to go?" Moving toward a goal is like having a target. If you do not set a target, you will never know whether you have hit it or not. Even if you miss it, then you can back off and say, "Well, is this even the right target?" Another analogy is that it is like climbing a ladder, and then learning that it is propped up on the wrong wall. Therefore, always have an evaluation, one that is culturally sensitive and appropriate to your programming. Otherwise, how will you know that the organization is getting where you think it needs to go?

In terms of your resource evaluation, you first have to decide what you have and what you need in relation to what you want to do. Then consider how to close the circle on those two things. Money is only one resource available to organizations. A lot of other resources are available, and sometimes they are far more valuable than money. However, you cannot run programs with no money at all. You are going to need resources for your programming and will have to consider budgets, expenses, income, and sustainability. In the United States, many foundations and corporations will give you start-up money, but from the very beginning you have to explain to them how you are going to sustain your operation, because they do not intend to keep doing that. Very few corporations and foundations will continue to give you funding year after year.

A Teachable Attitude

In networking, one should be discerning. It is important to talk to people, have eye contact, and listen carefully. Try and discern what relationships you are building, but continue to always consider yourself a resource. What you will find is that you are a tremendous resource.

It is important to have the right attitude in order to network. Ask yourself, "Do I have a teachable attitude?" Do I have this hungry willingness to learn from others, from other cultures, from other events? If I run across a piece of research that seems to negate what I think is true, am I willing at least to look at it? Are you open-minded enough to step back and consider an idea even though you may realize that you may reject it? Are you intellectually curious? Are you always looking for new ways, new ideas, new approaches?

Stephen Covey is a hugely successful consultant to businesses in the United States. He wrote the book called *Seven Habits of Highly Effective People.* He and the family division of the Covey organization have also written a book called *Seven Habits of Highly Effective Families.* One thing that Stephen writes about is looking at the world as a paradigm, and that sometimes we need to do paradigm shifts. We need to understand that some of our preconceived ideas are not accurate and need to be reevaluated.

Finally, do I have an internal perspective? Do we really believe that not only what we do counts in this world, but counts for the next? It is important for us to understand that we are connected to one another, and that we are connected to an eternal perspective that values humans and values our interaction with one another in a great way.

Networking Tools

Business cards are a really important tool, particularly now with e-mail. It makes life easier to always have business cards with you. People will cross your path, and if you are prepared with business cards, it is easier to make connections with them. It does not mean you cannot find their names on the internet or by looking them up, but it saves a lot of time. For conferences, business cards are extremely helpful, if not essential.

If you find you are wearing a couple of hats, you can put both of those on the card, so that the same card can be used for two different contexts. They can be designed so that there is a line separating the organization information either vertically or horizontally. Use your card as a key networking tool.

The internet is another invaluable resource. Some list-serves are free and others charge a fee. A large number of organizations focus on particular topics and put out weekly, even daily, information about legislation, funding, and other relevant subjects. At times subscribers to list-serves can exchange information within certain parameters.

There is a list-serve in the United States called charitychannel.org, which is analogous to an octopus because even though Charity Channel is the main part, or the head of the organization, there are legs to it. For example, you can choose which "legs" to sign up for, like grant writing, or resource raising, and so the discussions and the material that you receive will relate only to that particular subject.

There is another free list-serve in the US called jointogether.org that is primarily targeted toward trying to reduce substance abuse and gun violence in schools. However, that list-serve, just by the nature of the way it is developed, is very big. Many times you'll see mention of topics indirectly related, such as after-school programs and funding resources available for children's programs. Their thinking is that if kids are in after-school programs, they are not at home alone doing drugs. Therefore, list-serves can be very broad, or they can be very targeted.

Educational institutions sometimes have wonderful resources. In Michigan there is a professional organization of accountants that, as part of their service outreach, provides seminars on grant-writing and on evaluation. The United Way in the United States uses an evaluation model called the "logic model." It teaches people how to prepare an evaluation using this model, which some grantors like because it is easy to understand and makes it easy to see what you want to do and how you are going to do it.

Institutions of higher learning sometimes have classes or scholarship programs that you can consider in terms of doing necessary research for projects. For example, Calvin College in Grand Rapids, Michigan, and many other colleges all over the country, have a research design class. These are undergraduate students who generally intend to do graduate work and need to practically understand how to do research design. Part of the practicum for these students is that they have to go out and put their designs to work. Therefore, if you can partner with one of those classes, with a professor that sees the opportunity for his students to meet their goals of completing part of their academic assignment and at the same time do a service for you, it is a win-win situation. The students get their work done and you get some research done, which helps you evaluate where your program should to go, or whether there is sufficient interest.

If you can find a graduate student in an institution that has a graduate program related to what you do, see if maybe you can work out another win-win situation with them. They get their research done on something of importance, which gives them a greater chance that they will get published in some journal. That is good for their career, but at the same time gives you a credible source and some good information helpful to your work.

Civil society partnerships may not exist in every country. In the United States there are volunteer organizations such as the Points of Light Foundation, or faith-based organizations such as the Christian Medical and Dental Society, which have programs that provide education in return for students using their learned skills in humanitarian service programs. In the last several years the Christian Medical and Dental Society has had a program where they help American students in need of financial assistance attend medical school or dental school in return for their agreeing to go to the mission field for a period of two to three years. Similar programs in the United States send doctors, nurses, and nurse practitioners out to rural areas or to areas that are grossly underserved. It may be worthwhile to look at volunteer organizations and see if they are an answer for you.

Follow up right away, or within a few days after a conference, since immediacy is really important in networking. E-mail those people with whom you want to network. If you can do some work on the airplane going home from a conference, that is always helpful, whether it is organizing cards, recording impressions, or whatever. Remember, the purpose of information is that it is going to help you either develop a relationship with a person, to find out more about what they do, or get a specific piece of information from them.

Storing Information

I meet a lot of people at conferences. To help remember them, I will jot something on the back of the business card to remind me of what our conversation was about or something they said that will jog my memory later on. Then I file that away in my palm [handheld computer] or Rolodex under a topic, because as my files grow I will not necessarily remember the person's name unless I have had a reason to continue the relationship with them. I usually do the card work on the airplane going home while the meeting is fresh in my mind and I know with whom I'm going to network.

Sometimes you can find a volunteer—someone in your organization or who is associated and passionate about what you do, but who really is not an appropriate board member—who is flexible about time and has a computer. Think about the resources that you have and the people who might be able to help you, someone who could glean through and file those cards.

Instead of throwing out cards that initially I think I will not need, I will take them and put them in an envelope and mark them. In four months, five months, six months—when something triggers a need to find that information—I will pull those out again because things can change in six months. Sometimes things you did not think you needed at one time change, because circumstances change, and now that person that you did not think you would have anything to do with is maybe the one who could help you. But be discerning about what you want to do, and be on target.

Many times people bring papers to conferences. They may be very interesting but not be relevant to you. Do not clog up your briefcase with this material, or your file cabinet at home or whatever system you use. Work intentionally. Papers are great, but in terms of networking, the paper is only as good as the information that is on the paper that helps you get to the university—or get to the person—or get to the research institute that sponsored it.

Save conference information. It is a good reference source that has all the participants' names, the books they have written, the universities with which they are associated, or the programs that they run and the boards of which they are members.

I file conference information in folders so that if I am working on a project and need specific information from a conference, I can pull out a paper and find the contact person. For business cards I use a palm, which has been absolutely invaluable. When my networking contacts need information I can literally beam that information to them.

I am a file folder person. I file hard copies in folders. I also make files on my computer. For example, I will take my e-mails of listserves and file them under topics. I use Outlook Express, but whatever e-mail program you use should allow you to file and organize those pieces of information you get, such as from Charity Channel. Again, be very discerning. If you get a long piece of information and you only want part of it, do "cut and paste." Cut what you want, send yourself an e-mail, and then file it. I try to do that as I go through e-mail.

Networking in Developing Countries

Generally, developing nations do not have the same structures or channels to work through that exist in more developed parts of the world. NGOs that are well-established and are either connected to people in the political environment or to donors will network together. They all know one another. However, NGOs that are new do not have established relationships with donors and get squeezed out, ignored by the established NGOs because they are seen as competition for their funding or for political favor.

NGO leaders from Africa report that networking is very difficult there. For NGOs without these connections or resources, it is an unfriendly and sometimes hostile environment in which to build relationships. Those who have worked in developing countries acknowledge this lack of cooperation and collaboration, mainly caused by jealousy and competition for resources. There is a need for organizations like WANGO to intercede and help build models of cooperation among the various NGOs in these countries.

A possible source of funding to look at in developing nations is corporations and foundations that have investments—corporate or charitable—in these nations. Through the internet you can research corporation financial reports, grant guidelines, and information. Begin networking and building relationships with these people, since they are dependent on information about the country you are working in. You can be an information resource for them.

Part VIII
Excellence in the NGO Community

Award presenters and recipients (left to right):
Mr. Tajeldin Hamad, Dr. Noel Brown, Dr. Frederico Mayor Zaragoza, Dr. Chung Hwan Kwak, Rev. Sanford Garner, Mrs. Sheila Watt-Cloutier, Mrs. Wajeeha Al-Baharna, Shaykh Hassan Ali Cisse, Dr. Oscar Arias Sanchez, and Mrs. & Mr. Charles A. Ballard

Seven awards with hands holding a globe given to outstanding NGOs and individuals for service to humanity. Each award is engraved with a symbol representing the purpose for which the award is given.

Introduction

This section is devoted to recognizing certain outstanding NGOs and individuals who have demonstrated extraordinary effort, innovation, leadership, and excellence in providing service to humanity. These were all recipients of the 2002 WANGO awards, presented at an awards banquet in Washington, DC at the time of the WANGO annual conference. Some are internationally known organizations and figures. However, WANGO not only recognizes prominent NGOs but also the smaller, lesser-known NGOs in the least-developed countries, whose exemplary service and success may have gone unnoticed and under-appreciated on the international stage.

This section consists of an introduction by the chairman of the Awards Nominating Committee and presentations by those honored who represent diverse fields of activity and come from different regions of the world.

2002 WANGO AWARDS

Arias Foundation for Peace and Human Progress

African American Islamic Institute (AAII)

Inuit Circumpolar Conference (Canada)

Bahrain Women's Society

Institute for Responsible Fatherhood and Family Revitalization

Bishop William E. Swing and the United Religions Initiative

Dr. Federico Mayor Zaragoza

Presentation of the 2002 WANGO Awards

32

Human and Proud of It

NOEL BROWN

It is a privilege to be acquainted with a large number of individuals and organizations whose dedication and passion for human betterment, peace, and solidarity provide us with a new sense of hope. The threat of war hangs in the air and terrorism stalks the land, fostering in many people a new sense of fear and foreboding. Planetary degradation continues, and the abject poverty of millions in an age of abundance remains a permanent blot on our common humanity and sense of decency. But despite these somber headlines, there remain a few flickers of light on the horizon, which registers the fact that there are still those who are not content merely to lament the human condition and its predicaments, wringing their hands in a kind of callous resignation that there is nothing that can be done. This is not the WANGO spirit.

The people here are courageous enough to dare, to dare to make a difference, a reminder that in essence we are a problem-solving species. When we put our minds to it, we are capable of the most extraordinary achievements, which has led poets to describe us—as only poets can—in the words of Shakespeare: "What a wonderful piece of work is man."

Despite the bleakness of our times, the human species is not destined to self-destruct; nor is this present generation likely to be the terminal generation. History suggests that human beings are maybe nature's most efficient terminators of species, but this generation does not seem to be the terminal generation—far from it. Certainly, if space exploration is any guide, we are gearing up for the long cosmic journey among the stars. This is not the generation of the long good-bye, standing in the doorway. And our space station equipped for human

---

Dr. Noel Brown is president of Friends of the United Nations and former regional director for the United Nations Environment Program, North American Region. He also served as chair of the nominating committee for the WANGO Awards 2002.

habitation suggests that we are fast becoming an extraterrestrial species, another human marvel.

We celebrate those who feed us with a sense of wonder. We celebrate the fact that individuals can and do make a difference, and that excellence is both an ennobling and an empowering experience.

Therefore it is our hope that the honors bestowed upon the 2002 WANGO Award recipients will be a source of inspiration to all people to elevate their sights, redouble their efforts, and engage in those causes that make everyone proud to be human. A thought that could very well become a slogan of WANGO, "Human and proud of it."

WANGO has elected to recognize seven areas of human endeavor: peace and human progress, the human environment, education, human rights, family values, interreligious cooperation, and universal peace and security. One aspect that I think is very exciting about this enterprise is that a lot of people do not do these things because they are going to be recognized. They do them because of their inherent values and out of a desire to work for human betterment. Certainly the greatest award for a job well-done is having done it!

The Award Symbols

The WANGO Award is a crystal globe being held in the palm of a crystal hand. The seven award categories are represented each by an appropriate symbol—such as a dove with an olive branch for the Peace and Security Award—etched into the surface of the globe.

Crystal conveys a feeling of purity and endurance, and its transparency suggests that there is nothing hidden. This is characteristic of the WANGO spirit: openness, inclusiveness, and transparency.

The human hand holding the planet earth symbolizes our responsibility. Notably, the hand is not a grasping hand—but open and generous—caressing the globe in a sense of caring and affection. The earth is also precariously balanced, symbolizing our relationship with the natural world and our need for this balance to be maintained. This is one ball we cannot afford to drop!

Finally and above all, our symbol is a magnificent work of art. As Shakespeare once said, "A thing of beauty is a joy forever." In summary, this beautiful crystal creation reflects WANGO's desire to recognize and reward leadership and excellence.

WANGO Peace and Security Award 2002
Arias Foundation for Peace and Human Progress

A man whose reputation extends worldwide and who is an active part of our global vocabulary for peace and human progress is Dr. Oscar Arias Sanchez. Dr. Arias served as president of Costa Rica from 1986 to 1990, assuming office at a time of great regional discord. His vision of a Central America free from war, strife, and repression, widely known as the Arias Peace Plan, culminated in the Esquipulas II Accords.

On August 7, 1987, all of the Central American presidents met in Guatemala to sign these accords. For his efforts, Dr. Arias was awarded the 1987 Nobel Peace Prize.

In 1988, Dr. Arias furthered his vision of democracy and nonviolence by founding the Arias Foundation for Peace and Human Progress, with a mission of promoting just and peaceful societies in Central America and other regions.

The Arias Foundation has conducted innumerable programs, research projects, and educational initiatives devoted to such areas as: conflict prevention, demilitarization and permanent security, democratic governance and development, gender and human rights, law and civil society, and NGOs as advocates for social change. The foundation's continuing work is divided among three active and expanding programs: the Center for Human Progress, the Center for Peace and Reconciliation, and the Center for Organized Participation.

The foundation promotes pluralistic participation in the search for and consolidation of strategies to achieve lasting peace and security; and works to educate the public about women's rights—and toward the creation of a culture that respects these rights. The organization has conducted extensive studies in many topics of vital importance for peace, including civil-military relations in small democracies throughout the world, the challenges of demilitarization for leadership in Africa, the causes of conflict in Central America, the involvement of Central American militaries in business activities, and the construction of gender identity in Central American security forces.

In taking the decision to present the Arias Foundation for Peace and Human Progress with the WANGO Peace and Security Award 2002, the WANGO International Council recognized the many remarkable achievements and the continuing outstanding and sacrificial service of the Arias Foundation toward bringing about a world of peace and security for all.

WANGO Education Award 2002

African American Islamic Institute (AAII)

The African American Islamic Institute (AAII) was founded as a non-governmental organization in Senegal, West Africa, in 1988 by Shaykh Hassan Ali Cisse, chief imam of the Grand Mosque in Medina Kaolack, Senegal, and a respected Islamic scholar and leader. AAII has grown to be an international NGO headquartered in Senegal with affiliates throughout Africa—mainly in the sub-Saharan region, Europe, and North America. AAII's mission is to develop a capability for sustainable human and natural resource development that focuses on education as well as human rights, health care, peace studies, food and water availability, and alleviation of poverty.

As an institute of *Nasrul Ilm*, which means "Helping Knowledge," the teachings of Islam provide the foundation of AAII's educational and humanitarian activities. By generating greater understanding of Islam, the institute strives to inspire humanity to fulfill its purpose on earth, and to build bridges of understanding, compassion, and respect among nations and tribes. One of AAII's most significant functions is interpreting the goals of the international conferences of the United Nations within an Islamic context and disseminating vital information reflecting that perspective.

AAII's educational initiatives are extensive and diverse. It is particularly dedicated to universal education, with special commitment to the education of women and girls. The institute established the AAII Qur'anic School and the AAII American School, which provide religious and secular education to thousands of students. In cooperation with the Senegalese government, AAII established 17 classes for over 1,000 students—most of whom are adult women—to teach reading and writing in their local dialects. In addition to educational programs, AAII builds and operates schools and clinics for the provision of medical care. The institute also works for the alleviation of poverty through skill training.

Furthermore, AAII established the AAII Female Genital Mutilation Prevention Initiative to educate communities about the health and human rights issues surrounding this controversial practice. AAII, which holds General Consultative Status with ECOSOC, has assumed a leadership role in bringing smaller Senegalese NGOs together for the purpose of reflecting on annual DPI/NGO conference themes and providing a vehicle for their voices to be heard. AAII also organizes and convenes international Islamic conferences in Africa to address contemporary issues.

The African American Islamic Institute's commitment to education and its cooperation with numerous other programs in health care, human rights, peace building, and poverty alleviation serves as the basis for the awarding of the WANGO Education Award 2002.

WANGO Environment Award 2002

Inuit Circumpolar Conference (Canada)

The Inuit Circumpolar Conference (ICC) was founded in 1977 and has grown into a major international non-governmental organization representing approximately 150,000 Inuit of Canada, Alaska, Greenland, and Chukotka (Russia). To thrive in their circumpolar homeland, the Inuit realized they must speak with a united voice on issues of common concern and combine their energies and talents toward protecting and promoting their way of life. The principal goals of the ICC are to develop and encourage long-term policies that safeguard the Arctic environment; to strengthen unity among Inuit of the circumpolar region; to promote Inuit rights and interests on the international level; and to seek full and active partnership in the political, economic, and social development of circumpolar regions.

Under the guidance of its president, Ms. Sheila Watt-Cloutier, the ICC (Canada) has been in the vanguard of international efforts to negotiate and conclude a global agreement to address persistent organic pollutants (POPs), which end up and accumulate in the Arctic, contaminating traditional native food sources. Arriving from such regions as southern and eastern Asia, Latin America, and Africa, many POPs, such as dieldrin, DDT, and chlordane, arrive in the Arctic "sink" via air and water currents. These contaminates bio-accumulate and bio-magnify in the food chain and are ingested when Inuit and other indigenous peoples consume their traditional foods. This is not an abstract formula for the Arctic peoples. Women in the arctic have ten times as much PCBs in their breast milk as any other women in the world; and so the next generation, almost at birth, is impaired.

The global convention on POPs, finalized in South Africa in December 2000 and signed in Sweden in May 2001, singles out indigenous people and the Arctic as a fragile and vulnerable region—the first global convention to do so. ICC (Canada) is currently working to promote early ratification of the convention. WANGO considers the ICC (Canada)'s participation in the negotiation on persistent organic pollutants to be of historic significance, which may yet set a precedent for other indigenous peoples to be engaged in global discussions that affect their lives and livelihood. ICC participation signals a new kind of "indigenous statesmanship." Likewise, the Northern Contaminants Program, of which the ICC (Canada) is a key player, is a rarely heralded success story that deserves special recognition.

The Inuit provide a dramatic demonstration of life in harmony with nature and the ability to ensure that development activities do not undermine the environment. The Inuit have lived in the Arctic for forty thousand years and have never eliminated a single species because they live in harmony with nature. And perhaps the most telling example of this is the fact that in their language there is no word for war. They live at peace with themselves, and in peace and harmony with nature.

In taking the decision to present the Inuit Circumpolar Conference (Canada) with the WANGO Environment Award for 2002, the WANGO International Council was most impressed with the consistent commitment of the ICC (Canada) to the values of sustainability and the protection of the natural environment on which the lives and livelihoods of the Arctic peoples depend. WANGO recognizes the determination exhibited by the ICC (Canada) to protect the Arctic resource system from the many environmental assaults to this region, and applauds the ICC (Canada)'s efforts to focus global attention on the risk faced by the Arctic people from toxic chemicals, heavy metals, and other environmental hazards.

WANGO Human Rights Award 2002
Bahrain Women's Society

The Bahrain Women's Society (BWS) is a rare entity—one of the few women's organizations in this small Middle Eastern country and one that is pioneering the rights of women and children. Young, dynamic, and effective, it is one of most active social conscience organizations in the country, with five ongoing projects and two national campaigns.

Established in 2001 by influential and prominent women in Bahraini society, the BWS's goal is to integrate Bahraini women in particular and Bahraini society in general with desired contemporary, social, legal, cultural, and environmental norms. In this way Bahrain can share a greater role in global responsibilities and directions alongside leading nations.

BWS works to bring about the realization of the full value and significance of the Bahraini woman, to assist her in recognizing and practicing her civilian and social rights, and to help her to better utilize the opportunities present in a global era. BWS helps empower Bahraini women to share their views, extend their vision, and shift their intellectual paradigm beyond personal affairs toward global, societal, and environmental concerns.

The BWS assists Bahraini women who want to take advantage of a broader selection of modern and effective ways of raising children as well as enrich and update their child protection awareness. Their "Be-Free" project addresses the issue of child rights and is the first of its kind in the Middle East to deal with the issue of child abuse. The organization conducts a survey to assess the extent of the child abuse problem in Bahrain, and provides extensive mass media education and awareness programs targeting care providers, parents, officials, and children. The society is working to erect a specialized clinic to both physically and psychologically treat victimized children and the affected parents.

"Empowering a Village" is another ongoing program to educate village women with respect to their role socially, environmentally, and legally. And the "Gender Mainstreaming Project" works to enhance Bahraini women's participation in economic development and national growth.

Because of BWS's pioneering efforts for the rights of women

and children in Bahrain amidst difficult obstacles, and as part of a mission that also includes environmental citizenship, health, community service, and cultural affairs, the WANGO International Council recognized the society with the WANGO Human Rights Award 2002.

WANGO Family and Peace Award 2002

Institute for Responsible Fatherhood and Family Revitalization

The Institute for Responsible Fatherhood and Family Revitalization is a pioneer institution tackling a most fundamental challenge to individual and family well-being and happiness, societal health, and world peace: the growing trend of fatherlessness. Founded in 1982 by Charles A. Ballard with the mission of empowering and encouraging fathers to become comprehensively engaged in the lives of their children in a loving, compassionate, and nurturing way, the institute has grown to thirteen centers in nine states. This nonprofit organization has successfully helped thousands of fathers become responsible, healthy members of their families. Charles Ballard summarized the mission of the institute on the *Oprah Winfrey* television show: "The Institute works at one thing: giving children their fathers, and fathers their children."

Given that more than 24 million children in the United States live in homes where fathers are absent, and that the repercussions to the children, parents, and society at large are far-reaching, this is a critically important mission. The problem of absentee fathers is closely linked to family poverty, domestic violence, substance abuse, premature parenting, destructive behavior, lack of educational achievement, and unemployment. The institute provides an innovative, nontraditional, home-based service to fathers and their families, including one-to-one outreach, one-to-group outreach, and family outreach.

The institute is unique in its structure of employing married couples to operate each of its thirteen community-based offices. The couples live in the communities they serve, thereby modeling and reseeding the community with clear examples of a vibrant family, though living in a society that is experiencing widespread family disintegration. The institute targets a community in each city where the need is greatest by consulting that city's demographics of highest rates of female-headed households, out-of-wedlock births, teenage pregnancy, truancy, crime, drug and alcohol abuse, and domestic violence. The institute supports the belief that there is no substitute for a father who has the skill and desire to be an effective and present parent. Based on this premise, the institute prepares fathers to be strong, stable parents while working with the entire family to facilitate the father's reentry into the life of his child(ren) and that of the child(ren)'s mother.

In taking the decision to present the Institute for Responsible Fatherhood and Family Revitalization with the WANGO Family & Peace Award 2002, the WANGO International Council was impressed with the sacrificial effort, serious commitment, and substantial accomplishments of this NGO in addressing a most fundamental problem related to families and peace on all levels. The institute works in the most difficult communities, tackling the problems family-by-family. The sincere dedication of the founder, Charles Ballard, his wife Frances, and the institute's staff, and their continual service and follow-up with each family, has yielded most impressive results: reuniting fathers and families across the United States.

WANGO Interreligious Cooperation Award 2002

Bishop William E. Swing and the United Religions Initiative

For more than a hundred years, visionaries have been dreaming of a day when the world's religions could work together for peace. A day in which people of diverse religions, spiritual expressions, and indigenous traditions throughout the world—Hindus, Christians, Muslims, Jews, Zoroastrians, Buddhists, Shintos, Confucians, indigenous people, Baha'i, and many others—work together for a just peace that includes each other. The United Religions Initiative has been the culmination of just such a vision.

The United Religions Initiative (URI) began in 1995 and held its first global summit in 1996. Since then it has held five global summits and countless regional summits and consultations in all regions of the world. Since its inception, more than a million people in more than 60 countries have participated in URI activities, and the URI membership includes over 15,000 people in 47 countries, representing more than 88 spiritual traditions. The URI's purpose is to promote enduring daily interfaith cooperation, to end religiously motivated violence, and to create cultures of peace, justice, and healing for the earth and all living beings.

The URI recognizes that while nations have been working for peace through the United Nations for more than fifty years, religions lacked a daily global forum for dialogue, conflict resolution, and cooperative action. Under the innovate leadership of the Rt. Rev. William E. Swing, who since 1993 has been a primary catalyst for the creation of a United Religions Initiative, the URI has built support for a permanent forum similar in concept to the United Nations where all the world's religions are represented. This will be a place in which conflicts and disagreements can be discussed and mediated effectively.

The United Religions Initiative has been most timely and may yet lay the foundation for a kind of "United Nations" of religious leaders committed to building cultures of peace and justice, promoting planetary healing and the well-being of all living things. Clearly this work has special meaning for all humanity and yet provides the missing piece in global efforts to create a world at peace with itself, just in its transactions, tolerant in its relations, and in harmony with nature.

The URI's interfaith peace-building activities, its visionary initiatives for peace among religions, its Partners in Leadership Program, its Interfaith Education Project, and other innovative programs have broken new ground in the quest for interreligious cooperation and understanding. More important, at a time when the limitations of traditional political and military authority have become more obvious, it may be timely for the world to mobilize its moral and spiritual resources, thereby enhancing its moral capabilities.

In taking the decision to present Bishop Swing and the URI with the WANGO Interreligious Cooperation Award 2002, the WANGO International Council was most impressed with Bishop Swing's lifetime devotion to cultivating the best in the human spirit and in promoting cooperation among the world's religions, and the URI's concrete efforts toward fulfilling that vision.

WANGO Universal Peace Award 2002

Dr. Federico Mayor Zaragoza

Professor Dr. Federico Mayor Zaragoza is a rare individual in our times and one who has substantially impacted the world in which we live. For twelve years, from 1987 to 1999, Dr. Mayor served as director general of the United Nations Educational, Scientific and Cultural Organizations (UNESCO), where, among other important contributions, he advocated education in underdeveloped nations as an effective way to address fundamental problems of poverty, overpopulation, and disease. He tackled traditional areas, such as the need for a dialogue between scientists and society, and cutting edge issues such as the Human Genome Project and the problem of child pornography on the internet. He has been a courageous leader who has worked to revitalize and reaffirm free press principles, and he has advocated for important initiatives in terms of the environment, ethics, and democracy.

Dr. Mayor was born in Barcelona, Spain, and received his Ph.D. in biochemistry from the Universidad Complutense de Madrid. He has served as rector of the University of Grenada, directed the Department of Biochemistry at the Universidad Autonoma, and was cofounder of the Centro de Biologia Molecular, which was the cradle of several generations of biologists. Dr. Mayor's research on brain metabolism and prenatal biochemistry received international recognition and had significant social impact. And his promotion of a plan for the prevention of mental retardation is credited with saving and improving the lives of thousands of children. Dr. Mayor has also held positions of high responsibility in the first governments that paved the way for democracy in Spain, and he served as minister of science and education, member of Parliament, and chair of the Parliamentary Commission for Education and Science.

In taking the decision to present Dr. Mayor with its highest award to individuals, the Universal Peace Award, the WANGO International Council was most impressed with his distinguished leadership of UNESCO and the many innovative and creative initiatives he launched which have far-reaching global implications and which no doubt will significantly advance the cause of humanity. In this connection WANGO is especially grateful to recognize Dr. Mayor's role in spearheading the International Year for Tolerance, which has provided the world with a set of principles that will help guide human relations in a world awash with intolerance, racism, and various fundamentalisms. WANGO fully subscribes to that principle which reminds the world, "Tolerance is the virtue that makes peace possible."

WANGO can understand why UNESCO also would launch the Year for the Culture of Peace, which WANGO fully supports, and for which are planned a number of activities to promote the goals and objectives of the year during this, the International Decade of Peace and Nonviolence for the Children of the World. Other initiatives such as the Human Genome Project are especially important to the uniqueness and the future of the human race and will undoubtedly help inspire better ethics in our efforts to manage the mystery of life. For these and many other significant causes, WANGO is pleased to recognize Dr. Federico Mayor Zaragoza with the WANGO Universal Peace Award 2002.

Arias Foundation for Peace and Human Progress
Recipient of the WANGO Peace & Security Award 2002

33

Peace Begins with Each of Us

OSCAR ARIAS SANCHEZ

It is a great honor to receive the WANGO Peace and Security Award and to be recognized for my continuing efforts and those of the Arias Foundation for Peace and Human Progress.

Fifteen years ago I received the news that I had won the Nobel Peace Prize for bringing the presidents of Central America together to negotiate the regional peace accord. I was surprised by the announcement, but heartened that the eyes of the world were turning to Central America, its conflicts, and our efforts to resolve them. The quality of life in the region has improved in the years since these five Central American presidents rejected violence and agreed upon peace. I used the monetary award that accompanied the Nobel Peace Prize to establish the Arias Foundation for Peace and Human Progress in San Jose, Costa Rica, in 1988.

The foundation works on three different fronts to affect change. The Center for Peace and Reconciliation acts to further disarmament, demilitarization, and conflict prevention in all regions of the world. The Center for Organized Participation aims to strengthen the involvement and action of civil society in Central America and emphasizes the important role NGOs play in promoting democracy and equality. Finally, the Center for Human Progress focuses on promoting gender equity and equal opportunity for women in the region. I am very proud of the work that the foundation undertakes, and I know its diligent efforts to improve the well-being of the people of Central America and the world will continue in the years ahead.

Today more than ever the world needs to receive the message

Dr. Oscar Arias Sanchez, former president of Costa Rica and 1987 Nobel Peace Laureate, is founder of the Arias Foundation for Peace and Human Progress.

of peace. Cynics may tell you otherwise. Peace is not a dream. In reality, there is nothing glamorous, naïve, or idealistic about peace. Peace is hard work. It is a path that we must all choose and then persevere in. This means resolving even our small daily conflicts with those around us in peaceful ways. For peace begins not out there, but with each of us. Each of us can do something to create a better world. The poets must write peace. The politicians must legislate peace. The warriors must lay down their weapons. The teachers must pass on the legacy of peace to our schoolchildren, and the parents must lead by example. Our hope indeed is our children. However, this does not mean we should leave actions for a better future to tomorrow. The future begins today, with us, in our hearts, and in our homes.

Bobby Kennedy once said, "Few will have the greatness to bend history itself, but each of us can work to change a small portion of events, and in the total of all those acts will be written the history of this generation." Those words are as true today as they were in the 1960s. I believe each of us can, and should, and indeed must work to make this world a better place. As we step into the twenty-first century, let us all work to create a world with more solidarity and less individualism, more honesty and less hypocrisy, more transparency and less corruption, more faith and less cynicism, more compassion and less selfishness. In short, a world filled with more love.

My friend and fellow Nobel laureate, Elie Wiesel, once said, "The opposite of love is not hate, it is indifference." Whatever you choose as your part in creating a better world, do not let yourselves fall into indifference. It is a great danger in our age. We have so much information, and so little energy to care. In the face of indifference I implore you to let yourselves care, and to find a way, however small or large, to make your work serve the goal of peace. If we each contribute, the total of all those acts will lead us toward a future that is not bleak but bright, not marred by conflict but charged with hope.

African American Islamic Institute
Recipient of the WANGO Education Award 2002

34

Helping Knowledge

HASSAN ALI CISSE

It is a great pleasure and a great honor for the African American Islamic Institute to receive the WANGO Award of Education. This award is for Africans, and for Americans, and for Islam because our knowledge and all our activities are based on Islamic teachings. The first word the prophet Isli of Islam received in his revelation from God is the word *eckra*, meaning to "read." And when he ascended, all that Allah told him to ask for is knowledge. It is obligatory in Islam that men and women be educated. There is no excuse for a Muslim to be ignorant, because one cannot deal with an ignorant person. It is better to have a knowledgeable enemy than to have a friend who is ignorant. A friend who is ignorant, in trying to help you, may harm you; your enemy may end up benefiting you with his knowledge.

My grandfather, Shaykh Ibrahim Niasse, is the one who pushed us to be educated. I love my grandfather and I love my father, not just because they are my parents, but because they helped me to be educated. Education was highly regarded by my grandfather. He used to tell us about these three things: knowledge, wealth, and woman. If you start with woman, you may never have knowledge. If you start with wealth, you may have woman, but you will never have knowledge. But, if you start with knowledge, you may have knowledge, woman, and wealth. So this award is for him. If he were alive today, I would just receive it and pass it on to him, like I did when they wanted to name the future university in Dakar after my name. I asked that it be named after my grandfather.

All Senegalese, starting from President Abdoulaye Wade, are

Shaykh Hassan Ali Cisse is founder of the African American Islamic Institute (AAII), an international NGO headquartered in Senegal but with affiliates in Africa, Europe, and North America.

very happy that the African American Islamic Institute has received this recognition. The ambassador of Senegal to the United States, His Excellency Mamadou Mansour Seck, said he was asked by President Wade to represent him at the awards ceremony to show the president's pleasure and happiness that the institute received this award.

This award is for Africa, because within the institute one can identify more than twenty nationalities from Dakar in West Africa to Johannesburg in South Africa. It is for America, because our fellow Muslim Americans are here from different parts of the United States to show their support and pleasure that we are receiving this award. We thank WANGO for giving us this award, and we want to say that we will never let this globe [the crystal globe in the award] fall down. We will continue the great work that you have recognized in our activities.

The African American Institute, originally named after *Nasrul Ilm*, is a branch from the great association created back in 1944 by my grandfather. *Nasrul Ilm* means "helping knowledge." This is our work, and we are working on it day and night because we know that knowledge is everything—honor and greatness. We are ready to work side by side with you for knowledge. Knowledge, which will bring peace in our world today, is something we need badly. The same way that we are hungry and thirsty for knowledge, we are hungry and thirsty for peace.

Our religion, Islam, is a religion of peace. The Koran is a book of light. It is a book to guide you to the way of peace. Peace is very important. If there is no peace, there is no knowledge, there is no commerce, nothing can be done. World peace—and similar words—have been repeated in the Koran 133 times, while the word "war" is repeated only six times. It means that Muslims are being taught to be peacemakers, to live in peace, and to give in peace. That is part of our message. We will continuously work for that message, and for spreading knowledge.

35

Inuit Circumpolar Conference (Canada)
Recipient of the WANGO Environment Award 2002

The Circumpolar Arctic as a Barometer of the Globe's Environmental Health

SHEILA WATT-CLOUTIER

The Inuit Circumpolar Conference (ICC) was founded in 1977 by the late Eben Hopson of Barrow, Alaska, and has flourished and grown into a major international non-government organization representing approximately 150,000 Inuit of Alaska, Canada, Greenland, and Chukotka, the northern part of Siberia in Russia. The organization holds Consultative Status II at the United Nations. I am now the chair of the ICC, and it is certainly an honor for me to accept this on behalf of ICC Canada.

Environmental concerns were certainly at the top of the agenda twenty-five years ago, and they still are. Since I was a child in Nunevic, in northern Quebec, I have witnessed and experienced a lot of social and economic change. So much has changed in less than fifty years. During the first ten years of my life, my family and our communities traveled only by dog team; today, I fly jumbo jets to South Africa to help negotiate UN treaties.

Because it has been a very short period of time, we have remained very connected to our cultural way of life. We are a hunting, fishing, and gathering people, and we preserve and conserve the environment—which forms the very basis of our life still today. Until recently the circumpolar Arctic was, politically speaking, a forgotten region frozen in the Cold War. And until the late 1980s, Inuit Chukotka in Siberia were not allowed to attend any ICC meetings in North America, although they were fellow Inuit. We kept two seats unoccupied at all of our meetings to remind us that politics between nations

---

Sheila Watt-Cloutier is chair of the Inuit Circumpolar Conference and recent president of Inuit Circumpolar Conference–Canada.

were separating us as a people.

Tremendous change, much of it positive, has occurred in the circumpolar world, especially in the last ten to fifteen years. The region's many indigenous peoples meet regularly, and we help each other. We are flourishing in international debates and in new circumpolar institutions—such as the University of the Arctic, the International Arctic Science Committee, and the Eight Nation Arctic Council, of which we are very active participants. Our home is now starting to be seen as the barometer, or indicator, of the globe's environmental health.

Things are happening very quickly in the Arctic because we are a people so closely linked and tied to ice and snow, by our life and culture. We are starting to witness dramatic changes in our climate. All of these issues are drawing more attention from scientists, from NGOs, and from agencies of the United Nations.

Contaminants and Climate Change

Currently, Inuit indigenous wisdom and traditional knowledge about the Arctic barometer is being sought by many scientists and policymakers from around the world. This attention will intensify in part as a result of two global processes negatively impacting us now in our homelands. These are the contaminants issue and climate change.

Many of these persistent organic pollutants (POPs) end up in our traditional country food. POPs such as DDT and PCBs, from industrial and waste management processes, end up in the Arctic sink. Because we are a marine mammal-eating people, they end up in the fatty tissues of our food and bio-accumulate there; and, because it is so cold, they remain there and make their home in the Arctic sink.

We end up ingesting so much POPs because of the diet that we eat. Many of our women have an accumulation in their bodies ten times higher than people in other parts of the world, and these are very worrying health implications for us—especially for nursing mothers. Can you imagine the kind of world that we are creating today, where mothers of the Arctic have to think twice about nursing their babies as a result of chemicals that are used to protect the babies of others in Central America from malaria? Surely we can find other solutions to this sort of problem!

This is why we intervened with a great deal of commitment in the global negotiations that resulted in 2001 in the Stockholm Convention on POPs, the first to single out the Arctic and its indigenous peoples. It is because the future—certainly of my people—depends on the ratification and implementation of this convention. It is very important that the world starts to understand what this is all about, that what is happening in the Arctic—be it the contaminants issue or climate change—is the early-warning system for the rest of the world. We must remember that we are all connected as one, and whatever is happening in the Arctic is a snapshot of the future of the rest of the planet.

In the long term the circumpolar Arctic may well be altered fundamentally through human-induced climate change. In the Arctic, Mother Earth is melting. It literally is melting before our very eyes. People are in fact falling through ice. Where everything previously was based upon our indigenous knowledge and was extremely predictable, today changes are happening so quickly with our environment that everything has become unpredictable. The rules are all changing, and even the wisest of hunters and elders are falling through the ice—because it is starting to melt even from the bottom. This is quite serious and alarming.

Increased coastal erosion as a result of melting—which we have been reporting for years now—is also forcing many of our own communities to plan to relocate. For the Inuit, climate change is not a theory. It is not just about the thinning of polar bears. It is about a people behind the animals, and climate change and contaminants issues are about the cultural survival of a whole people. We are only 150,000 in the entire world, and often we wake up thinking that we, not just our animals, are an endangered species. It is important that we continue to let the world know what is happening in terms of the environment.

Politics of Influence Rather than Protest

We are committed to defending the environment upon which we so deeply depend. We are few in number but we are starting to exert influence, out of all proportion to our limited population, because of the message that we bring. As we engage in the politics of influence rather than the politics of protest, I think we have been able to let the world know what is happening, what it is doing to itself, and to start to take some action.

Developing partnerships is very important for us, as Inuit. We are a sharing people and this is very much a part of our culture, and we continue to do that. I think the world has a vested interest in keeping us on the land because we are the natural guardians of the environment. I think it is very important that, because we are there on the land every single day hunting, fishing, and gathering, and because we live on ice and snow, we are able to predict, see, and observe the minute changes that are happening to our environment.

We seek partnerships with organizations, NGOs, and individuals that we can work with to get the message out and try to save the environment and our planet. We are a people that are not just harping about the challenges that we have in the Arctic. We have always tried to work from the moral high ground—that it is all of us who are going to be negatively impacted. It is only a matter of time that the rest of the planet will be so negatively affected.

We must consider how this will impact the next generation. I am a grandmother. I have a grandson whom I would want to continue this wonderful, rich culture of the Inuit people in the Arctic. It concerns me that we may not be able to continue this culture much longer if major changes do not occur in terms of the world looking and seeing what should be done to reverse some of these negative impacts.

Bahrain Women's Society
Recipient of the WANGO Human Rights Award 2002

36

Women and Change: A Clear Message To Women of My Region

WAJEEHA AL-BAHARNA

On behalf of all the members of the Bahrain Women's Society, I sincerely thank the WANGO administration for their support and encouragement. We are honored and delighted to receive this WANGO award that acknowledges major milestones in the history of the Bahrain Women's Society. I am sure that each and every member of the Bahrain Women's Society and all the women in my beloved country will cherish it dearly.

Living in a world where the only constant is change, regeneration, and evolution, the members of the Bahrain Women's Society (BWS) believe that such a world makes no allowances for nations that lag behind. But lag behind the Bahraini women did—for decades—for a variety of reasons, reasons that all contributed and led to a sense of hopelessness among the women. However, during the recent era of democratic political reforms in the kingdom of Bahrain, the women have reassessed their appalling status and have determined to make a serious effort to catch up socially, legally, economically, and environmentally. And to organize and facilitate this process, the Bahrain Women's Society was established with a vision of ensuring that the Bahraini woman assumes her full rights, her full confidence, and a productive advocacy position alongside her contemporaries worldwide.

This vision is as undoubtedly ambitious as the challenges are difficult, while the resources are modest, and the support—in an inherently male-dominated culture—is next to nil. Yet the women of the Bahrain Women's Society have managed within one year of existence to research, devise, and launch four high-profile projects designed

---

Wajeeha Al-Baharna is founder and president of the Bahrain Women's Society.

to address a variety of demanding issues, namely: child rights and welfare, women's rights, and environmental issues. Through a committed participation in social concerns and by utilizing mass media to broaden the awareness of children's rights, women's rights, and environmental protection, the society has earned the respect of the Bahraini people, who have identified it as one of (if not *the)* most active women's groups in the nation. This reputation serves to pave the way for more public activities and more ways to reach out to the women of our country.

Children's Rights

An important anti–child abuse and antineglect project, Be Free, was launched by the BWS as a campaign to help a brutally abused child, who had run away from home, to return safely. Our plan was not only to help this eleven-year-old girl, Fatima, but also through the publicity generated raise critical questions for our nation, such as: What rights do our children have when they are subjected to abuse by relatives or strangers? What are the responsibilities of our courts of justice to protect and preserve our children's rights? What is the level of awareness in our nation with respect to the unspoken phenomena of child abuse? What type of support and rehabilitation infrastructure do we have in place to take care of abused children? And finally, was Fatima only the visible tip of the iceberg?

To effectively communicate our message to government officials and to our society that the child abuse issue should be a priority, we knew that the Fatima campaign had to have a strong impact. Therefore the BWS systematically bombarded the newspapers and the media with significant numbers of cases of abused children and with statistics from field studies that were conducted and published by the society. Radio and TV exposure was maximized, and through the internet we publicized Fatima's case and spread awareness of child abuse prevention. Furthermore, we distributed more than 1,000 flyers in public places offering a reward for her safe return, followed by another 17,000 flyers in multiple languages, inserted into all of the kingdom's newspapers.

The uniqueness of this campaign attracted the attention of the electronic media, and all of the country's newspaper and magazine journalists without exception. Several key figures started writing and publishing articles related to children's rights, which served to apply further pressure on the kingdom's officials to intensify their search for the missing girl. The campaign was classified as the biggest of its kind in the kingdom and the region. It drew so much attention to the Fatima case that his majesty, the king of Bahrain, personally aired a plea to the child to come forward, promising her his protection. The prime minister also publicly instructed officials to intensify their efforts to end the child's ordeal.

Unfortunately, Fatima remains missing, but her case has served to present the issue of children's rights to the nation's consciousness. The BWS will continue the struggle and will join hands together with all human rights activists everywhere to see that children assume their full contemporary human rights.

Gender Mainstreaming

The BWS project of Gender Mainstreaming is a means of uplifting Bahraini women's awareness and self-confidence by encouraging their participation in cultural and economic activities, which in turn contributes to women's productivity, overall growth, and poverty reduction. Our strategy and activities have been to establish direct communication links with middle-aged and older housewives in our villages—where women are the most unaware of their contemporary rights and roles. This project is most challenging, as it attempts to shift the cultural paradigm of a very traditional and conservative, male-dominated society. Though it is a difficult task, it can be done, and we will see to it.

Environmental Preservation

The BWS firmly believes that failing to create an ecologically balanced globe would render in vain all of our other endeavours. Therefore, the Environmental Citizenship project, and the Marine Environment Preservation project, together with the the Earth Charter campaigns are among the concerns of the society. Preserving the integrity of our environment is the responsibility of each and every member of any society. Our studies indicate that thus far the Bahraini public is not fully in tune with global environmental concerns, and that is mainly due to the lack of programs promoting awareness. The good news is that this situation can easily be rectified provided appropriate resources are invested in upgrading interaction levels on environmental issues. One of the steps the BWS is taking to tackle this issue is to conduct meetings with fishermen to discuss the long-term effect of stock depletion and sea pollution. The initial response is promising, and we are encouraged to further devise similar programs.

Though the BWS is a newly formed organization, the success of its projects prove that sincere devotion, clear vision, proper planning, and targeted marketing can get the ball rolling toward a better tomorrow. It is also worth noting that the biggest hurdle the BWS continues to have is typical cultural resistance to change. However, by gaining recognition and credentials from national and internationally recognized bodies of WANGO's caliber, the BWS is able to widen its perspective and thus market itself to government and society as a serious, well connected, and aware organization worth cooperation.

Receiving the WANGO Award for Human Rights in fact translates into a clear message to the women of my region in general, and to the women of my country in particular, that they are recognized to bear a major role in the progress, sustained development, and integrity preservation of their nations. Most important, they indeed can make a difference—if they put their heads and hands to it. There will be many hurdles in the way before we see things happen, but the good part is, there will always be the reward of making a difference.

Institute for Responsible Fatherhood and Family Revitalization
Recipient of the WANGO Family and Peace Award 2002

The First Battle Is a Battle of the Home

CHARLES A. BALLARD

We take our mission from the Word of God in the Bible, Malachi 4: 5–6. God said, "Behold, I will send you Elijah the prophet before the great and terrible day of the Lord comes. And he will turn the hearts of fathers to their children and the hearts of children to their fathers, lest I come and smite the land with a curse."

Look around our globe and you see bombs dropping all over the place. You see men and women, boys and girls dying of AIDS, starvation, and so forth, all because of fatherlessness. And not just absent fathers, because there are homes where there are fathers present, but the conditions are just as bad. "Fatherlessness" is a condition of violence, neglect, and abandonment that is created in the absence of a loving, compassionate, secure father. Our work is to stop the bleeding and help fathers, first in America and then eventually in all parts of the world, to become loving, compassionate, and secure men.

When I was eleven years old, boys and girls in Honolulu were playing in a playground, skipping rope and swinging, when suddenly bombs were dropped—which took the lives of those boys and girls. Around 1963, boys and girls were in a church waiting for Sunday school when a bomb went off in the church—and three girls lost their lives. I can go on and on. Around this country there is fear because somebody is going around killing people at random. I believe that unless we change how men think, the problem will only get worse. The first battle is a battle of the home. Before we can resolve problems internationally, we must first resolve problems in our homes. From the

---

Charles A. Ballard is founder of the Institute for Responsible Fatherhood and Family Revitalization.

home, boys and girls go out either to curse or to bless the world. From the home, boys and girls will leave to either to heal or to wound.

One well-ordered, well-disciplined, and nurturing family says more for peace than all the sermons and all the preaching in the world. The greatest evidence of the power of peace can be presented to the world in a well-ordered, well-disciplined, well-loving home and family. In fact, such a family in the sight of God our Father is more precious than all the gold in the world. We must create more homes in the world that are well ordered and well disciplined. Our work, given by God, is to go into inner-city communities, where boys and girls are dying of starvation, abuse and neglect, and women are being beaten to death, and turn the fathers' hearts to their children.

My wife and I have been married for thirty-two years and we have three children, all doing well, who believe their parents are the model parents. I think all of us want to have parents who are model parents. So the work we are taking on is to go to the worst communities where the problems are the greatest and change those hearts, and then move around the globe to do the same thing.

Someone has said that the greatest war in the world today is the one against fathers and mothers: Fathers and mothers, who are true and honest and not afraid to call a problem by its right name; fathers and mothers who will stand for what is right—though they themselves may be suffering.

A little boy came home from school and his father was watching a ballgame. He said, "Daddy, play with me." His father said "I will, in a minute." The boy kept coming back asking the father to play with him. Finally, the dad noticed a picture of the world map on a piece of newspaper. He said, "What I'll do is give you some tape, and I'll tear up the world and have you put it together again. Come back in half an hour and I'll play with you." But in five minutes his son came back holding up the reassembled picture of the world. Although not quite like it was originally, the world was together. The father was surprised, and exclaimed, "How did you do that?" The boy said, "Father, on the other side was a man. I got the man together, and then the world came together."

Bishop William E. Swing and the United Religions Initiative
Recipient of the WANGO Interreligious Cooperation Award 2002

38

Religions Together

A Common Vocation for Peacemaking

WILLIAM E. SWING

It was extremely difficult to take a deep desire for making peace among religions and turn it into a globally appropriate organizational design. It took three long years to unite a one-sentence purpose statement that would be the right cornerstone to build upon. It was terribly demanding for a few people in one place to learn how to create a vision-inspired presence throughout the world. It was a hard challenge to find the kind of people whose personal integrity and willingness to grow together would set the standard for authenticity at the center of the community. Nevertheless, it all happened. The right person has shown up at the right time. Always there has been a sense that we have been led by a power far, far greater than our tiny imaginations.

The emerging life of the United Religions Initiative (URI) has been a gift and a blessing to all of us who have been privileged to participate. Honor of the URI belongs to the mysterious urgency that has been seated in the hearts of yearning people throughout the world; people who know that religions together can have a common vocation for peacemaking among themselves.

I want to thank the World Association of Non-Governmental Organizations for its recognition of the United Religions Initiative. Our first principle declares that we are not a religion. Our last principle declares that none of us will be coerced to participate in any ritual or to be proselytized. Thank you for singing out the freedom that is in our heart and the radical inclusivity that is in our nature. In the future I hope that the people of all religions, indigenous traditions, and spiri-

---

Bishop William Swing is founder of the United Religions Initiative. This award on behalf of Bishop William E. Swing and the United Religions Initiative was received by Rev. Sanford Garner, a long time friend and colleague, who read aloud this letter from the bishop.

tual expressions can transform the energies now given to denominations and turn those energies for cooperation.

Federico Mayor Zaragoza
Recipient of the WANGO Universal Peace Award Award 2002

39

Transition To a Culture of Peace

FEDERICO MAYOR ZARAGOZA

First of all, I would like to thank the World Association of Non-Governmental Organizations, because non-governmental organizations are extremely relevant as we enter the new millennium. NGOs represent the voice of the people, and therefore WANGO, which is an association of many non-governmental organizations, is extremely important.

I would like to thank Dr. Chung Hwan Kwak, Dr. Taj Hamad, Dr. Noel Brown, and Dr. Thomas Ward for all their kindness, and to express my gratitude for this award, which has special significance for me because of my esteem for the other recipients. Dr. Oscar Arias, recipient of the WANGO Peace & Security Award, is one of the notable people in the world who had a vision and was able to persuade so many people that following the way of peace was feasible. We are living in what is called the "global village," and we need to talk. We need to make a transition from a culture of imposition and of force to a culture of understanding and of dialogue.

Solution Is Education

I would like to speak to you as an educator because I am a professor of biochemistry. I have been very honored in my country to be the minister of education and science. From my experience, I know that the solution is education: education for all, and education throughout life. In 1991, I requested Jacques Delors, who was the president of the European Commission of UNESCO, to chair the International Commission on Education for the Twenty-First Century, which was made up of a panel of educators from around the world.

This commission published a report in 1996 entitled: *Learn-*

Professor Dr. Federico Mayor Zaragoza served as secretary-general of the United Nations Educational, Scientific and Cultural Organization (UNESCO) from 1987 to 1999.

ing: the Treasure Within, which concluded that education throughout life takes place in many forms based upon four pillars of knowledge: learning to know, learning to do, learning to be, and learning to live together. These pillars cannot stand alone; without all four pillars, education would not be the same.

Therefore, if we know, then we can do. More important, we need to learn to be: to be ourselves, to have our own answers, to have time to think—because to think and to create are distinctive capacities of human beings. Finally, learning to live all together means we must learn to listen, we must learn to dare, and we must learn to better share. I think that the twentieth century has been the demonstration of our inability to share—not only material goods and resources, but also knowledge. I think that to share knowledge and to live together in this global village is what we must try to give to our children and to their children. It is the best gift we can give them.

Since one of the most important aspects of WANGO activities is related with the United Nations system, I would like to point out that the Charter of the United Nations, founded in 1945, begins with: "We the peoples of the United Nations, determined to save the succeeding generations from the scourge of war, which twice in our lifetime has brought untold sorrow to mankind…" The emphasis is on "We the peoples," not "We the states" or "We the winners" or "We the governments." It states, "We the peoples." This is a democratic view, and it is a preventive view—a way to avoid war and save future generations. There is no country so big that it has no lesson to learn. There is no country so small that has no lesson to give. Therefore all people must work together and transcend the moment of "We the powerfuls." We must try and we must love our best, in order to be able to say together, "We the peoples of the world."

Ethical Principles

We have these fantastic horizons of ethical values that represent the rights of human beings. All human rights are indivisible, but one human right that is requisite to the exercise of the other human rights. It is the right to life. Every day in our world, approximately twenty-thousand people die of hunger and poverty. This is a terrible shame. In my opinion this is the first mission in which we, the non-governmental organizations, have failed. We must show the world that it is unacceptable that people are dying of hunger while we spend $2 billion a day on armaments. We must recognize that all lives are equal. All human beings are born free and equal in dignity. We must not accept inequalities between different parts of our global village.

I like the phrase "culture of responsibility" because we always talk about rights but very seldom about responsibilities. To have this sense of responsibility will be extremely important in the future, because if one is responsible, then one is committed, one is involved. It is important for non-governmental organizations to have this sense of mission and responsibility. Governments should base their responsibilities on values and ethical principles. Therefore the discussion on how a "culture of responsibility" could be better implemented is a very important one.

In the transition from a culture of force and imposition to a culture of peace—which includes a culture of dialogue and a culture of understanding and compassion—there is one point I would like to emphasize. We have the capacity to prevent making the same past mistakes in the future. The past has already been written, but the future is still intact; we must not allow anybody to write the future because it belongs to succeeding generations.

In conclusion, as individuals and organizations we must not dismay. We must try every day, and if we fail one day, we will start again the next day. Sometimes we think, "Actually, we are a very little non-governmental organization. What can we do? We have no voice. They do not listen to us." On those days, we should remember the words of Mother Teresa, who said: "Yes, it is true that you are like a drop in the ocean. But if this drop doesn't exist, the ocean will miss it."

Part IX
Diversity of NGOs

Introduction

Since the end of the Second World War, civilization has experienced a dramatic increase in globalization. The European Age of Exploration in the sixteenth century and the Industrial Revolution in the eighteenth and nineteenth centuries were remarkable in terms of world integration. However, the extent of societal and cultural integration and interaction in recent years truly has been breathtaking. In short, the planet seems to be shrinking.

In conjunction with globalization, we have witnessed since the mid-twentieth century a dramatic increase in the number and diversity of NGOs. In 1956 the *Yearbook of International Organizations* listed 985 "international NGOs," with this category including organizations operating in at least three countries. By 1996 that number had swelled to more than 20,000. In the year 2000 the *Yearbook* documented almost 29,495 active international NGOs. With respect to national and local NGOs, we find that half of all European NGOs were founded in the past decade, and in the former Eastern bloc countries, more than 100,000 nonprofit groups alone were set up between 1988 and 1995.

The explosion in numbers of NGOs has been accompanied by an expansion in what they do and how they are oriented and organized. NGOs now espouse a wide variety of agendas, causes, and ideologies—from promoting research and education to human rights and aid-related activities, from environmental activism to health care. Furthermore, NGOs range in size from one volunteer with a fax machine and internet connection working out of his or her home to large, international organizations with offices in several nations.

The papers in this section exhibit some of that diversity of NGOs. Selected NGO leaders from different parts of the world present their organizations and the projects that they are involved in, giving a taste of the NGO experience.

Searching for a New Vision
Global Common Society

40

WOON HO KIM

The Graduate School of NGO Studies in Seoul was founded in the year 2000, the first of its kind in Korea. Specializing in civil movements and future governance, the graduate school seeks to develop an interdisciplinary program drawing widely from theories of humanity, social actions, and global communities. With a current enrollment of eighty students, the school offers three majors within the Master's degree program: Civil Society, Global Governance, and NGO Policy/Management.

The graduate school is administered by Kyung Hee University, the largest private university in Korea. The graduate school grew out of a seed planted over twenty years ago, in 1981, when Dr. Young Seek Choue, founder and chancellor of the Kyung Hee University System, proposed establishing a United Nations International Day and Year of Peace at the sixth triennial conference of the International Association of University Presidents (IAUP), held in San José, Costa Rica. With the help of the Costa Rican government, the proposal was delivered to the United Nations General Assembly and unanimously adopted, proclaiming every third Tuesday of September as the UN International Day of Peace, and 1986 as the UN International Year of Peace.

In 1999, Kyung Hee University together with the Conference of NGOs (CONGO), a membership organization of NGOs in consultative status with the United Nations, and the Executive Committee of NGOs, associated with the UN Department of Public Information (NGO/DPI), hosted the Seoul International Conference of NGOs under the title of The Role of NGOs in the 21st Century. The following year, the Graduate School of NGO Studies was established with the goals of educating responsible world leaders and citizens who can devote themselves to the cause of global civil society through active participation in NGO-related activities.

Dr. Woon Ho Kim is a professor and associate dean of the Graduate School of NGO Studies, Kyung Hee University, Seoul, Korea.

Community of Common Destiny

Though the modern world enjoys unprecedented affluence and all the conveniences of a scientific-technological civilization, many would agree that it is overly devoted to the pursuit of wealth, worldliness, and belief in the supremacy of science and technology to the extent that it alienates people and diminishes humanity. Of serious concern is the prevalence of inhuman and antisocial crimes in the midst of a general atmosphere of moral and cultural decadence and family breakdown.

Scientific development has transformed the world into a global village, which enables all of us on earth to live virtually in the same zone like partners in daily life and has created a community of common destiny. Thus, our human society has become a transnational, cross-cultural, and borderless society. The spirit of our time is now defined in words such as: globalization, democratization, humanization, scientification, and welfarization.

Human life is full of problems that are interdependent and therefore need to be addressed as a whole, such as: environmental distress, human rights, gender equality, peace and security, disease and hunger, refugees, the elderly and the weak, restoration of morality and family values, social welfare, and conflicts among religions, races, and cultures. We know that individual states and nations, or corporations and institutions, cannot solve them alone, and that those problems should be dealt with globally and transnationally. I came to believe that NGOs, which work with global perspectives, could deal more effectively with these problems. Therefore, NGOs should be regarded as important world players working in alternative ways to help find solutions for such gloomy situations and as critical organizations that should be supported by all.

NGOs as Alternative Paths

As we witness the phenomenal growth in the number of NGOs with the development of democracy and economy, the role and influence of NGOs all over the world are also dramatically increased, thereby building-up a "partnership" with governments and corporations. It is generally said that the raison d'etre of NGOs is to contribute to the realization of a vision, a better world pursuing public benefit and fulfilling the gap between reality and a desirable future. In that sense, what is in the minds of people working at NGOs becomes more important than ever. The question then becomes what concept of a better world do NGOs and their leadership share with the rest of the world; are they envisioning and preparing for the same future world?

With these questions in mind, the Graduate School of NGO Studies was initiated to address the need for raising future civil leaders equipped with a common vision and common goals. In order to do that, understanding proper roles for NGOs in this new millennium is essential. First, NGOs have an important role in this age of participatory democracy and should direct their activities accordingly. Second, NGOs have a role as guardians of keeping government for citizens and as partners of it in running public affairs. Third, NGOs have a role in promoting good governance by shaping healthy public opinion.

NGO activities should be based on mutual respect and cooperation while promoting the necessary conditions for a healthy human society where all of the members of the global village can coexist in an environment of coprosperity. Cooperation among NGOs will enable their respective tasks to be carried out successfully, and NGOs, by opposing extreme nationalism and ideological class struggles, and by supporting internationalism, democratization, humanization and welfarization, can provide leadership in creating a global common society.

In the course of carrying out these tasks, NGOs should always stand up against all forms of injustice or abuse of power from any source including governments, political parties, and corporate interests. At the same time, NGOs should be aware that opposition for the sake of opposition is counterproductive and undesirable. Participatory democracy is possible if governments and NGOs have shared goals and are working for the common good of human society.

Educating for Global Vision

With this view in mind, the Graduate School promotes the right understanding, judgment, and conduct for a shared global vision and the means to put these ideals into practice. Prior to taking action, however, we have to change our minds in the right direction. Therefore, the role of the Graduate School of NGO Studies is to research a new vision for mankind, a global common society, which will guarantee universal democracy for all people and all the nations of the world, based on common goals, common norms, and common tasks.

The curriculum is designed to enable students to receive a balanced education combining theory with practice. Students are expected to analyze NGO phenomena as expressions of humanity, compassion, and dedication, and to visualize governance programs as substantial products of collective social praxis. And it tries to contribute to the formation of an epistemic community on the tasks and means for the construction of a human-centered global common society toward global peace and coprosperity.

International Voluntary Service

Eighty Years of Promoting Peace by Teaching Nonviolence and Fostering a Culture of Responsibility

41

PETER COLDWELL

The first programs of the International Voluntary Service (IVS) emerged from war-torn Europe in 1920 and involved former French and German soldiers. This initial project planted the seeds for a movement that currently involves more than one hundred thousand volunteers every year. The IVS mission is to promote peace, justice, and greater understanding among people and nations through voluntary work.

Volunteers for Peace, based in Vermont, serves on the Executive Committee of the Coordinating Committee for International Voluntary Services (CCIVS), an international NGO created under the aegis of the United Nations Educational, Scientific and Cultural Organization (UNESCO) in 1948, which is responsible for the coordination of voluntary service worldwide. CCIVS currently has more than 140 member organizations around the world in over 100 countries. VFP helps promote civil society and supports the Earth Charter.

International Voluntary Service Experience

Most of the twenty-two hundred programs offered in the IVS network every year are short-term voluntary service programs of two to three weeks. These are known as international workcamps and are very affordable, with most programs costing $200 to $500, including room and board. Typically, teams of ten to twenty volunteers originating from at least five countries, who previously do not know each other, live and work together like a family while focusing on local projects toward the betterment of the host community. A wide range of projects is undertaken, which may involve the preservation of cultural heritage

---

Peter Coldwell is founder and president of Volunteers for Peace.

and the environment, or construction and renovation projects, or other projects that address various social concerns. Volunteers come prepared to pitch in and do whatever needs to be done.

Volunteers schedule vacation time or take time off work or school and pay for their own travel and expenses. They are strongly motivated to want to help others in the world and are willing to sacrifice personal resources to do so. People are from all walks of life, all ages, and from both genders—though more females (about 70 percent) than males take part. Volunteers tend to be relatively independent, with a sense of adventure, since they arrive in camp not knowing who else will be there and with whom they will be spending the next two to three weeks.

By living together as a family and sharing the same living space, volunteers learn about each other's cultures as they share the day-to-day tasks of food preparation and cleaning while creating their own forms of entertainment and recreation. Volunteers enhance their own understanding of what it means to be responsible world citizens by learning about the social, cultural, and political situations that exist around the planet.

Problems that may arise in the camp are solved peacefully through dialogue and compromise, through human understanding and humility. Participants learn to appreciate that genuine peace comes through mutual understanding, respect, trust, and by solving problems in a humane way. Through intercultural immersion they also learn that violence is counterproductive. Workcamps foster family values such as caring, sharing, and working for the sake of others.

Volunteers usually leave the program with a strong sense of achievement, knowing how well everyone, despite their differences, got along while having fun in the process. They leave feeling good because they accomplished some good. Workcamps are really small schools that teach the skills of conflict resolution and good citizenship, since democratic decision-making is an important part of the group-living experience.

One could say that this program succeeds because each camp is a microcosm of the human family, and humans at heart are innately family-oriented and tribal beings. People commonly enjoy each other's company through sharing ideas and experiences while working together to improve living conditions, all of which contributes to a positive atmosphere that brings out the best of the human spirit. Their overall experience demonstrates that people with diverse cultures and beliefs can get along—it seems to be the governments that cannot!

Workcamp participants are free to practice their religious faiths and other traditions customary in the cultures from which they come. However, the common faith that all volunteers share—regardless of religion or culture—is that international cooperation through voluntary service is one of the most important ways to ensure a lasting peace between peoples. As effective vehicles of intercultural education, workcamps clearly nurture a "culture of responsibility" because they promote the ethic of working for the sake of others.

Extending the Program of Peace

If the values learned at workcamps can be extended and applied in today's world, it would improve the security and well-being of our planet. America and all countries should invest in a proactive program for peace. Keeping in mind the well-known expression that an ounce of prevention is worth a pound of cure, America should consider establishing a "Department of Peace" to study the root causes of conflict and promote nonviolent solutions. It is a tragedy of our time that every year we are willing to pay one hundred times more on military spending than the entire annual budget of the United Nations.

The United Nations recommends that each developed country give 0.7 percent of its GNP toward foreign aid. At present the United States government averages about 0.1 percent, whereas countries such as Norway, Denmark, and the Netherlands pay their fair share and more. Though the United States did recently rejoin UNESCO after eighteen years of absence, it is revealing that this United Nations agency's initiatives to promote a culture of peace and the spirit of volunteerism operates on a budget of approximately $250 million. Compare that with the $200 billion development of next generation US fighter aircraft, which is over four hundred times the budget of UNESCO.

The United States has not been investing in peace. It should come as no surprise that the horror of terrorism accompanies the widening gap of rich and poor. According to UN sources, the cost of lifting the world's poorest 1.3 billion people out of poverty, providing them with safe drinking water, adequate food, education, sanitation, and health care, is a modest $34 billion a year. At the crossroads where America now finds itself, questions are raised of how we should approach the future. Should we continue consuming a disproportionate amount of the world's resources, live in fear of terrorism and in a state of perpetual war, or can we be a model of responsible world citizenship, paying our fair share and promoting the well-being of the human family and our planet?

Global Healing

Ethical Imperatives for Sustainable Development

42

DAVID W. RANDLE

In August 2002, just before the World Summit on Sustainable Development (WSSD) took place in Johannesburg, South Africa, the United Religions Initiative (URI) Global Assembly met in Rio de Janeiro, Brazil. Although the URI Global Assembly was hardly mentioned in the press, I believe that it was an event that brings much hope for our world. It was remarkable in its diversity of 300 people from every continent representing 47 faith traditions and indigenous tribes, and that this diverse body was able to unanimously agree on a Call to Global Healing. I would like to report on the URI Global Assembly's Call to Global Healing, including the ethical imperatives for sustainable development that it outlines.

The URI Global Assembly was titled Sharing the Sacred, Serving the World. Every day of the Global Assembly, a different region of the world shared some of its sacred tradition, beginning a day that later explored how URI could better serve the world.

The conference was held at the Hotel Gloria in Rio de Janeiro, Brazil. The site was symbolic because it had been the headquarters for the Global Forum of the Earth Summit, attended by some forty thousand people ten years earlier in 1992. It is also the founding site of the city of Rio de Janeiro, the location where Spanish explorers killed thousands of indigenous people to found the city. In this respect, it was appropriate that the URI Global Assembly began with a sacred ceremony of songs and dances from indigenous peoples from all over Latin America, featuring indigenous children from Brazil.

For five days the assembly learned how to better serve the

Dr. David W. Randle is president and executive director of the WHALE Center and environmental justice minister for the United Methodist Rocky Mountain Conference.

world and implement URI's purposes of promoting daily interfaith cooperation, ending religiously motivated violence, and advancing cultures of peace, justice, and healing for the earth and all living beings. Subsequently the URI held its first-ever Global Assembly Meeting of Members. This meeting was facilitated by the Rt. Rev. William Swing, founder of URI; Ms. Rita Semel, chair of the URI Global Council; and Charles Gibbs, URI executive director. It was at this historic meeting of the members that the Call to Global Healing: Ethical Imperatives for Sustainable Development was endorsed unanimously by the assembly.

Call to Global Healing

The Call to Global Healing calls for religions of the world to partner with the United Nations Environment Program (UNEP) to bring ethical and spiritual values to public policy decisions for sustainable development. Mr. Adnan Z. Amin, director of UNEP in New York, wrote the URI global participants: "On behalf of the United Nations Environment Programme, I would like to express my great appreciation to United Religions Initiative (URI) and commend the 'Call To Global Healing: Ethical Imperatives for Sustainable Development' that has been initiated by the URI Global Summit."

Key to the Call to Global Healing is the statement, "We understand that there can be no peace without justice, and no justice without sustainability." The Call to Global Healing also affirms the global agenda found in the UNEP publication *Earth and Faith: A Book of Reflection for Action.* This is an agenda for water, land, health, air, industry, and well-being.

The Water Agenda includes protecting freshwater sources, protecting oceans, coral reefs, coastal areas, and small islands. A critical item on this agenda is the negative impact of the movement to privatize water for commercialization.

The Land Agenda includes conserving biological diversity, combating deforestation, and desertification. A critical item on this agenda is the need to develop sustainable agricultural practices to protect biodiversity and address the problem of world hunger.

The Health Agenda includes protecting human health and quality of life, especially the living and working environments of the poor, from pollution and environmental degradation. Critical to this agenda are the negative impacts of pollution. One billion of the world's people are exposed each day to health-threatening air pollution.

The Air Agenda includes protecting the atmosphere by combating climate change and transboundary air pollution. Critical to this issue is the US ratification of the Kyoto treaty.

The Industry Agenda includes the management of biotechnology in an ecologically safe way and the management of hazardous wastes and toxic chemicals in an environmentally sound manner. Critical to this issue is the growing problem of hazardous wastes and toxic chemicals, including the problem of nuclear wastes.

The Well-Being Agenda includes the examination and change of production and unsustainable consumption patterns, and the analysis of the effects of globalization on the environment and a call to take appropriate protective measures. Critical to this issue is the need to move toward renewable energy and reduce, reuse, and recycle consumed items, particularly in the developed countries of the world. Also critical to this issue is not to allow trade agreements to degrade the environment, further increase the gap between the rich and the poor, and further threaten the extinction of species.

Key Principles

With this Call to Global Healing are key principles. The principles are as follows:

- *All life is sacred and has intrinsic value regardless of the value judged by humans.* The well-known Noah's ark story in the Bible makes this point quite well. In this story there is a crisis in the world that included greed, corruption, violence, and coming climate change. Things were so bad that the Bible actually says God was sorry that he ever made humans, an indication that other forms of life had worth even beyond human beings in some evaluations (Gen. 6:6). The story says that Noah was the one saving grace to save the human race. It was important to God, though, that in the process biodiversity be preserved. At the end of the story we are told that God made a covenant with the animals separate from human beings, again reminding us of the intrinsic value of other species in nature.

- *Conserving biodiversity is in the best interest of both humans and other species.* Science has taught us that human beings could not survive without the support of other plant and animal species. At the same time, it is quite obvious that other species would do just fine without the survival of humans. Some 60 percent or more of the medicines we use today, including ten of the twenty-five top-selling drugs, come from plant and animal sources. Some animal and plant species may hold the key to diseases for which we have no present cure and for diseases that are still unknown. Some 75 percent of the world's population rely on health care derived from traditional medicines that come from natural sources. Biological diversity also provides the biological basis for world food security and support of human livelihoods.
- *The human population must be stabilized to assure quality of life and protect the rights of future generations.* The recent UNEP GEO3 report states that increasing human population along with unsustainable patterns of consumption is the greatest threat to biodiversity. Population growth also is a key issue related to poverty, hunger, environmental degradation, and consumption of resources.
- *Economic focus on the quality of and appreciation of life as opposed to standard of living must become a new norm.* Unless we find a way to reproduce planet earth for habitation, the world's population cannot live at the developed world's standard of living. Currently, if everyone in the world lived the lifestyle of just the average US citizen, we would need five to seven more planet earths to support this level of consumption. More threatening is that we have recently surpassed the earth's ability to renew its resources, and we are in self-destructive pattern that can only be averted by moving to sustainable practices in society.

At the WSSD in Johannesburg, South Africa, on September 2, the following news story was reported: "Calling the present model of development 'flawed for many,' United Nations Secretary-General Kofi Annan said he hoped the World Summit on Sustainable Development in Johannesburg would mark the opening of a new chapter of responsibility, partnerships and implementation.

'Let us face the uncomfortable truth,' Mr. Annan said. 'The model of development we are accustomed to has been fruitful for the few, but flawed for the many. A path to prosperity that ravages the environment and leaves a majority of humankind behind in squalor will soon prove to be a dead-end road for everyone.'

"Urging action and implementation toward sustainable development, Mr. Annan said action starts with governments, and that the richest countries must lead the way. 'They have the wealth. They have the technology. And they contribute disproportionately to global environmental problems,' he stated.

"But he said governments cannot do the job alone, and civil society groups have a critical role to play, along with commercial enterprises. 'We are not asking corporations to do something different from their normal business; we are asking them to do their normal business differently.' "

- *Each person and segment of a culture has the responsibility to contribute in their own way to building a culture of global healing.* On Wednesday at the URI Global Assembly, I participated in a tour of a favela project in Rio. We toured the efforts of Viva Rio and the Methodist Church to assist the poor with programs, such as microcredit loans, legal services, employment centers, day care, community recreation centers with a variety of programs with youth, and so forth. During the tour a young boy from the favela continued to tag along following our group. At one point I gave the young boy a dollar to buy a treat at the Methodist canteen and also gave him a bumper sticker from the Conch Republic that simply states "Everyone around the world can share the Official Philosophy of Key West, Florida and spread the word—The truth is that we are all one human family." This young boy looked at the bumper sticker and obviously did not have a car to put it on, so he put it on his T-Shirt. This was his contribution to helping to build a culture of global healing. I thought to myself that if this young boy in the slums could so quickly and decisively find a way to contribute to the Call to Global Healing, how much more can each of us and the organizations we belong do.

In another part of the favela tour we visited a classroom in the Methodist Church, where many other children were eagerly waiting for an opportunity to contribute as well. They seemed to all know that together we can make a difference. This is in essence what the URI Global Assembly was about for me, a Call to Global Healing and a unique organizational structure through URI, where people can work together to make a difference.

The Call to Global Healing was sent to the World Summit on Sustainable Development, which took place the following week in Johannesburg, South Africa.

Ethics and Sustainable Development

The World Summit on Sustainable Development concluded its deliberations with both a 153-point implementation plan and a political declaration from the heads of state, or their representatives in attendance.

I want to reflect on a few select parts of these documents and the ethical imperatives that they raise for consideration.

This year UNEP published the *Global Environment Outlook 3 (GEO 3) Report* in preparation for the World Summit on Sustainable Development. The *GEO 3* report identifies four major divides in the world that need to be closed if the world is going to move toward sustainable development. These include:

1. The Environmental Divide—characterized by a stable or improved environment in some regions, for example Europe and North America, and a degraded environment in other regions, mostly the developing countries.
2. The Policy Divide—characterized by two distinct dimensions involving policy development and implementation, with some regions having strength in both and others still struggling in both areas.

3. The Vulnerability Gap—which is widening within society, between countries, and across regions, with the disadvantaged more at risk to environmental change and disasters.
4. The Lifestyle Divide—partly a result of growing poverty and of affluence. One side of the lifestyle divide is characterized by excesses of consumption by the minority one-fifth of the world population, which is responsible for almost 90 percent of total personal consumption; the other side by extreme poverty where 1.2 billion people live on less than a dollar a day.

The *GEO 3* report outlines four scenarios for the future, which are titled the Market, Policy, Security, and Sustainability Scenarios. Only the Sustainability Scenario holds much promise for the future, and even that scenario will face many challenges for the years to come as the result of environmental processes that have already been set in motion.

The *GEO 3* report further identifies the need for cultural change where the values of solidarity, reciprocity, sufficiency, and stewardship will guide public policy and implementation of programs toward a sustainable future. To the extent that it does not interfere with the above values, tolerance is also identified as a key value as well.

From that background, the WSSD plan was developed with an understanding that there are ethical imperatives related to Sustainable Development. In the very introduction of the WSSD Implementation Plan is the statement that: "We acknowledge the importance of ethics for sustainable development, and therefore we emphasize the need to consider ethics in the implementation of Agenda 21."

This may be one of the most important statements in the implementation plan, for it is an acknowledgment that for the past ten years this has been a key missing ingredient in the implementation of Agenda 21. It also provides civil society with an opportunity to significantly assist with the development of these ethics through such initiatives as the Call to Global Healing.

Poverty Eradication

The first section of the WSSD plan is titled *Poverty Eradication*. It reaffirms the UN Millennium Declaration goal to halve by the year 2015 the proportion of the world's people whose income is less than a dollar a day and the proportion of people who suffer from hunger, and, by the same date, to halve the proportion of people who don't have access to safe drinking water.

While this is a good starting point it raises some important ethical considerations, including but not limited to the following:

1. Is the goal of having 1 billion or more people by 2015 in conditions of unsafe drinking water, hunger, and less than a dollar a day income an acceptable policy? If we currently have 2 billion, or about a third of the world, in this condition, and we halve that amount but the population continues to grow, we may still have close to 2 billion people in this condition with that stated goal. Would it not be more ethical to have a policy with a timetable to not have anyone in the world in this condition?
2. Can we achieve sustainable development with one-sixth of the world in abject poverty? If you accept the premise of the Call to Global Healing that there can be no peace without justice, and no justice without sustainability, then one has to conclude that leaving one-sixth of the world or more in abject poverty, even if the goal is achieved, will not allow us to really live in a sustainable world. If poverty is one of the causes of a lack of sustainable development, then we will not have a sustainable society with one-sixth of the world in this condition.
3. Do nations of the world have the moral obligation to provide 0.7 percent of their GNP to assist developing nations, as recommended by the UN? The WSSD implementation plan will require a significant increase in resources if it is to be successful. For nations of the world not to achieve the small contribution of 0.7 percent of their GNP brings into question the ability of the WSSD plan to ever be successful. Should not the rich nations of the world be held morally accountable to contribute this minimal amount?

Changing Unsustainable Patterns

The second section of the plan is titled *Changing unsustainable patterns of consumption and production.* This section of the report provides another opportunity for civil society through its stated goal to: "Develop awareness-raising programs on the importance of sustainable production and consumption patterns, particularly among youth and the relevant segments in all countries, especially in developed countries, through, education, public and consumer information, advertising and other media, taking into account local, national and regional cultural values."

This is another opportunity for initiatives such as the Call to Global Healing to take action and for other NGOs to participate. This section of the report also raises some important ethical considerations such as but not limited to:

1. Is there a moral limit to how much more developing nations consume than underdeveloped nations? (The current rate is fifty times as much.) If we believe that justice and sustainable development are connected, then there ethically has to be a more equitable sharing of the earth's resources.
2. Does the protection of species from extinction override the desire to consume? Clearly, many faith communities would respond to this question with a resounding yes. In addition, those concerned with our health and well-being and the rights of future generations would also affirm. The ethical question of *how much is enough* needs to be addressed. Clearly the value of other species needs to be considered in our current patterns of consumption and production that are unsustainable.
3. Is there a point where clean air, water, and healthy soils are more important than our desire to consume? Whatever short-term gain can be achieved through unsustainable production and consumption patterns, the gains will be short-lived if we do not have clean air, water, and healthy soils in order to live. Not only is the need to protect these resources important for us today but also for future generations.

Renewable Energy Development

Key to this section was the debate on renewable energy development.

The WSSD, despite strong efforts from the European community to set targets for renewable energy, in the end set no timetables or specific goals. The US delegation led the opposition to this effort, along with Saudi Arabia and Iraq. The language in the report does state the goal to: "Develop and disseminate alternative energy technologies with the aim of giving a greater share of the energy mix to renewable energies, improving energy efficiency and greater reliance on advanced energy technologies, including cleaner fossil fuel technologies"

Some of the ethical considerations from this section of the plan include but are not limited to:

1. High-income countries, home to 20 percent of the world's population, account for about 60 percent of energy use, most of which is nonrenewable. Is there an obligation to future generations to save some of the earth's nonrenewable energy resources? Is it ethical for the present generation to waste energy the way that it does, to not use renewable energy when it can, and foreclose the options and potential needs of future generations?
2. Should the cost of nonrenewable energy include environmental losses in the price of this energy, so that renewable sources are more price competitive? At present nonrenewable energy such as oil and gas and nuclear energy receive heavy government subsidies while clean efficient renewable technologies struggle in the marketplace. It does not seem ethical to rob future generations of their opportunities and options just to support subsidized energy sources, who do not pay their real costs, when other renewable alternatives to move toward a sustainable society are available.
3. Is it ethical to continue with nuclear energy when there is no solution to nuclear waste disposal? In the October 2002 issue of *National Geographic*, seven major setbacks are listed in the world since the Earth Summit in Rio in 1992. One of them is the issue of nuclear waste, where it is noted that this year 440 nuclear reactors will create 11,000 tons of spent radioactive fuel, which poses both a risk in the form of accidental leakage and as a terrorist target.

In the United States, home to a quarter of these reactors, there is no final plan to deal with this waste. The tentative plan calls for the shipping of these wastes to Utah for temporary storage with the goal of eventually getting it to Yucca Mountain in Nevada. This means that nuclear waste from thirty-nine states minimum will travel to Utah with all the accompanying risks.

Since we have viable sustainable and renewable alternatives, if coupled with conservation measures, it seems unethical to continue with this source of energy.

Natural Resource Base

The fourth section of the WSSD plan deals with protecting and managing the natural resource base of economic and social development.

Some of the key components of this part of the plan include:

- invitation to join the Law of the Sea Treaty
- encouragement to ratify the Kyoto treaty
- cut in half by 2015 the number of people who suffer from hunger.

Some of the ethical considerations for this section include:

1. Does the United States economy have more moral and ethical value than addressing the issue of climate change? Many in the world are disappointed that the US has refused to join the international community in implementing the Kyoto treaty. Climate change is a global problem and needs global solutions. Is ethical for the US to play with the world's future just to benefit its own special interests?
2. Does any nation have the right to endanger the resources of the world's oceans in order to serve its own national interest? Just like the issue of climate change, protection of the oceans requires global cooperation. Is it ethical for one nation to destroy a global resource and foreclose on the options of future generations just to meet its own short terms needs?

3. Is the right to food a basic human right? This comes down to a question on how much we value human life. Certainly food and water are essential to anyone's long-term survival. It is not ethical to deny people food in order to prop up profits of multinational corporations, or to deny opportunities for sustainable agricultural practices that could feed people in order to grow crops like tobacco, as is the present case in Malawi Africa.

Globalization

The fifth area of the WSSD plan is on sustainable development in a globalizing world. The report states that globalization should be fully inclusive and equitable, and there is a strong need for policies and measures at the national and international levels, formulated and implemented with the full and effective participation of developing countries and countries with economies in transition, to help them to respond effectively to those challenges and opportunities.

Globalization is a very complex issue with some possible benefits as well as many dangers. Some of the ethical considerations of globalization include:

1. Poor nations need debt relief. When a poor African nation is paying three times the amount of interest on loans than the amount of development assistance they receive, the situation leads to increased problems, not less.
2. Genetic diversity needs to be preserved. Genetic diversity in food is necessary for food security. If all food is of the same genetic composition, it would only take one disease or other adverse condition to destroy food supplies worldwide.
3. Trade policies need to include environmental factors so that sustainable practices are promoted, not discouraged. If new trade policies do not promote sustainability, then any economic gains will be short-lived.
4. Economic policies should not promote consumption levels beyond the earth's capacity. The attempts of multinational corporations to create new markets in developing countries poses the question of how much consumerism the earth can sustain.

> At present the earth is not sustaining the existing population. What happens if we have 4 billion middle-class people consuming at current middle-class levels?

Health and Sustainable Development

The next section of the WSSD plan deals with health and sustainable development. The HIV pandemic is a major concern in this area. One of the stated goals of the WSSD plan is to: "Health and sustainable development: Implement, within the agreed time frames, all commitments agreed in the Declaration of Commitment on HIV/AIDS adopted by the General Assembly at its twenty-sixth special session, emphasizing in particular the reduction of HIV prevalence among young men and women aged 15–24 by 25 percent in the most affected countries by 2005 and globally by 2010, as well as combat malaria, tuberculosis and other diseases."

Some ethical considerations include but are not limited to:

1. Is it acceptable to allow people to die of HIV and for this catastrophe to spread simply because people are to poor to pay for health care?
2. What is the world's responsibility to youth who suffer from the impacts of HIV through no choice of their own? (i.e., parents ill or dead, poverty, education issues, etc.).
3. Is health care a basic human right? The United States, the wealthiest nation in the world, is one of the few developed nations without a national health care plan that provides for all of its citizens. Unlike the US, many of the world's citizens believe that health care should be a basic human right. In developing countries, particularly in southern Africa, it is more a question of resources than public policy that prevents access to health care. More and more people are building an ethical consensus that health care should be a basic human right.

Small-Island Developing States

The seventh section of the WSSD plan addresses sustainable development of small-island developing states. Here the ethical issue is stated quite well in the UNEP book *Earth and Faith* by H.E. Kinza Clodumar, president of the Republic of Nauru. President Clodumar states:

> For more than 5,000 years, my people have inhabited what the ancient mariners called "Pleasant Island." Rain forests once abounded on Nauru, anchored by the Tomano tree and decorated by hanging orchids. Hundreds of bird species, including our treasured Noddy bird, made Nauru their home.
>
> But the 20th century has not been gentle with our island. First we lost our land; 80 percent of my country has been destroyed by phosphate mining, initiated by colonial powers. My people have been confined to the narrow coastal fringe that separates this wasteland from our mother, the sea. And now we face a new threat: the emission of greenhouse gases in distant lands is warming the Earth and causing the sea level to rise. The coastal fringe where my people live is but two meters above the sea surface.
>
> The willful destruction of entire countries and cultures with foreknowledge would represent an unspeakable crime against humanity. No nation has the right to place its own, misconstrued national interest before the physical and cultural survival of whole countries.

Ethical Choices

The WSSD goes on with specific proposals for Africa and the other regions of the world and for the financial needs for implementation.

The bottom line is, though, that unless government leaders are persuaded by civil society to make ethical choices in their policy decisions, unless multinational corporations are called into ethical accountability, and unless each of us is willing to make ethical decisions to build a sustainable society, then there is little hope, especially for the poor, our children, and for future generations.

The heads of state made the following points in their political declaration:

1. We, Heads of State and Governments, assembled at the World Summit on Sustainable Development in Johannesburg, South Africa, 2–4 September 2002, declare our commitment to build a humane and caring global society in pursuit of the goal of human dignity for all.
2. We reaffirm our commitment to the achievement of sustainable development.
3. As representatives of the world's peoples, we assume a joint responsibility to advance and strengthen the three inseparable pillars of the protection of the environment, social, and economic development at the local, national, regional and global levels.
4. From the African Continent, the Cradle of Humanity, we declare our responsibility to one another, to the greater community of life, and to future generations.
5. Meeting in the great city of Johannesburg, which bears testimony to how industrial activity can change the environment in a matter of decades, we recall the great social and economic divides we have seen.
6. This is a mirror of our global existence. If we do nothing, we risk the entrenchment of a form of global apartheid. Unless we act in a manner that fundamentally changes their lives, the poor of the world may lose confidence in the democratic systems to which we are committed, seeing their representatives as nothing more than sounding brass or tinkling cymbals.
7. We pledge to implement a global sustainable development program that gives absolute priority to bridging the deep fault lines that divide human society into the rich and the poor.

53. Recognizing the importance of building human solidarity, we urge the promotion of dialogue and cooperation among all the world's peoples and civilizations, irrespective of race, disabilities, religion, language, culture, and tradition.

54. We respect human diversity and recognize it as a cause for celebration.
61. To achieve our goals of sustainable development, we need a democratic system of global governance with enhanced and accountable international and multilateral institutions.

We know what we need to do. Real people are depending on us to make the ethical choices. Let us respond accordingly.

Estonian Association Anti-AIDS

43

Twelve Years of Activity

LJUDMILLA PRIIMÄGI

The Estonian Association Anti-AIDS is a nonprofit organization involved in the prevention of HIV infection and other sexually transmitted diseases and the promotion of healthy lifestyles. In September 1990 the association was formed by a volunteer group of physicians, scientists, teachers, cultural workers, religious leaders, and youth workers prior to the existence of any national HIV-prevention program in Estonia.

The association actively participated in developing a new public health strategy in Estonia, which formed the basis for the first state AIDS prevention program approved by the government in 1992. As a result, new methods of prevention, evaluation, and quality control were implemented. The association was the first organization to introduce internationally adopted views about HIV/AIDS and the means of prevention to Estonian society.

In the beginning of the '90s, members of the association considered the prevention of the sexual transmission of AIDS to be of great importance and utilized mass media to convey this message to a wide audience. The mid-'90s was the main period of publishing preventive educational materials, which totaled over thirty publications. The promotion of healthy behavior was the focus through the end of the twentieth century and into the beginning of the new millennium.

The original message of only preventing the transmission of HIV/AIDS has expanded to include the promotion of healthy sexual behavior. In recent years we have added a drug prevention program with youth as the main target group. Our training programs encourage teenagers how to say "no" to drugs.

Dr. Ljudmilla Priimägi is chairman of the board of the Estonian Association Anti-AIDS.

Nine Projects

During the last five years the association has carried out a total of nine projects, with two ongoing, on HIV/STD prevention and the promoting of safer sexual behavior among adolescent students and army recruits. The projects were financed by PHARE programs of the European Commission, the Soros Foundation, Family Health International (USA), Tallinn city government, and others. Over 5,000 teens ages thirteen through eighteen, 1,100 army recruits, and 250 schoolteachers were trained. Interactive learning workshops lasted anywhere from four to twelve hours, depending on the group.

The training materials were based on World Health Organization (WHO) and United Nations Educational, Scientific and Cultural Organization (UNESCO) materials, *Manuals for School Health Education to Prevent AIDS and STD,* and on the programs of the Netherlands Institute for Health Promotion and Disease Prevention. A variety of methods of interactive learning (small and whole group discussion, role playing, brainstorming, individual work, videos, etc.) were used during the workshops. Use of creative tools such as drawing and composing allowed younger teens to express themselves and promoted a self-learning approach. The workshops were carried out not only in schools, but also in out-of-school settings such as youth summer-camps.

Innovative training materials in the Estonian and Russian languages were developed and distributed among teachers who participated at the workshops. The second edition of a methodological manual for teachers, youth workers, counselors, psychologists, and social workers was created. To relay the message more effectively to youth, an interactive approach was also adopted to promote healthy sexual behavior and prevent HIV/AIDS and other sexually transmitted infections. Questionnaires, completed before and after the workshops, demonstrated young peoples' interest, active participation, and improvement in their self-esteem. Teachers taking part in the workshops expressed their confidence in this model by repeating it in their own classes.

In January 2002 the Third National AIDS Prevention Program was adopted by the Estonian government, with members of the Association of Anti-AIDS participating in its composition. Beginning in April 2002, a new project for schoolchildren was financed by Family

Health International (USA). Later that year, in September 2002, the United States embassy in Estonia financed a project to educate fifteen hundred military personnel of the Estonian Defense Forces. The association continues to work in close collaboration with many state organizations and NGOs in Estonia. Thus, for the past twelve years, the Estonian Association Anti-AIDS has been able to serve the population of Estonia through these helpful public programs.

The Democracy School

44

RUTA PELS

[Editor's note: *Toward the end of the 1980s, Estonia underwent what has been called the "second national awakening." It was a time when the national consciousness became very pro-Estonian throughout society and a new emphasis was placed on educating and speaking in the Estonian language rather than the language of the Russian occupants. The Estonian Singing Revolution happened throughout these years (1987–90). The population had a renewed interest in journalism and politics, and various societies and professional organizations were established. The Estonian sense of identity experienced a new level of confidence. This national awakening led Estonia to regain its independence in August 1991 after enduring Soviet control since immediately after the Second World War. Free democratic presidential and parliamentary elections took place in September 1992.*

Estonian civil society was reestablished beginning in 1988, and by 1994 over three thousand different organizations, societies, and fellowships were established, involving approximately 10 percent of the total population. After so many bleak years under Soviet domination, the concept of pluralism and freedom to choose activities and interests brought a surge of life into the Baltic nation. ARS]

The People to People Estonia NGO began in 1993 with a group of eleven Estonian and Russian men and women ranging in ages from seventeen to fifty-seven. Over the following year, this founding group defined the key elements of the PTP Estonia mission as promoting mutual understanding and creating programs for youth. Combining their varied interests, the first project was an international youth conference, *Living in a Multicultural Democratic Society—From Tolerance to Mutual Understanding. Fifty* participants from nine countries participated together with twelve guest speakers.

Ruta Pels is president of People to People, Estonia.

The idea of the Democracy School arose from this successful conference. In March 1995, PTP Estonia organized the first ten-day course in three cities in Estonia and a one-week course in Denmark. Interest in these programs increased and further follow-up activities were discussed. By August 1995, PTP Estonia organized a six-day study trip to Sweden for young people. Students visited some organizations and institutions (Swedish Parliament, a Swedish daily newspaper, Stockholm University and Uppsala University, and a school for immigrants). One of the scheduled activities was organizing a number of meetings with People to People Sweden and with a committee for youth organizations, the LSU. The trip included a cultural program and a visit to the Stockholm Water Festival. After this trip there was sufficient interest to continue the Democracy School project as an annual one.

Interest in the Democracy School continued to grow, and we held a conference in Narva, Estonia (Historical Heritage—Historical Responsibility), a workshop on civics in Estonia, several other seminars about mass media and journalism in a democratic society, and study trips to Denmark. Important seminars on conflict resolution and mediation techniques, which provided practical and philosophical training, were offered for students in Estonian and Russian schools in Estonia. The seminars also included elements of leadership development. The numbers of young members steadily increased. The most successful programs for young people combined educational projects, communication, and having fun! Program areas continued to expand to include civic education, anti-AIDS, human rights, and development.

Every year PTP Estonia has traditional camps for teenagers during the summer, and sometimes during school vacations at Christmas and Easter. Usually the participants discuss achievements, make plans for the future, and have fun. Each year the program is varied to include new elements. The first youth camp included English as a second language program as well as civics; the following year focused on our multicultural society, which included folk dances and songs of nations living within the nation. Future years will involve cooperating with the New Age language school and have students living in "home stays" in the capital of Tallinn.

Additional Programs Offered

Travel Club for Teenagers is part of the Democracy School as a soft integration program to bring non-Estonians to Estonian society. Travel Club has meetings with different themes: history, culture, journalism, practical aspects of traveling, lessons on psychology and astrology, and discussions on specific projects.

Educational Exchanges. We've made student exchanges in the German language with Augsburg and Berlin, as well as a student's exchange with Petersburg (Russia); internship programs for students of the University of Missouri-Kansas City in Estonia; and internship and direct students exchanges with the People to People US sister chapters and PTP Europe chapters (PTP Angouleme). High school students and teachers in civics enjoy study trips to Latvia and to the bilingual center in the Riga Classical Gymnasium.

Family Club. Youth and adults are participating in traveling and receiving guests as part of a homestay program, which is popular in PTP Estonia chapters. We've had guests of all ages from many European countries and the United States.

"Simurg" Association of the Culture of Azerbaijan

45

FUAD MAMMEDOV

The Association of the Culture of Azerbaijan "Simurg" (ACA) is the first diversified cultural NGO in Azerbaijan. Founded in April 1990 to help form a democratic and civil society in Azerbaijan, "Simurg" strives to achieve its mission through progressive structural changes in the development of Azerbaijan society, its democratization, and modernization. The association establishes programs and projects aimed at strengthening democratic values, education and enlightenment, stable development, and cooperation between nations.

Among the hundreds of individual and group members are experienced, well-known specialists in various fields—culturists, sociologists, economists, lawyers, political scientists, engineers, medical doctors, diplomats, and theologians as well as talented youth. Many "Simurg" ACA members are highly qualified experts in the fields of management and marketing, the sciences, education, market economy, and political and strategic studies. Among the foreign honorary members of the association are such prominent diplomats, scientists, and public figures as Paolo Lembo, Michael Schmunk, Tomas Yang, Valter Shoniya, Pear Ulvevadet, Olaf Berstad, and Eliezer Yotvat.

In accordance with programs aimed toward the formation and development of civil society culture, the association implemented a variety of projects with grants provided by ISAR-Azerbaijan, UNESCO, the Budapest Institute of Open Society, and the Norwegian embassy in Azerbaijan, among others. "Simurg"ACA held approximately fifty seminars, conferences, and training and focus groups. It has issued dozens of scientific and educational articles concerning cultural policy and democratic culture. Dozens of specialists were educated

---

Fuad Mammedov is president of the "Simurg" Association of the Culture of Azerbaijan (ACA).

and trained about "culturology" in projects initiated by the association such as management and business school and nursing school. In November 2000, "Simurg" ACA took part in an international conference entitled Upbringing in the Spirit of Peace and Nonviolence sponsored by the Interreligious and International Federation for World Peace (IIFWP) and the World Association of Non-Governmental Organizations (WANGO) in Baku, the capital city of Azerbaijan.

One of the current projects of the Association is the School of Civil Society Culture. This school serves to train participants in forming a civil society culture, which includes structures management, cultural resource centers in the capital and regions, the Center of the Culture of Democratic Elections, and "culturological" trainings for office workers, youth, and social groups in the country. The strategic goal of the project is the creation of a Civil Society Culture Forum that is supposed to coordinate efforts of the NGOs and government and business structures so as to gain stable development, peace, and security in the southern Caucasus. The association also intends to establish a feature magazine about peace culture and the world cultural experience in the interest of solving global, regional, and national problems of modern development.

"Simurg" ACA welcomes the cooperative partnership model WANGO endorses with colleagues from different countries in the interest of achieving international and interreligious harmony, the realization of a humane philosophy of unification, the ideals of a peace culture, and the goals of achieving global civil society.

Action on Disability and Development (ADD): Cambodia

46

SREY VANTHON

Action on Disability and Development (ADD) is one of the few British-based organizations supporting rights-based development work with groups of disabled people in Africa and Asia. Since its founding in 1985, ADD has supported over seventy-five thousand disabled people in their self-help activities and their fight for their rights and equal opportunities. ADD programs have been established in Bangladesh, Cambodia, Sudan, Uganda, Tanzania, Zambia, Ghana, Mali, Burkina Faso, and Côte d'Ivoire. ADD has also partnered with organizations in India and Zimbabwe.

The ADD vision of the world is one where people who are called disabled can participate at every level of society as fully as they choose. To achieve this, the organization partners with networks of disabled people in some of the poorest communities in the world and helps them campaign for their rightful inclusion in society. Disability is viewed as a human rights or social issue related to attitude and access to equal opportunities rather than an impairment of an individual, for example. ADD embraces the social model of disability as opposed to the medical model.

Fighting for basic human rights remains a priority for disabled people's groups to ensure that they are included in policymaking, legislation, and access to basic services. Only 7 percent of disabled children receive any sort of education in developing countries. Many parents still believe that sending their children to school is a waste of resources. Therefore, ensuring that educational and training opportunities and information are open to disabled people is another of ADD's main concerns. ADD works with disabled people's organizations to challenge attitudes that turn impairment into problems that exclude disabled children and adults.

ADD works with self-help groups of disabled people as they

Srey Vanthon is the Cambodian National Representative of Action on Disability and Development (ADD).

gain the skills to fight discrimination and understand the causes of poverty and exclusion. With increased confidence and strength in numbers, they can then start influencing policymakers. Groups form networks, and networks link into national and international organizations of disabled people, thus forming strong alliances.

ADD in Cambodia

ADD Cambodia started in 1995 and facilitated the formation of small groups where disabled people could find better ways to take care of their needs. Self-help groups were formed based on information generated from field visits and by studying the situation of people with disabilities. Informal group meetings were set up to receive feedback and understand how self-help groups could best benefit disabled people, and counseling sessions helped build up their confidence. These self-help groups at the village level have generally helped raise people's awareness about what it means to be disabled. The groups encourage confidence in all the members so that they can speak out about their problems and advocate changes on the family and community levels. Today, 140 self-help groups (SHGs) have been formed through the facilitation of ADD, with an additional fifty SHGs set up by other organizations learning from the ADD example.

At the commune level, village SHGs have joined into a federation managed by a governing board, which works on a voluntary basis. The role of the federation is to link the groups at the village level to the disability movement on the provincial and national levels. This federation employs commune workers, who work closely with the groups in order to exchange information. At this point ADD has facilitated three such federations.

To specifically address the needs of disabled women, a forum was established where they can discuss the problems that cannot be raised or solved in the group or federation.

At the national level, ADD is working closely with the Cambodian Disabled People's Organization (CDPO). CDPO represents people with disabilities and plays an important role in training, awareness-raising, and advocacy, and influences activities at national and international levels. So far the disability movement has initiated and drafted disability legislation that is now waiting for approval from council ministers before being submitted to the National Assembly.

International Recognition

ADD was awarded the United Kingdom's highly esteemed International Aid and Development Award at the Charity Awards 2002, considered the most prestigious award for the voluntary sector. The award was given for ADD's groundbreaking work in Bangladesh, Ghana and Zambia, through which disabled people gained the fundamental right to vote. In these countries, inaccessible polling booths and the lack of tactile ballot papers prevented disabled people from voting independently or, as in most cases, from being able to vote at all. As a result, many people with disabilities did not believe they had the right to vote. ADD's project raised the awareness that disabled people do have the right to vote and helped them campaign for this right through media coverage and discussions with electoral officers and governments. ADD worked in partnership with the International Foundation for Electoral Systems to train over four hundred disabled people as election monitors. Disabled people did not just gain the right to vote, but were also able to actively partake in the whole election process.

A highlight in Bangladesh in 2001 was the passage of the Bangladesh Disability Welfare Act, which was a direct consequence of advocacy, campaigning, rallies, and demonstrations by the disability movement that followed a wheelchair march in 2000.

In Ghana, a school for children who act as guides for their blind parents was opened with an initial forty-five children enrolled. These children can go on to mainstream education in the future. Another great achievement was in Sudan, where after much lobbying from disabled people's organizations, the government announced that all disabled children will be entitled to a free education from 2002.

Contributors

Wajeeha Al-Baharna

Ms. Wajeeha Al-Baharna is President of the Bahrain Women's Society (BWS), one of the most active social organizations in Bahrain. The BWS pioneers the rights of women and the child in Bahrain, and has as its goal the integration of Bahraini women in particular and Bahraini society in general with desired contemporary social, legal, cultural, and environmental norms. Ms. Al-Baharna is also a marine biologist and the author of *Fishes of Bahrain*, published by the Ministry of Commerce and Agriculture, Directorate of Fisheries, State of Bahrain.

Oscar Arias Sanchez

Dr. Oscar Arias is former President of Costa Rica and the 1987 Nobel Peace Prize Laureate. As Costa Rica's president from 1986 to 1990, Dr. Arias' vision of a Central America free from war, strife, and repression, widely known as the Arias Peace Plan, culminated in the signing of the Esquipulas II Accords by all of the Central American presidents. Dr. Arias holds a doctoral degree in political science from the University of Essex, England. He founded the Arias Foundation for Peace and Human Progress in 1988.

Alexandra Arriaga

Ms. Alexandra Arriaga serves as Director of Government Relations for Amnesty International USA. Previous posts include Senior Fellow and Director of Legislative Affairs for the Inter-American Dialogue; Special Assistant to President William Clinton and Chief of Staff to the Special Envoy for the Americas at the White House; Special Coordinator for External Affairs for the Bureau of Democracy, Human Rights and Labor at the US Department of State; Executive Director of Secretary Albright's Advisory Committee on Religious Freedom Abroad; US Delegate to the UN Commission on Human Rights; Chair of the Bureau's Working Group on Women's Human Rights; and Director of the Congressional Human Rights Caucus.

Charles A. Ballard

Mr. Charles A. Ballard is Founder of the Institute for Responsible Fatherhood and Family Revitalization. The Institute was founded in 1982 in Cleveland, with the mission of empowering and encouraging fathers to become comprehensively engaged in the lives of their children in a loving, compassionate, and nurturing way, and has grown to thirteen centers in nine states. The Institute is unique in its structure of employing married couples to operate each of its thirteen community-based offices.

Noel Brown

Dr. Noel Brown is President of Friends of the United Nations and Vice Chair of WANGO's International Council. Previously he served as Director of the United Nations Environment Program (UNEP), North American Regional Office. Dr. Brown is also Chairman of the International Institute for Peace Through Tourism and Chairman of the Rene Dubos Center for Human Environments Dr. Brown holds a Ph.D. in International Law and Relations from Yale University. He is Editor of *Ethics and Agenda 21: Moral Implications of a Global Consensus.*

Hassan Ali Cisse

Shaykh Hassan Ali Cisse is founder of the African American Islamic Institute (AAII), an international NGO headquartered in Senegal but with affiliates in Africa, Europe, and North America. He also serves as Chief Imam of the Grand Mosque in Medina Kaolack, Senegal, and is a respected Islamic scholar and leader. He holds a B.A. degree from Ain Shams University in Cairo, Egypt, and a Master's degree from the University of London.

Mei Cobb

Ms. Mei Cobb serves as Senior Vice President of the Points of Light Foundation. Founded in 1990 by former US President George H. W. Bush, who serves as Honorary Chairman, the Points of Light Foundation is a national nonpartisan, nonprofit organization that promotes volunteerism, and is one of the nation's leading advocates for and authority on volunteering. Ms. Cobb has designed and conducted trainings on Volunteer Center development in numerous countries in North and South America, Europe, Asia, and Africa.

Peter Coldwell

Mr. Peter Coldwell is President and Founder of Volunteers for Peace (www.vfp.org), which has exchanged over twenty-one thousand volunteers since 1982. He also serves on the Executive Committee of the Coordinating Committee for International Voluntary Service (CCIVS) at UNESCO offices in Paris. Mr. Coldwell has traveled to over fifty countries in his work.

Donald B. Conroy

Dr. Donal B. Conroy serves as President of the North American Conference on Religion and Ecology (NACRE), a nonprofit educational and eco-action organization. Dr. Conroy also heads up the administration of the International Consortium on Religion and Ecology (I-CORE), a network of organizations working on ethical and development projects resulting from Agenda 21. Dr. Conroy has served as an ethical adviser to the World Bank's Environmental Division and is founding director of the National Institute for the Family. He received his doctorate from the University of Pittsburgh.

Lorne W. Craner

Mr. Lorne W. Craner is US Assistant Secretary of State for Democracy, Human Rights and Labor. In this position, he coordinates US foreign policy and programs that support the promotion and protection of human rights and democracy worldwide. Prior to this appointment, Mr. Craner was President of the International Republican Institute (IRI), which conducts programs outside the US to promote democracy, free markets, and the rule of law. Secretary Craner has also served as Director of Asian Affairs at the National Security Council and Deputy Assistant Secretary of State for Legislative Affairs.

Mihaela Dimitrescu

Professor Mihaela Dimitrescu is vice president of the Romanian Association for European Integration and Democracy (RAEID)

Megan Epler Wood

Ms. Megan Epler Wood is Founder and former President of The International Ecotourism Society (TIES). Ms. Epler Wood has taught Ecotourism Planning and Management for George Washington University and is author of *Ecotourism: Prin-*

ciples, Practices, and Policies for Sustainability (UNEP). She also is overseeing a global consultation process for the United Nations' International Year of Ecotourism as well as managing the establishment of a new national tourism fee generation program in partnership with local organizations in Belize. Epler Wood has also worked for World Wildlife Fund-U.S.

Gary Gardner

Mr. Gary Gardner is Director of Research at the Worldwatch Institute, a nonprofit research organization devoted to the analysis of global environmental and resource issues. He has authored several Worldwatch Papers and select chapters in the Institute's *State of the World* annual publication, and he coauthored *Beyond Malthus: Nineteen Dimensions of the Population Challenge*. Mr. Gardner has also served as project manager of the Soviet Nonproliferation Project and authored *Nuclear Nonproliferation: A Primer*.

V. Mohini Giri

Dr. V. Mohini Giri serves as Chairperson of the Guild of Service, a social service organization. She is also Founder/President of the War Widow Association and Founder/Trustee of the Women's Initiative for Peace in South Asia. Among other positions she has held are Chair of the National Commission for Women and Chair of the Delhi State Social Welfare Advisory Board. Dr. Giri is the daughter-in-law of Shri V. V. Giri, former President of India. Her publications include *Kanya: Exploitation of Little Angels* and *Emancipation and Empowerment of Women*.

Tajeldin I. (Taj) Hamad

Mr. Taj Hamad is Secretary-General of the World Association of Non-Governmental Organizations (WANGO). Among previous posts he has held are International Executive Director of WANGO, Secretary of the Executive Committee of DPI-NGOs at the United Nations, Executive Director of the Interreligious Leadership Seminar, and Executive Director for Interdenominational Christians for Unity and Social Action. Mr. Hamad also serves as Chair of the Middle East Alliance for World Peace.

Margaret E. Hayes

Dr. Margaret E. Hayes is President and Principal Consultant of MEH Associates, a consulting firm to nonprofit and faith-based organizations. She is a former Dean of College Development at Bergen Community College and has served as Executive Director of Jobs for Youth and Vice President of Professional Services at the First Occupational Center of New Jersey. Dr. Hayes is also the founder and past president of the New Jersey Coalition of 100 Black Women and past president of Christian Women's Alliance.

Melissa Hopkins

Ms. Melissa Hopkins is President of The Hopkins Group, Inc., a communications company. Previously, she served as vice president of media relations for JAB & Associates. She spent several years working with a variety of corporate and nonprofit clients to help articulate their message and earn media coverage of their cause. Ms. Hopkins also managed the media relations office for the *Washington Times* newspaper and served as the newspaper's spokesperson. Ms. Hopkins entertainment experience includes serving as a casting assistant on the films *Batman Forever* and *True Lies* and acting roles on television shows.

Shireen T. Hunter

Dr. Shireen T. Hunter is Director of the Islam Program at the Center for Strategic and International Studies (CSIS). She previously served as Director of the Mediterranean Studies program with the Centre for European Studies in Brussels, Deputy Director of the Middle East Program at CSIS, and Research Fellow at the Harvard Center for International Affairs. Dr. Hunter is the author of many books, including *The Future of Islam and the West: Clash of Civilizations or Peaceful Coexistence?* She holds a Ph.D. in political science from the Institut Universitaire des Hautes Etudes Internationales in Geneva and an M.A. from the London School of Economics and Political Science.

Woon Ho Kim

Dr. Woon Ho Kim is Associate Dean of the Graduate School of NGO Studies, Kyung Hee University in Seoul, Korea. He is also a Board Member of the Korean Association of Nonprofit Organizations Research (KANPOR), and a Steering Committee Member of the Christian Ethics Movement. He was Executive Program Director for the Organizing Committee for the 1999 Seoul International Conference of NGOs.

Leonid Makarovich Kravchuk

H.E. Leonid M. Kravchuk is the first President of independent Ukraine (1991–94) and President of the Ukraine Peace Council. He has also served as Chairman of Ukraine's Supreme Soviet (1990). He was the Ukraine's first popularly elected president. President Kravchuk has since served as a National Deputy in the Ukraine Parliament and is a member of the Committee on Foreign Relations. He is author of the books *State and Authorities* and *We Have What We Have* as well as over five hundred articles on Ukraine's internal and foreign policy.

Chung Hwan Kwak

Rev. Dr. Chung Hwan Kwak serves as Chair of WANGO's International Council. He also is Chairman of the Board for the University of Bridgeport, Chairman of the Board for the World University Federation, and Chairman of the Interreligious and International Federation for World Peace. Reverend Kwak is the former Publisher and President of the daily newspaper *Segye Times* of Seoul, Korea, and currently serves as Chairman of the Board of News World Communications, the parent company that publishes the *Washington Times* and other newspapers and magazines.

Fuad Teyub Mamedov

Dr. Fuad Teyub Mamedov is President of "Simurg" Association of Azerbaijan Culture. He also serves as Professor of History for the Academy of Public Administration of Azerbaijan. Dr. Mamedov, who holds a doctorate in history, previously served as Chief of the Science Department of the Museum of Azerbaijan History, Chairperson of the History Department of the Baku Institute of Public Administration and Political Science, and Chairman of the Association of Azerbaijan Culture.

Paul Marshall

Mr. Paul Marshall is Senior Fellow and Coordinator for the Survey of Religious Freedom of Freedom House. He is General Editor of *Religious Freedom in the World: A Global Report on Freedom and Persecution* (2000). Mr. Marshall is also the author of a best-selling survey of religious persecution worldwide titled *Their Blood Cries Out* (1997), and is the author or editor of twenty-one other books and booklets including

Islam at the Crossroads, *The Talibanization of Nigeria*, *God and the Constitution*, and *Massacre at the Millennium*.

Federico Mayor Zaragoza

Dr. Federico Mayor is the former Director General of the United Nations Educational, Scientific and Cultural Organization (UNESCO), where he served for twelve years, from 1987 to 1999. Dr. Mayor received his Ph.D. in Biochemistry from the Universidad Complutense de Madrid. He has also served as Rector of the University of Grenada, directed the Department of Biochemistry at the Universidad Autonoma, and was co-founder of the Centro de Biologia Molecular. He has held the posts of Minister of Science and Education of Spain, Member of Parliament, and Chair of the Parliamentary Commission for Education and Science.

Laurie Mylroie

Dr. Laurie Mylroie is adjunct scholar at the American Enterprise Institute, publisher of *Iraq News*, and a consultant to the US Defense Department on terrorism. She is the author of *Study of Revenge: Saddam Hussein's Unfinished War Against America* (published in paperback as *The War Against America*), and her previous book, *Saddam Hussein and the Crisis in the Gulf*, was a number one *New York Times* bestseller. Dr. Mylroie received her Ph.D. in Political Science from Harvard University. She was an Assistant Professor in Harvard's Political Science Department prior to becoming an Associate Professor in the Strategy Department at the US Naval War College.

John O'Sullivan

Mr. John O'Sullivan is Editor-in-Chief of United Press International (UPI), an international news service formed in 1907. He also serves as Editor-at-Large of *National Review*. His previous posts included Special Adviser to Prime Minister Margaret Thatcher, Editorial Consultant to Hollinger International, Associate Editor of the *London Times*, Assistant Editor of the *London Daily Telegraph*, and Editor of *Policy Review*. Mr. O'Sullivan is Founder of the New Atlantic Initiative and serves on the board of several nonprofit organizations. He was made a Commander of the British Empire in the 1991 New Year's Honors List.

Ruta Pels

Ruta Pels is president of People to People, Estonia.

Ljudmilla Priimägi

Dr. Ljudmilla Priimägi is Chairman of the Board and Vice President of the Estonian Association of Anti-AIDS. Holding a doctorate in virology, Dr. Priimägi also serves as Head of the Virology Department for the Institute of Experimental and Clinical Medicine. Previously she has served as Director of the Institute of Preventive Medicine, and Head of Laboratory for the Tallinn Research Institute of Epidemiology, Microbiology and Hygiene. Dr. Priimägi has over two hundred scientific publications and serves on the Editing Committee for *Probl. of Virology*.

David W. Randle

Dr. David W. Randle is President and Executive Director of the WHALE Center, and Environmental Justice Minister for the United Methodist Rocky Mountain Conference. He is a leading authority on the link between spiritual disciplines and environmental issues, and on advancing faith communities as partners in addressing environmental challenges. The first ordained environmental minister in the United States, Dr. Randle served as program development coordinator for John Denver's Windstar Foundation and chaired the Chaplain Committee for the Salt Lake Olympic Committee.

Jerry John Rawlings

H.E. Flt. Lt. Jerry John Rawlings served as President of the Republic of Ghana from 1981 until 2000, overseeing the transition from a military government to democratic elections. He was democratically elected President in 1992. The 1996 elections marked the first time in Ghana that an elected government completed its term in office, had an election, and secured a renewed mandate in a democratic manner. Flt. Lt. Rawlings also served two terms as Chairman of the Council of Heads of State of the sixteen-nation Economic Community of West African States. In 2001, Flt. Lt. Rawlings was designated by UN Secretary-General Kofi Annan as a United Nations Eminent Person for International Voluntarism. He is the joint recipient of the 1993 World Hunger Prize.

Seriah L. Rein

Dr. Seriah L. Rein is Chairman of the Council on the American Family. Since 1998, Dr. Rein has also served on both the Advisory Council on Adolescent Pregnancy and the Governor's AIDS Advisory Council. Dr. Rein cofounded Samaritans AIDES, a faith-based outreach to families and individuals struggling with AIDS. Dr. Rein has previously served as State Director of Concerned Women for America of New Jersey, the largest women's organization in the United States.

William Reuben

Mr. William Reuben is Coordinator of the NGO and Civil Society Unit at the World Bank and is the World Bank's Senior Civil Society Specialist. Dr. Reuben has managed and coordinated regional networks for Latin American NGOs for the last twenty-three years and is founder of the NGO networks Asociación Latinoamericana de Organizaciones de Promoción (ALOP), Fondo Latinoamericano de Desarrollo (FOLADE), Concertación Centroamericana, and Centro de Capacitación y Promoción para la Democracia (CECADE). He holds a Ph.D. in Social Sciences.

Theresa Rudacille

Ms. Theresa Rudacille serves as Director of Development for the Empowerment Resource Network and is a fundraising consultant, trainer, and special event coordinator for nonprofit organizations. In 1999 she authored *Raising Resources: A More-Than-Fundraising Handbook*, which is being used as a training resource by the Office of Faith-Based Initiatives in the White House. Ms. Rudacille has written innumerable successful grant proposals and solicited major gifts up to $1 million. She holds a Certificate in Nonprofit Management from Duke University and is a 1986 graduate of the US Military Academy at West Point.

Phillip V. Sanchez

Ambassador Phillip V. Sanchez is Publisher of the hemispheric Spanish-language newspaper *Tiempos del Mundo*, Vice President of the *Washington Times*, publisher of *Noticias del Mundo*, and former Chairman of the Board of Nostalgia Television. Ambassador Sanchez also serves on the board of several universities. His appointment as

National Director of OEO (War on Poverty) made him the highest-ranking Hispanic appointee in the history of the United States government at that time. Ambassador Sanchez has served as US Ambassador to Colombia and to Honduras.

Anne Ranniste Smart

Ms. Anne Ranniste Smart is the WANGO Publications Director and Africa Regional Coordinator. She worked previously as Director of Creative Projects and Office Manager with Bridges to Community, Inc., an American-based NGO that takes groups of volunteers to developing nations for service and relief work. Together with her husband, Robert, they serve as the North American representative volunteers to Guinea, West Africa, for the Family Federation for World Peace International. In 1986 she was one of a group of editors who began *The World and I*, a monthly magazine published by the Washington Times Corporation. Born of Estonian parents living in Argentina who later immigrated to Canada, she studied at York University in Toronto.

Frederick A. Swarts

Dr. Frederick A. Swarts is Assistant Secretary General for WANGO. He is also President of the Waterland Research Institute for Water and Land Resources, a research, education, and conservation organization primarily active in the Paraguay River Basin in Brazil, Bolivia, and Paraguay. Since 1998, Dr. Swarts has served as Secretary-General of the World Conference on Preservation and Sustainable Development in the Pantanal. He is the editor of *The Pantanal: Understanding and Preserving the World's Largest Wetland.*

William E. Swing

The Rt. Rev. William E. Swing, Episcopal Bishop of California, has been a primary catalyst for the creation of a United Religions NGO since 1993. He is Founding Trustee of the United Religions Initiative, which began in 1995 and held its first Global Summit in 1996, and which has involved more than a million people in its activities and has a membership of over 15,000 people in 47 countries, representing more than 88 spiritual traditions. Bishop Swing has traveled extensively in Asia, the Middle East, and Europe, seeking commitments from many of the world's religious leaders.

Mary Evelyn Tucker

Dr. Mary Evelyn Tucker is Professor of Religion at Bucknell University. Her published works include *Worldly Wonder: Religions Enter Their Ecological Phase*, and she coedited *Worldviews and Ecology*, *Buddhism and Ecology*, *Confucianism and Ecology*, *Religion and Ecology*, and *Hinduism and Ecology*, among others. She and her husband John Grim directed a series of ten conferences on World Religions and Ecology at the Harvard University Center for the Study of World Religions. They are coordinating the Forum on Religion and Ecology and edited a book series on *Ecology and Justice*. Dr. Tucker is a committee member of the Interfaith Partnership for the Environment at UNEP. She received her Ph.D. from Columbia University.

Srey Vanthon

Mr. Srey Vanthon is Country Representative for the Action on Disability and Development in Cambodia. Previously he produced video documentaries for NGOs. He also worked five years with one of UNDP's projects CARERE (Cambodia Rehabilitation and Regeneration Project), in the department of Information and Documentation, promoting information strategy on the decentralization policy of the government on planning, financing, and rural development.

Alexa Fish Ward

Ms. Alexa Fish Ward serves as President of the Women's Federation for World Peace USA and Vice President of the Women's Federation for World Peace International (WFWP). Holding NGO general consultative status with ECOSOC of the United Nations, WFWP facilitates partnerships among women. Ms. Ward also served as executive director of the Eleanor Roosevelt Center at Val-Kill in New York, and on the board of directors of the American Red Cross.

Thomas J. Ward

Dr. Thomas J. Ward is Vice President for International Programs and Dean of the International College of the University of Bridgeport. Prior to this, he served as Assistant to the Provost and as a Visiting Professor of International Studies. Dr. Ward assisted Dr. Stoyan Ganev, 47th President of the United Nations General Assembly, in creating the University's New England Center for International and Regional Studies. Dr. Ward has also served as the Human Rights Commissioner in Dutchess County, New York.

Sheila Watt-Cloutier

Ms. Sheila Watt-Cloutier serves as President of the Inuit Circumpolar Conference (Canada) and Chair of the Inuit Circumpolar Conference (ICC). The ICC is a major international NGO representing approximately 150,000 Inuit of Canada, Alaska, Greenland, and Chukotka (Russia). Ms. Watt-Cloutier also serves as Vice President of the national Inuit organization, Inuit Tapirisat of Canada. She has been an effective spokesperson on a wide range of Arctic and indigenous issues and has made presentations before governments and international bodies such as the United Nations.

Ruth Wedgwood

Ms. Ruth Wedgwood is Professor of International Law at Yale Law School and Director of the Program on International Law and Organizations at the School of Advanced International Studies at Johns Hopkins University. In 2002 she was elected to the UN Human Rights Committee, the implementation body for the International Covenant on Civil and Political Rights. Ms. Wedgwood also is director of the project on international organizations and law at the Council on Foreign Relations. She was an independent expert for the International Criminal Tribunal for the Former Yugoslavia and a member of the advisory group to the Special Representative of the UN Secretary-General for children and armed conflict. Among her works are *After Dayton: Lessons of the Bosnian Peace Process* and *American National Interest and the United Nations.*

James Weidman

Mr. James Weidman is Director of Public Relations for the Heritage Foundation, a public policy research organization. Mr. Weidman previously served as Deputy Director of Regional Media Communications for the National Federation of Independent Business (NFIB). During his sixteen years at NFIB, Weidman handled public relations for the NFIB Education Foundation and also worked as Manager of Media Relations and Manager of State Media Relations. Before working at NFIB, Weidman was a project director at the National Public Research Institute.

Claude E. Welch

Dr. Claude E. Welch is Director of the Human Rights Center of the State University of New York at Buffalo as well as Director of the University's Program on International and Comparative Legal Studies and is Distinguished Service Professor of Political

Science. He is the author of *NGOs and Human Rights* and *Protecting Human Rights in Africa: Role and Strategies of NGOs*, and numerous other books related to human rights and politics. Dr. Welch also has served as Dean of the Division of Undergraduate Education, Associate Vice President for Academic Affairs, and Chair of Political Science. Dr. Welch completed his doctoral degree at Oxford University.

Richard G. Wilkins

Dr. Richard G. Wilkins, J.D., is a Professor of Law at the J. Reuben Clark Law School and Managing Director of the World Family Policy Center at Brigham Young University. The World Family Policy Center was established by the David M. Kennedy Center for International Studies and the J. Reuben Clark School of Law to provide worldwide democratic input and educate the United Nations on pro-family and other value-based issues, and it is one of the main conveners of the World Congress of Families. Dr. Wilkins is a former Assistant to the Solicitor General, US Department of Justice.

Karen M. Woods

Ms. Karen M. Woods is Executive Director for The Empowerment Network (TEN). She also is a certified Empowerment Resource Network (ERN) trainer for Raising Resources, an adviser to a state legislator for Individual Development Account Partnership legislation and program development, chairs the public affairs committee of the Muskegon Community Health Project, and is a member of Working Group II, an advisory group to the Rockefeller Institute and SUNY. Ms. Woods has served as a peer reviewer for federal IDA grants, is a board member for New Focus, National, and is an advisory board member of Christian Business Network, International.